"One should resist the temptation to proclaim the prospect of a wired brain an illusion, something that we are still far from and that cannot really be actualized: such a view is itself an escape from the threat, from the fact that something new and unheard-of is effectively emerging. Even if it will be realized in a much more modest way than today's grandiose visions of Singularity, everything will change with it. But how will things change? It is here that Jan De Vos points to the role of the mainstream psy-sciences and their simple, cardboard psychological models informing the design of our avatars and 'smart environments'. Are we doomed or is there a prospect for a more emancipatory digital technology? Jan de Vos approaches this question, carefully avoiding the fascination by New Age post-human dreams. His book is simply for everyone who cares about their destiny—if you will ignore it, you will do this at your own risk."

—Slavoj Žižek *is International Director at Birkbeck Institute for Humanities (Birkbeck College, University of London) and Senior Researcher at the Department of Philosophy, Faculty of Arts, University of Ljubljana, Slovenia*

"Jan De Vos's *The Digitalisation Of (Inter)Subjectivity* provides a trenchant critique of the very terms by which contemporary debates about artificial intelligence and the neurobiological model of the human mind are waged. De Vos shows convincingly that reductive forms of ego psychology ('psychologization') provide the basis for merging machines and human beings in a smooth calculus of late capitalist subjectivity. De Vos throws the sand of psychoanalysis into the well-oiled gears of this machine, providing a stark vision of the human species in the grip of its self-destructive drives. Against this dark picture he offers a renewal of radical left politics that overturns the game board, fractures the screen-based transparencies, and short-circuits the neuralinks that promise utopias of communication and consumer gratification."

—W. J. T. Mitchell, *editor of* Critical Inquiry *and author of* Iconology, Picture Theory, What Do Pictures Want?, *and* Image Science, *teaches at the University of Chicago, USA*

THE DIGITALISATION OF (INTER)SUBJECTIVITY

This book explores the responsibility of psychological and neuropsychological perspectives in relation to the digitalisation of inter-subjectivity. It examines how integral their theories and models have been to the development of digital technologies, and by combining theoretical and critical work of leading thinkers, it is a new and highly original perspective on (inter)subjectivity in the digital era.

The book engages with artificial intelligence and cybernetics and the work of Alan Turing, Norbert Wiener, Marvin Minsky, Gregory Bateson, and Warren McCulloch to demonstrate how their use of neuropsy-theories persists in contemporary digital culture. The author aims to trace a trajectory from psychologisation to neurologisation, and finally, to digitalisation, to make us question the digital future of humankind in relation to the idea of subjectivity, and the threat of the 'death-drive' inherent to digitality itself.

This volume is fascinating reading for students and researchers in the fields of critical psychology, neuroscience, education studies, philosophy, media studies, and other related areas.

Jan De Vos holds an MA in psychology and a PhD in philosophy and is currently affiliated to Ghent University and University College Ghent, Belgium. He is author of several monographs, amongst others, *The Metamorphoses of the Brain. Neurologisation and its Discontents* (2016) and *Psychologisation in times of Globalisation* (2012).

THE DIGITALISATION OF (INTER)SUBJECTIVITY

A Psy-critique of the Digital Death Drive

Jan De Vos

LONDON AND NEW YORK

First published 2020
by Routledge
2 Park Square, Milton Park, Abingdon, Oxon OX14 4RN

and by Routledge
52 Vanderbilt Avenue, New York, NY 10017

Routledge is an imprint of the Taylor & Francis Group, an informa business

© 2020 Jan De Vos

The right of Jan De Vos to be identified as author of this work has been asserted by him in accordance with sections 77 and 78 of the Copyright, Designs and Patents Act 1988.

All rights reserved. No part of this book may be reprinted or reproduced or utilised in any form or by any electronic, mechanical, or other means, now known or hereafter invented, including photocopying and recording, or in any information storage or retrieval system, without permission in writing from the publishers.

Trademark notice: Product or corporate names may be trademarks or registered trademarks, and are used only for identification and explanation without intent to infringe.

British Library Cataloguing-in-Publication Data
A catalogue record for this book is available from the British Library

Library of Congress Cataloging-in-Publication Data
A catalog record has been requested for this book

ISBN: 978-1-138-05304-5 (hbk)
ISBN: 978-1-138-05305-2 (pbk)
ISBN: 978-1-315-16735-0 (ebk)

Typeset in Bembo
by codeMantra

CONTENTS

Acknowledgments xi

PART 1
Introduction 1

1 The digital death drive 3

PART 2
Learning machines: digitalisation and its psy-antecedents 23

2 Alan Turing, artificial intelligence, and its psy-fantasies 25

3 Cybernetics and the war of the psychologies 52

4 Towards a psy-critique of the digitalisation of intersubjectivity: two case-studies 79

PART 3
Educating the people: digital deadlocks 107

5 Digitalising education and parenting: the end of interpellation? 109

| 6 | The digital (no)future of education | 136 |
| 7 | Digital mass effects | 159 |

PART 4
Conclusions 187

| 8 | What digitality should not think. A guide to imagine the end of the world | 189 |

Index *217*

"Que sei eu do que serei, eu que não sei o que sou?" (What do I know of what I'll be, I who don't know what I am?)

(Fernando Pessoa, 1972)

ACKNOWLEDGMENTS

I am wholly indebted to the following people for their comments on early versions of the chapters from this book: David Bates, Erica Burman, Alfie Bown, Neil Cocks, Jairo Gallo Acosta, Carlos Gómez Camarena, David Gunkel, Karin Lesnik-Oberstein, Ian Parker, David Pavón Cuéllar, Mandy Pierlejewski, Stefan Ramaekers, Glenn Strubbe, Cindy Zeiher, and Hub Zwart.

I am also incredibly grateful to Chris Higgins from Francis Hardie Academic Services for his scrupulous and thoughtful language editing. Special thanks to Ghent University (especially Tom Claes) and University College Ghent for financing the language correction.

Some parts of this book are based on previously published work. Chapters 1 and 2 are partly based on my book *La psicologización y sus vicisitudes. Hacia una crítica psico-política*, 2019, Paradiso Mexico City. All rights reserved. © Jan De Vos. Chapter 4 is partly based on *Which subject for the digital? A critique of digitalization's roots in (neuro)psychologisation*, Etkileşim, 1, 2018, pp. 20–34, Üsküdar University. All rights reserved. © Jan De Vos. Chapter 5 is partly based on *The neuroturn in education: between the Scylla of psychologization and the Charybdis of digitalization?* in M. Vandenbroeck (Ed.), *Constructions of neuroscience in early childhood* education, 2017, Routledge. All rights reserved. © Jan De Vos. Chapter 6 is partly based on *Digital Therapeutic Culture* in Daniel Nehring et al. (eds.), *Routledge Handbook of Global Therapeutic Cultures*, 2020, Routledge. All rights reserved. © Jan De Vos. And lastly Chapter 8 is partly based on, *Fake subjectivities: Interpassivity from (neuro) psychologization to digitalization*, Continental Thought & Theory, 2(1), 2018, pp. 5–31. University of Canterbury. All rights reserved. © Jan De Vos.

I dedicate this book to all of those people who have inspired me, supported me, and put up with me over the course of this long process of writing the book, which required significant (free) time and effort–Vera, you are, of course, the first person that comes to my mind here!

PART 1
Introduction

1
THE DIGITAL DEATH DRIVE

Introduction: what will become of us?

What will become of us? This is the question that humankind is forced to pose to itself when faced with events that have the potential to change both the world and ourselves. In such moments, one foresees that the world, oneself and, in some instances, humankind itself will never be the same afterwards.

Regardless of whether these major events—such as a global catastrophe, or, on a more personal level, losing one's job and source of income—truly engender fundamental changes, the question of *what will become of us* nevertheless carries significant weight. Human beings have a strange capacity to reflect upon themselves as somehow being different or as being something else entirely. This raises the question of whether the human subject is ever simply what it is? Or, phrased otherwise, if to be human is to be able to imagine oneself as being different, then does this not signal that one never simply coincides with oneself, that one is always already other to oneself?

Consider, in this respect, the man or woman who strolls through the city streets in the early hours of the night. He or she encounters various scenes of everyday life through the illuminated windows of houses and apartments, and thinks to themselves, 'this could be my house, my apartment, my wife, my husband, my children, my life, etc.'. Hence, in contradistinction to common-sense notions of identity that conceptualise it as a stable entity, human subjectivity, in fact, appears to be predicated precisely on our capacity to imagine ourselves as being somebody else. For example, what would my life have been like if I had been born a woman rather than a man, or vice versa, or any other alternative scenario one can imagine? How would my life had ended up if I belonged to this particular social class group, rather than this one, or if I lived in this or that region of the world? From this perspective, then, the human subject not simply is, but rather imagines its being, precisely through the act of imagining itself as different.

Indeed, even in the very moment that we whisper through bated breath, *what will become of us?*, we have already changed. This is because the very attempt to foresee forces and events over which we have no control necessarily presupposes picturing ourselves on the other side of them. Even when, or perhaps precisely when, one is not able to consider the consequences of an event—for example, *I cannot imagine how I would cope with the loss of my father*—one is already necessarily on the other side, inasmuch as one is already living with the thought of their dead father.[1]

In this way, the question of *what will become of us?* might be the quintessential mode of what I am calling here *subjective (self)interpellation*.[2] That is, the exemplary interpellative call through which we subjectivise ourselves takes the form of us imagining the loss of our identity and being placed in a state of limbo: *if this or that would happen then what would become of us?* Confronted with, among other things, the (expected) death of our loved ones, one's own ageing or impending death, along with the manifold potential major social, political, economic, and ecological shifts, leads us to experience a mode of desubjectivation. At the very least, when presented with cataclysmic events, which strike us as both inevitable and unthinkable, we know that in no way will things ever be the same and neither will we.

Today, the question of *what will become of us?* imposes itself most prominently vis-à-vis the so-called process of digitalisation. Digitalisation, so it has been argued, has the potential to engender truly fundamental change, both at the social and subjective levels. Undoubtedly, digitalisation has profoundly changed the spheres of production and consumption, governance and policing, as well as how we present ourselves to others (and ourselves) and interact with others (and ourselves). Moreover, digitalisation has been a key driver in globalisation; indeed, today's global hyper-financialised economy would be unfathomable without the digital technology that makes it possible for money to produce more money through multiple automated transactions that are realised in fractions of a second. In this respect, it would appear that capitalism has finally managed to surpass both its material boundaries and the need for concrete people. While materiality and concrete people still play a predominant role in the new digital economy, I will argue over the course of this book that it is precisely digitalised subjectivity that ultimately serves the virtual process of money producing more money. That is to say, it is the commodification of subjectivity via digitalisation that constitutes the backbone of the new digital economy and its key processes of expropriation and alienation.

In light of this, does this not mean that the aforesaid question of *what will become of us?* involves envisaging the end of the human subject as we know it? Has the anthropocenic age given way to the *digicenic age*, the age of coding? In this age, it is not the human being that is the measure of things, but rather codes and algorithms which propel, apparently autonomously, the course of things. Here, the question of *what will become of us?* takes the following forms: what will happen to us when the majority of work is performed by robots or by Artificial Intelligence (AI)? What will become of us as human subjects when our lives play out ever more in virtual environments? What will it mean when each and every one of us is directly connected (neurodigitally) not only with each other, but with everything (e.g. the so-called Internet of Things)? Will we be reduced to mere nodal points in the global network of the hypermarket?

A key question concerns whether these aforesaid issues should be the domain of psychologists (what does digitalisation do to the individual?), neuroscientists (what does digitalisation do to the brain?), or even for psychoanalysts, who might approach the matter from a more sophisticated perspective (e.g. conceptualising the subject as that which can imagine itself differently)? The problem with each of these three explanations, however, as I will argue in this book, is that they are incapable of mounting a neutral vantage point from which to view this issue. This is because, I would contend, the theories and models of psychology and neuroscience—and perhaps even psychoanalysis—already inform digital technologies. Hence, when considering the ways through which codes and algorithms have come to shape and model the new subjectivities and modes of sociality, one should look for the neuropsy-models and theories that are overtly and covertly utilised in the pre-formatting of (inter)subjectivity. Consequently, if at first glance the psy-sciences appear to offer explanations, this book argues that they are, in fact, integral to that which has to be explained.

Consider the title of a recent book by Stephens-Davidowitz (2017): 'Everybody Lies. Big data, new data and what the Internet can tell us about who we really are'. If it is truly the case that Big Data can reveal the core of our personality, then would the Internet not be a treasure chest for psychologists? This is what Stephens-Davidowitz seems to imply: with the so-called data-trails people leave behind when surfing the Internet, he claims, for the first time we can really see 'in the interior of people' (cited in Illing, 2017). What Stephens-Davidowitz overlooks, however, is that psychology and its attendant concepts and methods do not enter the fold only at a subsequent moment (i.e. when researchers reveal the psychological truths and various idiosyncrasies hidden within people's Internet search histories), but, rather, digital platforms like Google, Facebook, and others function fundamentally via heuristics that are informed by psychology. Indeed, Silicon Valley companies' principal interest is to know who and what you are via your searches, clicks, likes, or, to use another term, via your desires. In this way, they proceed as if they were psychologists, or even psychoanalysts to be more precise, for whom subjectivity is almost entirely synonymous with desire. In this respect, is the Internet not then a psychologist? This appears to ever more be the case especially since the launch of the so-called interactive and participative Web 2.0, which, above all, serves as an amphitheatre for our psychological life, that is, our thoughts, images, emotions, memories… at the very moment that they present themselves. Perhaps the reader may recognise in the latter formulation the basic rule of psychoanalysis, namely, the principle of free association. Of course, while social media and the like do not allow indecent or explicit content, there are obviously other virtual places for that. At the very least, these digital and virtual spaces are designed to host the psychological, and, as such, it is no surprise, as Davidowitz implies, that it is the psychological which emerges out of the digital. Consequently, as this book will argue, the very theories and models that are used to explain the Internet are the very ones that were used to build and design it in the first place.

In this respect, one could go as far to say that it is precisely here that the virtual realm and virtuality will always elude our grasp and be ahead of us. For does not the very question of *what will become of us if/when?* itself not bear a structural resemblance to an algorithm? This is where neuropsy-models would be applied in order to compute the potential outcomes of the various mutations of subjectivity. Moreover, given that the act of imagining ourselves as different already touches upon the dimension of the virtual, one is rapidly and unnoticedly entering a hall of mirrors when one claims to have a vantage point, be it a psychological, neuroscientific, or a psychoanalytic one, from which to explain (the effects of) digitalisation.

Hence, in the remainder of this introductory chapter, I will outline the key themes of the book by delineating in greater detail the main pitfalls, which, I argue, lead to us getting prematurely lost in digitalisation by uncritically adopting a psy- or neuropsy-perspective on the matters at stake. At the very least, my contention is that psychologists, neuroscientists, and, for that matter, psychoanalysts should proceed tentatively and disentangle how their very own (neuro)psy-theories and models are reflected within digitalisation and digital technologies themselves. This is the purpose of this book, all the while fully acknowledging the stickiness of the terrain and the fact that one cannot *not* evade psychologising digital matters. This book adopts a (critical) psychoanalytic perspective to approach this issue, because, as I explain further in Chapter 3, one cannot circumvent psychoanalysis if one hopes to conduct a fundamental critique of psychology and psychologisation. Hence, psychoanalysis can be understood to be the *via regia* for any psy-critique of the digitalisation of (inter)subjectivity.

It is expedient to begin our journey here by turning to the words of *digitalistas* themselves, not because they (nor their neuropsy counterparts) necessarily have the right answers, but because their perspectives can help to hone our questions, or, to be more precise, their conceptions of the digital and the virtual help us to more accurately trace the contours of the aforementioned hall of mirrors. Our bad guide on this journey—one always needs bad guides who with their treacherous lamps illuminate above all their own problematic position—will be Elon Musk, as he is emblematic, or perhaps even symptomatic, of how the key question of *what will become of us?* is invariably misunderstood. More specifically, I would contend that both his vision of how the digital signals the death knell for humanity and his heroic plans to save us all from it are the exemplification of what I am designating in this book as the digital death drive, which, rather than leading to the death of humanity necessarily, turns us all into undead digital zombies.

Elon Musk's digi-apocalypse

Elon Musk, the co-founder of, among other companies, PayPal and Tesla, perhaps more so than any public figure, has expressed his fears about AI and warned of 'a fleet of artificial-intelligence-enhanced robots capable of destroying mankind' (Elon Musk cited in Vance, 2015, p. 3). Here, the question of *what will become of us?* reaches its ultimate expression: what will become of us when the digital threatens to finish off humanity.[3]

Even at this early stage, in order to understand what the digitalistas themselves overlook in their fascination with the end-of-the-human theme, we must draw upon psychoanalysis. Sigmund Freud argues that human beings cannot think or even conceive of their own death, and that unconsciously everyone is convinced of their immortality (Freud, [1915]1957). One way to reformulate this point might be to say, if we cannot even imagine our own death, then perhaps the only way to deal with this is to ask ourselves: what will be of us when we are dead? It is precisely this that Elon Musk is unwittingly engaging in with his vision of a digi-apocalypse, which is merely another fantasy through which to think about humankind and its precarious existence.

However, it is important to follow the Freudian thesis to its logical end by supplementing it with the thought of Jacques Lacan, specifically his ruminations on the theme of death. Lacan (1981) tells us that we require the conviction that we are going to die in order to be able to live and to be present in the world ('to be able to cope with this comedy'). Hence, Freud's notion that we cannot imagine our own non-presence from a state of presence should be amended: in fact, it is only from a presupposed, imagined (and thus virtual) non-presence that we can think about and construct our presence. At the very least, this means that the question of our presence, our being here as it were, is an altogether problematic and convoluted issue. It is here that one can already surmise that psychoanalysis is not another form of psychology as it is sometimes mistaken to be; rather, psychoanalysis constitutes a radical critique of psychology (and psychologisation), in terms of its various conceptualisations of the unidimensional human whose feelings of presence are merely neuropsychologically conditioned. Musk's position is reflective of the latter point, in that it appears to be crystal clear to him what kind of presence, what kind of human, is in need of protection from the nefarious AI-fleet.

One way to explain this further is by opposing Musk's perspective to the profound words of the poet Fernando Pessoa: "Que sei eu do que serei, eu que não sei o que sou?" (Pessoa, 1972, p. 381), "What do I know of what I'll be, I who don't know what I am?" In contradistinction, Musk claims to know very well what we are: given that he considers AI to be an existential threat, he would appear to have definitive ideas about what the precious human *agalma* is, and that we should at all costs protect and preserve it from the onslaught of digital technology. One particular way through which Musk proposes to preserve humankind is to colonise Mars, with the red planet serving as a place of refuge for the kernel of humanity in the event that AI goes rogue and turns against us (Dowd, 2017). While commentators including Demis Hassabis are quick to respond that AI would simply just follow humans to Mars, Elon Musk has other options up his sleeve: to combat the risk of AI making humankind redundant, Musk proposes having 'some sort of merger of biological intelligence and machine intelligence' (cited in Dowd, 2017). This should be taken as literal, inasmuch as Musk's *Neuralink* project aims to design a 'neural lace', an injectable mesh that would connect the brain directly with a computer. In so doing, one would be able to directly communicate with both the machine and the Internet itself, in order to both upload and download information. For Musk, this represents the only way through which humans could keep up with AI, remain in charge, and not be turned into AI's house cat (cited in Muoio, 2017).

It is somewhat perplexing that, while Musk thinks that the *Neuralink* project will arm humankind against AI and, in turn, preserve their essential human essence, he does not devote any time to considering the danger that this very process would grant computers full access to humankind, and allow them to potentially domesticate them if they saw fit. Hence, while Musk evokes the Wagnerian point that it is only the spear that caused the wound that can ultimately heal it, Neuralink constitutes perhaps the prime example of how reusing the spear can produce an even more fatal wound. With Neuralink, at least one could say that the spear that wounds and the lancet that cures are held by the same hand, in that it is Silicon Valley that both controls the space and the available modes of resistance. The most problematic of Musk's claims, however, is that he knows what should be defended, what should be kept safe from digitalisation. This is the fundamental fantasy he shares with the developers of AI, as they design technological intelligence based on what they consider to be the established and unproblematic theories of what human intelligence is (which is arguably a model, a choice for a particular vision and perspective, which is always contestable). Consequently, both parties stand in radical opposition to the non-psychological positions of Freud, Lacan, and Pessoa: they who do not know what will become of us, as we do not know what we actually are.

Having said this, am I not using this 'we' here paradoxically, inasmuch as I am problematically shifting from the singular to the plural? The following anecdote should make this clearer: once I introduced a workshop on the processes of neurologisation by saying that *we* know less and less about what humans are (alluding to a phrase from one of my other favourite writers),[4] and thus that we need to urgently think about our *unknowledge* so as to be able to oppose the hegemony of, for example, neuro-discourses that do claim to know what human beings are. Immediately following this point, a colleague from my department picked up on my use of the word 'we', retorting *"but who is this 'we'"*, before proceeding to profess how annoyed she gets when people use the word 'we'. While, of course, she was right to both ask this question and flag-up the fact that, given that I claimed that for structural reasons we do not know what the human is, the 'we' I summoned was also problematic, I could have retorted (but I did not, as I am always too slow in such matters) that, while, of course, this 'we' does not exist as such, it does nevertheless come to life in the very interpellation to think about our predicament. That is to say, of course, the invocation of any notion of 'we' is problematic, but so is the invocation of the 'I' or the Ego, and it is precisely here that the 'we' inevitably steps in and, indeed, must necessarily step in. At the very least, invoking a sense of the 'we' is a critical way through which to oppose digital pundits, such as Elon Musk and Mark Zuckerberg, who via both their invocations of individual sovereignty and philanthropical endeavours claim to already know what is best for individuals.

The fantasy of stopping (a bad guy with) AI with (a good guy with) AI

Perhaps it is this precise issue of the 'I' and 'we' revolving door, that is, this parallax of subjectivity and sociality, that constitutes the central issue to examine in relation to digitalisation. One need only consider, here, how the digital sphere has rapidly become the sphere through which we are both present and present ourselves to and with others. In this respect, it is significant that #Iam (most commonly proceeded by a name or a proper noun) is invariably mobilised by social networks in the aftermath of disruptive events, like natural disasters, social or political calamities, and terrorist activities in order to express our compassion, support, and solidarity. Via #Iam individuals forge a (group) identity based on an identification with a (fatal) victim, proclaiming that in our collective empathy, we at least are still safe and sound and, above all, alive.

One of the first major events in which #Iam gained prominence was the terrorist attack in 2015 in Paris at the headquarters of the satirical magazine 'Charlie Hebdo'. As a result of having previously published cartoons featuring Mohammed, a group attacked the editorial office and killed 12 persons and one police officer who responded to the attack. Soon after the event, the phrase 'Je suis Charlie' (I am Charlie) began to circulate on social media, signalling both solidarity with the victims and defiance against the perpetrators. After a while, 'I am Ahmed' (the name of the dead Muslim police officer) also began to circulate online, in order to make clear that one was not a racist. Through the use of these various hashtags, people were seeking to assert both their own identity and a sense of sociality, which is to say that the use of 'I am' was also supposed to constitute membership of a group.

Perhaps we should contrast the '#Iam' with a slogan that used to be popular in pre-digital times: 'I love X', with the prototypical example perhaps being: 'I love NY'. These slogans, no doubt invented by marketers, were meant to both capture and incite desire for a particular city or product. It would not be a stretch to say that this slogan perhaps represented a prototypical version of the like function on social media, albeit there the emphasis in 'I like' tends to lie more with the 'I'? That is to say, when I wore products that affirmed 'I love NY' or 'I love Coca Cola' these products took central stage, only in a secondary movement did they transfer a bit more of their gleam to the I (by turning the latter into a 'cool' person). With 'I like', what the objects are is of minor importance, what matters is above all that they are elevated to match the dignity of my Ego. In other words, whereas 'I love' still evoked a desire for a commodity that was seen as being separate from the 'I' so to speak, in the case of 'I like' the commodity is nothing but the 'I', as opposed to the thing which is liked. Hence, the commodification of the I turns everybody into an entrepreneur whose product is their self, while, simultaneously, social media companies harvest our I-data to drive their main business: selling personal profiles to advertisers.

The question here is whether this 'I am' also contains the potential for resisting this process of commodification, along with holding out the promise for emancipation via the reintroduction of empathy and solidarity? In other words, could it, in fact, be the case that digitality is indeed both the spear and the lancet, the poison and the cure? More specifically, can the alienation and social fragmentation produced by digitalisation be countered by digital means themselves? Can the digital provide the path via which both subjectivities and sociality can (re)establish themselves perhaps in new ways?

Undoubtedly, the volatility of the digital sphere has transformed the I into an ever-shifting issue, in the sense that the 'I' that surfs the digital waves can like what it wants and ostensibly be what it wants (while, simultaneously, unknowingly being frozen in profiles). In this sense, is the 'I am' then not an attempt to give weight to the ephemeral digitalised 'I'? Is #Iam thus a way through which to overcome the atomisation and virtualisation of social networks, so as to once again become a 'real' person? However, despite the fact that the major events that engender the '#Iam' campaigns concern events in the supposedly real world, that is, in concrete, material reality, the standard confirmation of '#Iam' cannot but come from the virtual world, by virtue of the fact that its purpose is to harvest virtual and ephemeral 'likes'.[5]

In this respect, one could also argue that, above all, '#Iam' concerns a dead person. We identify with a victim or a hero, by pinning them down and isolating them in their death, and in so doing we fabricate a mask, a death mask, to give form to our own ephemeral, deadly (if not zombie-like) virtual existence. As alluded to earlier in the chapter, is there not an element of jubilation involved in the use of '#Iam'? I identify with the dead, while, at the same time, being alive myself, thus using the death as a means through which to escape our mortifying virtual existence? However, having done so we cannot but then observe that our outcry '#Iam' does not have long-lasting effects, and so we must repeat it at regular intervals in order to re-establish our sense of an 'I' and a temporary 'we'. In this respect, there appears to be little chance that these '#Iam' comments truly bring people together in a social and political 'we' that is capable of both transcending its ephemerality and engaging in an (inter)subjective act.

Here, it is expedient to draw upon a third poet, Arthur Rimbaud, who proclaimed: 'Je suis un autre' (Rimbaud, 1954, p. 268), 'I am an other', which Lacan takes to mean that alienation is the core of our subjectivity (Lacan, 1966, p. 213).

Hence, in the end, this basic bottomless subjectivity that can be understood as the very condition of subjectivity, is not only always already negated or even obfuscated within the sphere of digitality, it also gets lost in '#Iam' in the attempt to supersede digital alienation. In short, the paradox here is that, while alienation is denied in the digital sphere (as the latter demands or even pre-fabricates the full closure of subjectivity and sociality, which is an issue in which '#Iam' is also caught up), it produces yet another form of alienation, albeit one which cannot be subjectivised or socialised within the digital itself? We will return to this issue at various instances in this book, but, suffice to say for now, it is my contention that this is precisely the same thing that was overlooked in Elon Musk's attempt to save humankind from AI with AI. What Musk foregoes is precisely that human subjectivity cannot but establish itself via a mode of negation, that is, humanity, as such, can only be said to exist when people invoke the end of humanity. Musk, negating this dialectical movement, erects an essentialist image (or even fantasy to use psychoanalytic language) of human beings, an 'I am' that he claims humans are. Consequently, in his futurist vision of human annihilation via digital technologies, he fails (or refuses) to see the modes of alienation and mortification of subjectivity and sociality that are already at work within extant forms of digitalisation.

In this respect, one could here refer to Lacan's mirror stage of child development (which occurs between 6 and 18 months), whereby the child overcomes its 'motor impotence and nursling dependence' (Lacan, 2007, p. 76) by way of identifying with the image of itself in the mirror, which according to Lacan is the precise instance in which the 'I' sees light. In this stage, the child overcomes the state of 'the fragmented body' by means of a misrecognition with the specular reflection of its wholeness. If one accepts, albeit only to a certain extent, that similar processes of individuation take place via social media and other virtual spaces, then this might be useful for explaining some of the peculiarities of digital presence. For Lacan, the specular image of unity is both ambiguous and alienating, in that it promises the child a unity which it itself does not possess. The same could be said for our avatars and virtual personas in cyberspace, which also profess a form of unity and substantiality that we ourselves do not possess, and, in so doing, confront us with our lack of being. Musk and his Neuralink project can thus be said to be lost in the hall of mirrors insofar as they overlook the alienation that, paradoxically speaking, is constitutive of subjectivity and sociality. Indeed, insofar as he himself puts forward a specular image of the human being and what he wants to preserve and protect from rogue AI, he is only repeating the conditions of alienation.

To be clear, many other commentators reject Musk's fantasy about AI going rogue. For example, Sebastian Spence points out that a far more worrying and likely scenario pertains to concrete humans themselves using AI and other digital technologies in a *bad* way, if one will forgive such an expression. As Spence himself notes: "The tragic reality is that we are still more likely to destroy each other before technology destroys us. This, perhaps, should be our primary focus"

(Spence, 2019). Spence refers to the use of 'robot soldiers', 'autonomous submarines', and 'digital clairvoyance' that monitor and combat social unrest and other forms of resistance. However, does Spence's line of reasoning here not suggest that the only way to stop a bad guy with AI is to arm the good guys with AI? In response to this, I would argue that both Spence and Musk share a psychologising and individualising approach. While the essence of Spence's argument is that we all know what people are like, so we should be concentrating our energy on combating people going rogue with AI, what he is not willing to consider seemingly are more systemic forms of rogue behaviour. This points towards a larger problem in the arguments of both those who fantasise about technological systems eventually dominating and enslaving humanity (Musk) and those who instead focus on the dark side of human nature itself (Spence), which is that we are already living under such conditions of systemic control and unhuman violence. I am referring here, of course, to the domination and enslavement of the larger part of humanity by capitalism, which feeds on humankind like a gigantic parasite. Moreover, despite the fact that a limited amount of people are benefiting from this socio-economic system, one could still argue that they also are merely cogs in the system, replaceable and eventually redundant. Hence, Spence's position runs the risk of slipping into a psychologising approach that attributes the evils of technology as deriving from human nature, which could, in turn, quite easily lead to the demand to use technology to counter the inherent egoistic and dominative urges of humans: if we have sophisticated technology capable of monitoring and even steering entire populations which is currently being misused, then should we not use it for 'good causes'? This is where the fantasy of Spence meets the fantasy of Musk: the notion that what is needed is to bring in a *Dr. Yes*, a visionary expert who knows what human beings are, and, because he is a *good guy*, will use technology as he sees fit in order to bring joy, happiness, equality, empathy, solidarity, and more to all of us (for a more extensive discussion of the myth of neutral technology being used for good causes, see Chapter 7).

Psychoanalysis and the true dystopia

At this juncture, we must return to the starting point of this chapter and the book as a whole, which is that psychological theories and models inform both the design and architecture of the digital realm. The central question here is, if psychoanalysis constitutes the most expedient critique of how the psychologistic infrastructure of digitality is compliant with, and even fundamental to, what one might designate as digital capitalism (which will be demonstrated over the course this book), then could psychoanalysis also offer an alternative for a different mode of digitality? Given that this question will recur throughout the book (or one might say even haunt it), it is instructive to briefly delineate the stakes of this debate in this introductory chapter.

From the outset, it is evident that, albeit for different reasons, both the Internet and the digital sphere itself do not function according to the complicated, twisted, and paradoxical logic of psychoanalysis that I touched upon above. Rather, they are grounded in, what I consider to be, naturalising and simplifying mainstream neuropsychological theories and models (which can quite plainly be understood as antithetical to psychoanalysis). Even if at first glance one would think that psychoanalytic models that stress the centrality of the unconscious and the importance of sexuality would be the paradigmatic model for data mining, it should be evident by this point that the aforementioned alienated nature and radical negativity of the psychoanalytic subject would make it untraceable and untrackable. Hence, psychoanalysis by its very nature would not appear to be an especially expedient model for turning subjects into commodities. It is here that social media and its variants, in their express purpose to extract from us a sellable profile, turn to the psychologised *subconscious* and its attendant array of positive psychological categories. In digitalisation, psychoanalysis' *aporia* of subjectivity must be traded for essentialist theories and models from extant hegemonic neuropsychological discourses, as it is only through recourse to these models that digital companies can realise their business model, which comprises extracting data from people and commodifying subjectivities and forms of sociality. Despite the fact, and this is the disconcerting part, that psychoanalysis is the discipline that provided the conditions of emergence for the digital age—in this book I will show how some seminal figures in the history of digital technologies referred to Freudian psychoanalysis—the naturalising and essentialising models of (neuro)psychology were ultimately required to turn the digital and the virtual into a profitable and exploitable sphere. This can be discerned in the fact that the digital sphere is not an empty space for our free associations, but rather is a pre-structured space. Consider in this regard the way in which Facebook incites us to post messages if we have not been active in a while: *what are you thinking? what do you feel? please select the appropriate emoticon*. In this way, social media necessarily anticipates and preforms our subjectivity through recourse to psychological theories and models, the latter of which inform the algorithms that bring our subjectivities into the marketplace.

The consequence of this is that any critique of the digitalisation of (inter)subjectivity must proceed very carefully. For if one wants to pose as the rescuer or defender of subjectivity, then is one not always tempted to draw upon the very same essentialist and naturalising neuropsy-theories and models through which commodification itself is actualised? Let us return to Elon Musk again, and ask that if Neuralink seeks to provide a fusion between the 'biological intelligence' of humans and the intelligence of machines, then is the central question not which psychological model will operate as the interface for the two? One need only consider the fact that Musk argued that Neuralink would offer clinical advantages, such as enabling paraplegic persons to walk again or allowing for the treatment of disorders such as epilepsy or major depression (Muoio, 2017). To begin with, is Musk justified in bringing together these three issues? And, above all, which theory of depression is Musk drawing upon here: the conceptualisation of depression in psychoanalysis, the one from behaviourism, that of cognitivists, or the one proposed by neuroscientists (for whom there is but one model of depression, the neurobiological one)? Here, it appears that Musk conceives of the depressed person within the same paradigm as the paraplegic person: that is, of someone *who must learn to live again*. Now, if one accepts the idea that depression is about not knowing anymore how to live, then is this not precisely the very position from which humankind lives its life as such, that is, without anyone knowing what the proper way to live is? Hence, what would be the consequences of Neuralink and its idea of connecting humans to machine if it sets out from a straightforward idea about what humans are and what the proper way to live is? Would this not signal the closing down of a free space, of not knowing how to live? A not-knowing which might be constitutive of how we in fact live? Or could it also be the case that this very same form of not-knowing could also be algorithmically preconfigured? Here, the crucial question becomes, if one really could digitalise the kinds of aporias conceived of by psychoanalysis, then what would be the effect of this? This is where the question of *what will become of us?* would return in full force.

As such, the least one can say is that, rather than living in dystopian times per se, we are in fact living in a period in which dystopian fantasies have reached their peak, to the extent that that we perhaps truly are entering a different era and an alternative episteme. Seemingly, digital technologies fundamentally and structurally alter our ways of understanding ourselves, others and the world, as well as our ways of being with ourselves, others and the world. Consider how, for example, the basic idea of Musk's Neuralink is that it would allow for direct thought communication, not only between humans and computers but also between people themselves. Tim Urban posits that brain-machine interfaces would thus make it possible to skip the translation of 'thought' into words and discourse and instead allow for a direct form of exchange. Urban's example is that of watching a horror movie: while in pre-Neuralink times we have to simplify and narrow down our experience to a "few simple low-res buckets—'scary' or 'creepy' or 'chilling'" (Urban, 2017) if we want to articulate our experience to somebody else, with Neuralink we would be able to transmit and share the entire experience without any translational loss. However, as the psychoanalytic philosopher Slavoj Žižek perspicuously comments regarding this issue, Elon Musk's Neuralink overlooks the fact that thoughts are so closely, if not inextricably, related to language. Žižek argues that, while language does indeed simplify, it is only by virtue of this limitation that the actual richness of thought arises. That is to say, it is precisely the reduction of thought to linguistic categories that creates the subtleness of deeper meaning, the unsaid, nuance, etc. (Žižek, 2019a).

So, what would be transmitted between digitally neura-linked actors then? Here, Urban's example is a telling one: it would concern the neuropsychological realm, of affect. Hence, instead of the aforesaid simplification of thought into linguistic categories, would we not simply see the same translation and reduction of thoughts into the limited vocabulary of neuropsychology? We would have to be content with the following options: 'seeking, rage, fear, lust, care, grief (...) and play', which, according to Jaak Panksepp, map out the entire affective realm (which are allegedly all concentrated in ancient subcortical regions of all mammalian brains) (Panksepp, 2005). Would we then not be justified to cry out *the horror!*, to remain within the confines of the aforementioned example of Urban's? This is how I would understand Žižek's argument that devices such as Neuralink are signalling the entry into a post-human era and that this 'may spell [an] end to humanity as we know it' (Žižek, 2019b).

The digital thus risks us no longer being children of Logos, and instead becoming nodes in the transmission of neuropsychological codes. So, yes, while I would agree that we are already cyborgs in the sense that Elon Musk notes vis-à-vis phones already being practically part of our body, we are also more cyborgs in a more profound sense in the psychological fantasies of digital pundits and venture capitalists, who seek to reduce the human from a speaking being to a mere functional position in the informational network. This might be where the very subject who is driven or propelled to speak, to address another subject (perhaps precisely because there is something which cannot be said?) will be replaced by an avatar, a virtual psychological animal, who communicates with other avatars or the network itself.

However, on the other hand it is also important to stress, if this were not clear already, that Logos, as such, always already concerned virtualisation, and, hence, that the virtual did not only come into being with digital technologies, coding and algorithms. This is because, as speaking beings, we always already made present that which was not present as such: through language we open up a virtual space in which we can symbolise the not-now and the not-here. Moreover, as Jacques Derrida put it, by speaking we are already *tele* (removed) from ourselves (Derrida, Stiegler, & Bajorek, 2002): we turn ourselves into others, avatars if you wish, about whom we speak, and whom are spoken about by others. One could even go as far to say that, as a consequence of language, we are always in a way outsourcing our lives, in that we live our lives through and in language. Technology can be said to make this outsourcing more explicit and bring it into the open: if one could argue that we let language do the thinking and the knowing,[6] then with respect to writing and later printing, it is clear that we handed over the task of thinking, knowing and remembering to these technologies. Digital technologies should thus be understood in terms of this genealogy, but technological pundits themselves often fail to understand this history. See, for example, Tim Urban's point on Neuralink:

> This flow of information between your brain and the outside world would be so effortless, it would feel similar to the thinking that goes on in your head today.
>
> *(Urban, 2017)*

In response to Urban, I would argue that thinking never went on in our head, but rather always took place in Logos. Hence, what I am claiming that Musk and others of his ilk precisely misunderstand is human beings' desire to do things without effort, which technologies respond to and try to make use of. The issue of outsourcing the things we do (or think we do) to Logos and technology, could be seen as something which traditionally opened up a subjective space: it freed up the hands of the subject by letting Logos do the thinking and letting technology perform the labour. It is here that the issue could become, is digital technology, by stepping into this tradition, not also stepping over it? That is to say, the question is, as I will consider in greater detail later in the book (see especially Chapter 8), will digital technology eventually not lead to the closing down of the non-engaged subjective sphere (as a consequence of the freed-up subject having outsourced its daily tasks and chores) precisely by drawing this outside sphere into the dynamics of technology and, in turn, expropriating it? Consider here the musings of Tim Urban on the future possibilities engendered by brain-machine interfaces such as Neuralink:

> You'll think about wanting coffee and the coffee maker will get that going. As you head to the fridge the door will open and after getting what you need it'll close as you walk away. When it's time for bed, you'll decide you want the heat turned down and the lights turned off, and those systems will feel you make that decision and adjust themselves.
> *(Urban, 2017)*

Apropos Urban's above point, one could argue that technology used to secure a distance from the world, in that you were no longer obliged to forage or hunt in the meadows or woods, but today digital technologies appear to annul even the most minimal form of distance: just think of something and it is there. If we lived in such a world, why would one even bother to continue thinking for oneself, if even that could be outsourced; indeed, would a complex system not know better than you whether you needed a coffee or had to go bed? Would such a frictionless existence not lead to the disappearance of the subject however, as every single aspect of it would be outsourced and taken care of technologically?

The tell-tale sign of the death of subjectivity might be precisely the point at which the fantasy of immortality comes in. Just think of Ray Kurzweil, one of the first public figures who claimed that it would become possible to upload your personality into a computer so that one would be immortal. While I will return to this fantasy later in the book, it suffices to say a few words about it now by way of another novelist, this time Simone de Beauvoir, who wrote in her book *All Men Are Mortal* (De Beauvoir, 1992) about a figure who became immortal. Although it is not a particularly good book, the image of the immortal figure she depicts is useful for my purposes here: the main protagonist, having seen and experienced everything without needing to wage his time or his life anymore, sinks into a deep and profound lethargy. One is reminded of Lacan's aforementioned point that one needs the assurance that one is going to die in order to be able to cope with the comedy of life.

Towards a psy-critique of dangerous fantasies

The aforementioned theme of immortality also appears in Musk's public statements, albeit that it takes on an element of horror and is situated on the side of the machines.

> If one company or small group of people manages to develop god-like superintelligence, they could take over the world. (...) At least when there's an evil dictator, that human is going to die. But for an AI, there will be no death – it would live forever. And then you would have an immortal dictator from which we could never escape.
>
> *(cited in: Thompson, 2018)*

It is both astonishing and frightening (this is perhaps the true horror) that fantasies such as those expressed by Elon Musk above (to be haunted by a monster you cannot kill) play such a central role in the designing and modelling of the world where we all (are going to) live in? One could be tempted here to call the psychoanalysts in again. Consider Elon Musk's solution to his nightmare:

> AI is definitely going to vastly surpass human abilities. To the degree that it is linked to human will, particularly the sum of a large number of humans, it would be an outcome that is desired by a large number of humans, because it would be a function of their will.
>
> *(cited in: Urban, 2017)*

Hence, the whole idea of Neuralink is to link people directly to AI, so that the ultimate direction that AI takes will be steered and controlled by people themselves, or, in Tim Urban's words: AI "made by the people, for the people". Elon Musk also speaks of the need to democratise AI:

> Essentially, if everyone's from planet Krypton, that's great. But if only one of them is Superman and Superman also has the personality of Hitler, then we've got a problem.
>
> *(cited in: Urban, 2017)*

One should not be distracted here by the rather infantile and fantasmatic character of Musk's utterance or the idea that this is just Musk trying to make his ingenuous thoughts and plans palatable to a wider audience. Indeed, what one should not miss here is the fact that Musk is actually not pleading to bring AI under democratic or political control, but, rather, he is claiming that by linking humans up to the digital sphere, AI itself would become a function of the aggregated human will. In short: AI itself would be democracy in action, that is, that democracy would be embodied in technology. However, paradoxically, would this not culminate in the outsourcing of democracy, in that people would be left to lean back, relax, and enjoy themselves? At the very least, we should always be wary when told to relax, because in the digital age, it is precisely then that we are most controlled, steered, and nudged via all kinds of algorithms.

The crux of this argument in this book will be that this de-politicisation of subjectivity intertwined with an unprecedented commodification of subjectivity and sociality leans on certain neuropsychological theories and models of the human being. And while I would not hesitate to call these models fantasies, I would go a step further yet still and describe them as dangerous fantasies, due to the fact that they fuel a technology that is capable of changing both the face of humanity and the world. This would not be the kind of horror one experiences when a fantasy becomes a reality, but, rather, it would be more accurately understood as the horror of a fantasy becoming virtual.

If the task ahead of us is thus to formulate a psy-critique of the digital, then, as already noted, the recurring question in the book will be whether the critical form of psychoanalysis that informs the analysis presented in the book can serve as an alternative to the prevailing mode of the digital that is based on 'bad psychology' (bad in the sense that it does not depict humans as they are, but, rather, reproduces a fantasmatic construction that fits the prevailing contemporary political-economical model). Is my contention then that we need forms of AI that are based on a better version of psychology, or, for that matter, on psychoanalytic insights? Indeed, again, at first glance, psychoanalysis would appear to be fertile conceptual territory for technology and AI developers. Consider the musings of Tim Urban on what it would mean when Neuralink connects me neuro-directly with other people:

> I asked Elon a question that pops into everyone's mind when they first hear about thought communication:
> "So, um, will everyone be able to know what I'm thinking?"
> He assured me they would not. "People won't be able to read your thoughts—you would have to will it. If you don't will it, it doesn't happen. Just like if you don't will your mouth to talk, it doesn't talk." Phew.
> *(Urban, 2017)*

At the very least, psychoanalysis could bring in the insight that people can wish for something without really wishing it, as best exemplified in the Freudian slip of the tongue, where a person can betray what he or she is thinking, without actually wanting to give it away to other people. Could this insight in and of itself not inspire AI-developers to design additional features? Hence, could psychoanalysis, or, for that matter, any alternative theory or model of the human being, be used to devise alternative forms of AI or other technologies? Or, alternatively, should we uphold the idea that (inter)subjectivity will not be digitalised? While this question will necessarily rear its head at various points in the book, it is perhaps a superfluous question. That is to say, will we be not eventually be overtaken, not by virtue of the end of humanity as Musk and others fear, but, rather, as a result of the *digital death drive* pushing humanity to its digital 'undeath'? One is reminded, here, of Slavoj Žižek's explanation about how the Freudian death drive has nothing to do with craving a return to the inorganic absence of any life-tension, but rather:

> The paradox of the Freudian 'death drive' is (...) that it is Freud's name for its very opposite, for the way immortality appears within psychoanalysis, for an uncanny excess of life, for an 'undead' urge which persists beyond the (biological) cycle of life and death ... The ultimate lesson of psychoanalysis is that human life is never 'just life': humans are not simply alive, they are possessed by the strange drive to enjoy life in excess, passionately attached to a surplus which sticks out and derails the ordinary run of things.
> *(Žižek, 2006, p. 62)*

Being human is thus always necessarily related to the limit of the unhuman, a zero-level of subjectivity from whence human subjectivity is necessarily constructed. From this, the question becomes, is this external vantage point now not also on the verge of being incorporated into digital networks? This is the digital death drive, which entails the end of humanity, the end of humanity as we know it. In light of this, the true question might eventually become: will our non-humanity, or better yet still, our un-humanity end up being digitalisable or not?

This question serves to guide the development of the next chapters. The first of these addresses the historical lineage of the digital turn, by examining some of the seminal writers that constitute the backbone of extant digital technologies. Next, the book turns to the theme of education, which allows for closer scrutiny of the vicissitudes of subjectivity and sociality under digitalisation. Across all these chapters, I will scrutinise the contribution of neuropsy-theories and models to the digital death drive, and examine what, if any, role that critical psychoanalysis can play. The final chapter reiterates the latter theme, addressing the quasi-algorithmic tendencies in Freud, but above all in Lacan, in order to engage in the far from straightforward endeavour of imagining the end of the world.

Notes

1 If this appears to be the ultimate psychoanalytic example, then perhaps a more basic one would be to say that *I cannot imagine myself dead*. One could argue that, while imagining one's own death is the very condition to have a life as such, the problem in the meantime is that, according to Freud, one actually cannot imagine one's own death (Freud, [1915]1957). I will return to this issue later in the chapter.
2 Here, of course, I am alluding to the term coined by Louis Althusser (1971), see also further in this book.
3 Regarding the centrality of the Armageddon theme within digitalization, see also my discussion on Norbert Wiener and his understanding of entropy in the next chapter.

4 "We will know less and less what is a human being" (Saramago, 2008).
5 Freud wrote in his Group Psychology and the Analysis of the Ego (Freud, [1921]1955) that the identification of each group member with the leader allowed for the creation of a shared and, more or less, stable social reality. At the very least, in this virtual age, our social reality is less and less stable and less and less shared. For more on the effects of the shifts from symbolic forms of identification to imaginary forms of identification, see Chapter 7.
6 Consider how Lacan replaces 'I think' with 'it thinks' (Lacan, 1977, pp. 35–36): this might be recognisable for anyone doing philosophy or thinking as such: you let the concepts, the theories and the models do the hard work of thinking.

References

Althusser, L. (1971). Ideology and ideological state apparatuses (notes towards an investigation) (B. Brewster, Trans.). In *Lenin and Philosophy and Other Essays* (pp. 127–186). London: New Left Books.

De Beauvoir, S. (1992). *All men are mortal: A novel*. New Yorik: WW Norton & Company.

Derrida, J., Stiegler, B., & Bajorek, J. (2002). *Echographies of television*. Cambridge: Polity Press.

Dowd, M. (2017, April). Elon Musk's billion-dollar crusade to stop the A.I. apocalypse. *Vanity Fair*. Retrieved from https://www.vanityfair.com/news/2017/03/elon-musk-billion-dollar-crusade-to-stop-ai-space-x

Freud, S. ([1915]1957). Thoughts for the times on war and death. In J. Strachey (Ed.), *The standard edition of the complete psychological works of Sigmund Freud: Vol. XIV* (pp. 273–300). London: Hogarth Press.

Freud, S. ([1921]1955). Group psychology and the analysis of the ego. In J. Strachey (Ed.), *The standard edition of the complete psychological works of Sigmund Freud: Vol. XVIII* (pp. 67–143). London: Hogarth Press.

Illing, S. (2017, Octubre, 9). Persuasive proof that America is full of racist and selfish people. What millions of Google searches reveal about our national psyche. Retrieved from https://www.vox.com/conversations/2017/6/13/15768622/facebook-social-media-seth-stephens-davidowitz-everybody-lies

Lacan, J. (1966). *Ecrits*. Paris: Editions du Seuil.

Lacan, J. (1977). *The four fundamental concepts of psychoanalysis* (A. Sheridan, Trans.). London: Hogarth Press.

Lacan, J. (1981). La mort est du domaine de la foi. Conférence à Louvain, le 13 octobre 1972. *Quarto*, 3, 5–20. Retrieved from http://aejcpp.free.fr/lacan/1972-10-13.htm

Lacan, J. (2007). *Ecrits: The first complete edition in English* (B. Fink, Trans.). New York: Norton.

Muoio, D. (2017, Marzo 27). Elon Musk has launched a company that hopes to link your brain to a computer. *Business Insider UK*. Retrieved from http://uk.businessinsider.com/elon-musk-neuralink-connect-brains-computer-neural-lace-2017-3?r=US&IR=T

Panksepp, J. (2005). Affective consciousness: Core emotional feelings in animals and humans. *Consciousness and Cognition*, 14(1), 30–80.

Pessoa, F. (1972). *Obra Poética*. Rio de Janeiro: Aguilar Editóra.

Rimbaud, A. (1954). *Oeuvres completes*. Paris: Gallimard.

Saramago, J. (2008). *Death with interruptions*. London: Harvill Secker.

Spence, S. (2019). The birth of AI nationalism. *New Statesman*. Retrieved from https://www.newstatesman.com/science-tech/2019/04/birth-ai-nationalism

Stephens-Davidowitz, S. (2017). *Everybody lies: Big data, new data, and what the internet can tell us about who we really are*. New York: HarperCollins.
Thompson, C. (2018). Elon Musk warns that creation of 'god-like' AI could doom mankind to an eternity of robot dictatorship. *Insider*. Retrieved from https://www.businessinsider.nl/elon-musk-says-ai-could-lead-to-robot-dictator-2018-4?international=true&r=US
Urban, T. (2017). Neuralink and the brain's magical future. *Whait But Why*. Retrieved from https://waitbutwhy.com/2017/04/neuralink.html
Vance, A. (2015). *Elon Musk: Tesla, SpaceX, and the Quest for a Fantastic Future*. New York: Harper Collins.
Žižek, S. (2006). *The parallax view*. Cambridge, MA: MIT Press.
Žižek, S. (2019a). The digital police state: Fichte's revenge on Hegel. *Journal of Philosophical Investigations*, *13*(28), 1–19.
Žižek, S. (2019b). Mind-reading AI may spell end to humanity as we know it, but not because it will enslave us. *RT*. Retrieved from https://www.rt.com/news/468228-mind-reading-computer-humanity-zizek/

PART 2
Learning machines
Digitalisation and its psy-antecedents

2
ALAN TURING, ARTIFICIAL INTELLIGENCE, AND ITS PSY-FANTASIES

Introduction: will the signature of life become digitalised?

In 1931 Vladimir Jankélévitch wrote:

> With a perfect machine there never really are any deceptions, but there are also never any surprises. There are none of the failures but also none of the miracles that are, in a way, the signature of life.
>
> (Jankélévitch, 2015, p. 10)

It is precisely this that was subverted by Alan Turing in his ground-breaking and fecund work, which was so seminal to the development of digital technology and AI. Namely, in his famous essay "Computing Machinery and Intelligence (1950)", Turing argued that the question "can machine think?" cannot lead anywhere, and thus should be replaced by another question: could a machine successfully deceive a human opponent into making him or her believe that it is human? Or to put it in Jankélévitch's terms (to whom Alan Turing did not refer), a machine does not have to possess 'the signature of life', but, rather, only has to convincingly pose as if it does. Hence, contra Jankélévitch, Turing believed that deception and surprise do lie within the reach of the machine. It is in this context that Turing conceived of his notorious 'imitation game', the best known version of which features a person engaging with an opponent (either another human or a machine) via typescript, so that they cannot see his or her interlocutor: at the end of the conversation the person is asked whether they were conversing with a human or a computer.

In so doing, Turing can be said to have deconstructed the 'signature of life', or, alternatively, paraphrasing Fernando Pessoa's famous words which I referred to in Chapter 1:[1] *what do I know of what an intelligent machine would be, I who don't know what human intelligence* is. While this is a move that one may endorse, my basic argument in this chapter is that Turing refrains from fully thinking through the aspect of deception as such; for if deception can be said to constitute the very signature of life, then should the imitation game not be based on the redoubling of this: should the challenge for the machine not be to deceive the human opponent into believing that it is capable of deception?

However, prior to conducting a close reading of Turing's essay, and before we get lost in the various redoublings, let me first spell out the stakes of the debate by stating more explicitly the issue that is raised by Jankélévitch. Simply put, the key issue is: *will the human become digitalised?* In this respect, it is instructive to recall Elon Musk's Neuralink project that I discussed in the previous chapter, which aimed to connect the human to the digital. This immediately raises the question: can all things human be digitalised? That is to say, if one dreams of aligning the human and the machine, then the central issue would appear to be: if I as a human can download things directly into my brain, then what about the reverse movement: can I myself be uploaded into the digital realm? This question then rapidly raises a further one, namely: is it possible to completely digitalise a human being? Are all the things we consider as the core of our being (our personality, our thoughts, our feelings, and so on) translatable into the digital? Having said this, can we even be sure of what this core is, or what the signature of human life is? Is it not precisely here that one invariably regresses into seeing the psychological realm as that which can be considered to be untranslatable into the digital? Or, to put this argument another way, is there simply too much richness in human psychology for the digital realm to handle? Such thinking is emblematic of the common idea that digital technologies are grounded in a mechanistic and reductionist perspective far removed from the creative, unpredictable, and even twisted configurations of the human mind.

However, this is what David Bates rightfully argued against in his proposal to develop a critical history of automaticity. For Bates, criticising automaticity is not the point, as plasticity and even pathology were rapidly incorporated into the theories and technologies that underpinned automatisation. As he writes:

> The human brain was understood to be a special kind of genuinely open system that determined itself yet was also capable of defying its own automaticity in acts of genuine creativity.
>
> *(Bates, 2016, p. 198)*

At the very least, digital technology can thus be said to have started out from the human factor, if not always already from human psychology. In fact, the rationale has always been to make the technology work in conjunction with the human factor, that is, to incorporate human psychology within the economy of the machine.

However, here, of course, the following question is immediately raised: does digital technology work because its theoreticians and designers rightfully understood the psychology of the human? In other words, must we contend with the fact that cyberneticists, for example, who put forward an open model of the human (as plastic, inventive and creative), developed and used a model that accurately described the human being? From here, one could proceed to praise also those designers who do not solely rely on simple psychological models, but, rather, also take into account the darker aspects of human psychology, namely, symptomatology and psychopathology. It is precisely the latter approach that we encounter in the history of cybernetics, for, as David Bates writes, the early cyberneticists considered intelligence to be the consequence of disorganisation and unpredictability, or even potentially as a pathological disorder that allowed for leaps of genius (Bates, 2016, p. 202).

However, it is precisely here that psychological discourses are quickly traded in for ostensibly more tangible ones: neurobiological and neuropsychological frameworks. Indeed, when one conceives of pathology as forming the basis for intelligence, then is the next logical step not to understand this as some kind of material glitch in the brain? This is precisely what the history of the development of digital technology indicates. In other words, while the starting point for Turing, Wiener, McCullough, and others was psychology, ultimately, they all sought to ground this in neurobiology. Hence, rather than there being *too much psychology for the digital*, what we have here instead is neurobiology or 'material reality' neatly projected onto technology. If we slide from psychology to neurobiology, then the human and the technological appear to be more straightforward to align. It is here that the digital and technological aspects become naturalised as quasi-biological realities. The fact that this has become the predominant form of thought today should truly surprise us. For, at our historical juncture where we are ever more dwelling in virtual spaces, and hence more than ever before witnessing the power and the reach of the symbolic order (with only two symbols, I and O, immense virtual and real realities are structured), we nevertheless are more inclined to take recourse to ostensibly materialist, naturalising, and essentialist explanations.

This raises a critical question: while the neurobiological turn (hypothetically) allows for the full translation of the 'signature of life' into the digital realm, is there not in the process of the symbolic folding over into the virtual a form of excess, a surplus, a too muchness?

Given this, rather than seeking to identify precisely this "too much for the digital" (qua psychological/psychologised *too muchness* that resists digitalisation), should we not instead consider that there is "too much *of/within* the digital realm itself?" Indeed, it is evident that the issue of digitalisation compels us to think about the signature of life, the signature of intelligence, and that which can be said to be specific to human subjectivity up to the point where this all becomes a blur. In this respect, perhaps a closer look at Alan Turing's imitation game can help us to see things more clearly, more specifically, to see why this aforesaid blurring is inevitable and structural.

Turing's imitation game as a foundational fantasy

To begin with, it is interesting to note that Alan Turing himself put forward an argument that went against the aforementioned tendency, in matters of digitality, to naturalise and essentialise both the human and the machine itself. David Bates writes that when Turing proposed an analogy between the computer and the brain, he was nevertheless arguing that the operation of the digital computer was governed by its logical organisation rather than its physical organisation. For example, Turing denounced the argument that human thinking could be narrowed down to neuro-electrical phenomena that could subsequently be linked to machines using electricity:

> The feature of using electricity is thus seen to be only a very superficial similarity. If we wish to find such similarities we should look rather for mathematical analogies of function.
>
> *(Turing, 1950, p. 439)*

Ultimately, Bates writes, for Turing the physical substrate of the machine was irrelevant to its logical operation (Bates, 2016, p. 206). Hence, can one not say in a similar vein that, if the human is a machine, then he is a machine of logic, a machine that works according to the logic of Logos.[2] From this, should we then proceed to argue that *the physical substrate of the human is irrelevant to its logical operation?* In so doing, perhaps we can reinterpret the dream of Turing and cyberneticists to design digital intelligence in accordance with the leaps of human intelligence, which themselves were the result of mental disorganisation or pathological disorder. That is to say, does this not mean that the surplus, the pathological (and its potential consequences), must not be looked for in the physical substrate, but, rather, in the operations of logic itself?

It is precisely here that we can situate the fundamental problem of the hegemonic mainstream psy-sciences, which is that it has trouble thinking about the pathological in psychological terms: they have always sought the psychopathological within a different domain than the psyche itself. More specifically, the pathological is ordinarily understood as either a mechanical or chemical breakdown (relating to the inner or outer world), or as a cognitive structure that does not (or no longer) adapt to external reality. Hence, it never considers the pathological as residing within the level of the psyche itself. Of course, one could object here that the psyche is but the mere relationship between the inner and outside world (to be clear, this is also Freud's first conception of the subject), and so if there is something wrong, then this is due to a glitch in either the somatic or the cognitive relation to the inner or outer world. However, what psychology cannot consider is that the relationship of the subject itself to the inner or outside world is by definition something which is pathological, since it can be said to be characterised, in the first place, by primal maladjustment. Or, phrased otherwise, given that the human being relates to the inner or outer world via language, that is, via a representational medium, it no longer has a direct relation to both these worlds. It is in this sense that the human can be said to relate to both the inner and outer worlds in a primordially twisted, and thus maladapted, way: *I am poorly adapted, therefore I am*. It is precisely because our relation to the world is mediated through language, that there cannot be a full closure of our relationship with the inner or outer worlds. In Lacanian terms, there is no Other of the Other, that is, there is no signifier that could ensure the final closure of meaning. Hence, the relation of the speaking being to reality is one which is marked by failure, by a gap that is constitutive of subjectivity. Of course, all of this is in stark contrast to mainstream psychological approaches that consider poor adaptation not as something primordial and constitutive of subjectivity, but, rather, as something bio-cognitive, which, in turn, can be overcome.

If the psy-sciences thus are characterised by a 'vulgar materialism', then Turing's initial starting point in devising intelligent machines was to transcend the physical substrate and attend to the logical operations themselves. However, does the central question not then become the following: can the internal logic of the human as the speaking being be considered in terms of the same logic as the algebraic machine? Can one truly say that Turing's machine could function, or, perhaps better yet, malfunction, in the same way as the human subject? To put it differently yet: did Turing have a better and truer psychology to implement when constructing intelligent machines?

However, this is where things get even more complicated, due to the fact that Turing, in his seminal essay, leaves behind this very idea to construct a machine that would behave *as a human*. He ultimately considered the question of "can a machine think?" to be an unproductive one, and thus replaced it with the question: could a machine act *as if it were a human in such a way that deceived a real human into thinking it were human*?

At this juncture, it is perhaps useful to point out that the Turing test, although generally considered to be a key seminal text within the field of AI, is not believed to be of much relevance today. Marvin Minsky, himself a key figure in the development of AI (see also Chapter 3) purports that the Turing test is above all a joke, arguing that Turing himself would not have taken the test seriously (Danaylov, 2013). In the same vein, Dylan Evans (2001) writes that AI research proceeds with very little reference to Turing. Moreover, Evans argues that the main predicament today does not concern us facing an interlocutor without knowing whether it is a computer or a program, but, rather, pertains to us leading our on/offline lives without realising that it is all taking place within a computerised 'intelligent' environment. In other words, we are largely unaware that our (inter)subjectivity is shaped and controlled by intelligent machinery. Or, as Timothy Snyder notes, the efficiency of today's digital governance is not based on machines posing as human agents, but, rather, on silent and invisible bots and algorithms (Snyder, 2019). What we do on the internet and in virtual environments is, above all else, based on everything going smoothly so that we do not know how we are being guided, nudged, and steered. From this perspective, then, the computer is not deceptively posing as a human, it is simply hidden and deceiving us (i.e. luring us into doing and pursuing things, whilst making us believe that we wanted or desired them).

Apropos various authors' claims that Turing's imitation game is no longer relevant and only an amusing joke, should we not consider the fact that in psychoanalysis jokes are always to be taken seriously and warrant closer scrutiny? As such, Turing's rejection of the question "can machines think?" signals that Turing himself understood that there is no science capable of conclusively positing what a human is. It is in this respect that Turing can be said to have rejected a psychologised approach to 'the signature of life'. Hence, if in a way Turing also thought that there was *too much human* for the digital to copy or replicate, then this was not due to some excess, but, rather, due to a lack: a lack in our knowledge about what exactly the signature of life is. It is here that Turing's creative move began, which was to propose: can a machine successfully mimic a human so that a human could be fooled by it? Let us not devise a humanlike machine, but, rather, a machine which could convincingly mimic a human being. The judge of this could not be a scientific expert but could only be you and me in our capacity as non-experts.

Many commentators on Turing's imitation game miss this central point. Illustrative, in this respect, is Ben Goertzel's claim that the Turing test is not relevant for AI: he calls the actual attempts to create such AI: "theatrical constructs, which generate responses that simulate understanding, but don't actually understand what they're talking about" (Goertzel, 2014). Is Goertzel implying here that 'really existing AI' either does or would be able one day to truly understand the human being? In Turing's initial proposition this would not make sense, in that he was not attempting to design an AI which would truly understand humans, but, rather, to create an AI that would make human beings feel like they were understood. Does this not come close to what Evans and Snyder are concerned with: the whole array of AI bots and such like which we do not even notice? We do not notice them precisely because of how well they understand us, which means that they can stay under the radar while, simultaneously, nudging and steering us. Perhaps this is the contemporary Turing test: whether machines can pass unnoticed and create an environment which we consider to be normal, natural, and a true fit for humans; that is to say, an environment where the things we are offered to do and pursue appear to derive from our own desires.

At the very least, I would argue that Turing's attempt to bypass an essentialist approach (to devise computers who actually are humanlike) and instead opt to design computers that could successfully fool humans into thinking that they are human, raises manifold questions and issues which hitherto have been only partially addressed. Resultantly, what I aim to demonstrate in this chapter is that, even if on a practical level, Turing's imitation game has not been directly guiding AI development, one could argue that rather than it being a frivolous idea that accompanies the development of bots and data governance, it is, in fact, a truly founding fantasy of the AI field. No doubt, Turing's essay is something of a rollercoaster, with manifold twists and turns that appear at times irrelevant, and thus it is worthwhile to conduct a careful reading of the text to discern why this text is so central to the development of AI.

Deception, the woman, and the sex of C

In 'Computing Machinery and Intelligence', Turing introduced his famous test by means of another test that involved only humans. This first test concerned the determination of the sex of two persons with whom communication was solely conducted via messages. The situation is as follows: man A and woman B answer questions from a third person C who cannot see or hear A or B. C has to decide the sex of A. As Turing writes: "It is A's object in the game to try and cause C to make the wrong identification" (Turing, 1950, pp. 433–434). Various interpretations have been made which frame this as an issue of 'gender', for example, by focusing on the situation of a man posing as a woman. However, what is seldom commented on is the fact that the actual imitation game itself (opposing a human person to a computer) was preceded by a variant of the first test: namely, the A figure (the male) is substituted for a computer. Here, we have a rather intriguing situation of *a machine posing as a man posing as a woman*. How to understand this? Does this not primarily mean that posing and even deceiving is a constituent element of human subjectivity? That is to say, a human is not simply a human; rather, we always have to play, show, and convince others, and hence ourselves, that we are human. Being human thus involves an element of deceit, which, as Turing's first scenarios showed, concerns the centrality of being designated as a member of a specific sex.[3] It is within this double scheme of deceit and sex that Turing based his quest to develop intelligent machinery.

Concerning the first element, the element of deceit, it can be noted that today, in the realm of digital virtuality, humans being deceived appears to be par for the course: we are bombarded with spam or phishing emails, lured by clickbait, and nudged to buy this or that or to vote for this or that. Turing's deceiving machine has thus become ubiquitous. However, at the same time we are also told that we ourselves cannot deceive the machine, for, so the argument goes, Big Data knows our innermost thoughts up to and including our innermost desires. As Brian Brackeen, CEO of Kairos, a facial recognition company, said in an interview: "AI can tell you anything about anyone with enough data" (cited in Levin, 2017). And if one wishes to believe research from Michal Kosinski and Yilun Wang, then AI is capable of accurately guessing whether people are gay or straight, based on photos of their faces (Wang & Kosinski, 2018). Simply put, AI has seemingly out-deceived humans, in that humans have now allegedly become as transparent as glass, denuded of our deceiving veils. This brings us back to Turing's initial game that featured a man posing as a woman.

Hence, concerning the second (more obscured) element of the Turing constellation, the element of sex, the key question would appear to be: leaving aside Turing's well-known biography, why does AI need to start from the male-female opposition? Does this not mean that thinking (i.e. what Turing set out with was the question of whether machines can think) is centrally related to gender and sexuality? To briefly sketch out this Freudian proposition in a simplified and intuitive way: if thinking uses language, and language is based on pairs of opposites (day/night, here/there, up/down, etc.), then, arguably, the basic pair is male/female, which constitutes the 'signature of life'.[4] At the very least, if the male/female opposition signalled Turing's point of departure, then how can we understand this in relation to the development of AI?

One potentially important point is that Turing placed the male in the deceiving role, and not the woman. Would the reverse situation, that is, a female posing as a male, not have been more in accordance with the psychiatric tradition of understanding the female as the hysterical deceiver (e.g. the hysteric who poses as sick whilst not having an organic disorder, thus trying to deceive the male doctor)? However, Turing's reversal, that is, placing the male in the deceiver's role, might point to the fact that, although Freud's central enigma was *Was will das Weib?* (what do women want?), this does not mean that being male is a comparatively unproblematic and straightforward issue. In other words, even though the male can be said to be a categorical being, who can anchor his being in the fact that he is the possessor of the phallus, his being a man is inevitably linked to the enigma of the woman. Or, phrased otherwise, the fact that men once asked in all seriousness, can a woman think? above all points to something problematic in male thinking itself: the inability to think that a woman could think or the inability to think of what she thinks about.

At the very least, there are a lot of themes resonating in Turing's intriguing and Romanesque set-up of his imitation game, as he basically introduced the computer into the male/female dichotomy. As the computer initially replaced the male A-figure, the question 'can a machine think'? can be said to shift initially to: "can a computer think as a male who tries to think as a woman?" But, of course, given that Turing already redirected his inquiry away from the question of 'can a machine think'?, the aforementioned question is perhaps better stated as 'can a computer pretend (in communicative exchanges) to be a male who performs (in communicative exchanges) in such a way that makes his gender indeterminable'?[5] Hence, from here, one could ask whether the machine would be a better deceiver, or even, would it be a better psychologist, would it be better in understanding women, precisely because it has no psychology/sexuality in itself?[6] That is, if one will forgive me for putting it in slightly psychologising terms, the male figure A could be bothered or hampered in his imitation by his own questions or doubts concerning gender and sexuality, while the machine would suffer from no such misgivings. Or, alternatively, does one require a body, more specifically, a phallus to be more or less successful in such an endeavour? Here, the crucial question would appear to be, can a computer, based on the binary and categorical logic of the digital, imitate the non-categorical dimension which appears to be at the heart of the distinct logic of human subjectivity? This returns us yet again to the question of whether there is not too much human for the digital? Is there not a fundamental incompatibility between the logic of the digital machine (with its binary logic of 0 and 1) and human logic with its twisted binary of male and female? The latter might constitute the precise reason why Turing's essay rapidly moves away from the male/female opposition. So, we might not only attribute to Turing a creative and fecund move (transcending the deadlock of the question of whether machines can think), but also a founding act of repression. Or, should we put these points together as follows: the creative and fecund move by Turing was to introduce the question *can a machine pose as a human* via the issue of sexual difference, only to then drop and repress it, because keeping it would have blocked the development of 'intelligent machinery'?

In any case, let us not forget that sexual difference for Turing was essentially coupled with the element of deception. However, this should not be merely interpreted in terms of the issue of *performativity,* that is, ostensibly involved with sex and sexuality. Megan Foley, for example, argues that Turing's landmark thought experiment called into question the ontological difference between humans and computers by comparing it to the performative character of sexual difference (Foley, 2014). However, the fact that Turing dropped the sex issue while retaining the issue of deception –remember that Jankélévitch also considered deceit to be a central human issue that could not be replicated by a machine—should prompt us to inquire further into this aspect, before too readily reducing it to the notion of performativity.

I take this issue up further in this chapter, as we still need to deal with the third figure, figure C in Turing's initial set-up, the one who must judge whether a deception has occurred. As aforementioned, this figure is not a scientific expert, but, rather, a layperson, he or she who is genuinely fooled or otherwise. However, remarkably, this figure is itself not assigned sex. Although arguably the sex of C would play a role, certainly in the first versions of the game, as if a man or a computer is mimicking a woman, then surely a male or female interrogator would assess this differently. Having said this, perhaps the sexless nature of the interrogator can be explored from another angle. Timothy Snyder describes 'C' as such:

> Turing proposed the interrogator, C, as an ideal human thinker, but did not tell us enough about C for us to regard C as human. Unlike B and A, who talk about theirs, C does not seem to have a body. Because Turing does not remind us that C has a corporeal existence, we do not think to ask about C's interests.
>
> *(Snyder, 2019)*

However, while Snyder proceeds to state that a (real) human being has the particularities and characteristics of both A, B, and C, I would argue against such a view and ask instead whether this sexless, bodiless C testifies to the very position of the human subject, as that which is positioned between two other sexed and embodied persons (think of Oedipus in this respect)? Hence, C, purely a mind, without a self and sexless, who is caught up in the riddle of *what is a human?* can thus be said to stand for the figure of the human subject itself. Figure A attempts to mimic a woman, while B suffices to just be herself. I would argue that it is only with C that the human figure who ponders, negotiates, and struggles with sex and gender comes into play. Indeed, it is C who is forced to ask themselves: *what would a man or a computer say that a woman would say?* Hence, it is only in this redoubling of perspectives that the true human factor comes to the forefront.

In this way, I think Snyder is right at this point to make mention of Turing's biography:

> Turing was a creature of his sex, as his creation C is not; and he was prey to the revelation of his passions, as C could never be. The British state that Turing served during the Second World War was perfectly capable of killing him when it emerged that he had the normal human quality of the desire for love. Turing lived in a certain sexual imposture, like A; in court he told the truth about himself, like B.
>
> *(Snyder, 2019)*

However, I would reformulate this somewhat: the deceiving (and its redoubling) does not merely relate to how sexuality and sexual identities either can or cannot exist within certain cultures or during specific historical junctures, but, rather, I claim, it is the very base of sexed subjectivity as such. Moreover, and in relation to this, what Turing's figure C shows us is that the default base is the sexless position: if the figure of C stands for the human subject as such, then this means that the latter occupies in the first instance the position of the audience, the position of the interrogator, who actually shares its lack of body and sex with the machine. To put it in simplified terms: to be a man or a woman and to have a body must involve the enunciation: *I am a man or a woman, I have a body*: which means that there is an 'I' that itself transcends sexual difference and the possession of a body.

Hence, with regards to Turing's goal of designing an intelligent machine, the central question is what happens to the C figure when Turing drops the initial sexed situation (in order to, I would argue, be able to develop a machine and the technology)? The first thing to notice here is that the C figure is turned into something more than just a layperson. It is instructive to refer to Isaac Asimov's story 'Evidence' (1946) here, in which the person who must decide whether someone is a human or a machine is a psychologist (Asimov, 1965). Indeed, does the scenario of an interrogator who cannot see his interlocutor not closely resemble the couch configuration in psychoanalysis? Be that as it may, as I argue in the next section, cutting out the sex issue also signals in yet another way the return of psychology (after its initial rejection by Turing when sidestepping the question of *can machines think?*) in regards to the issue of mimicking.

From sexual difference to mimicking, or the return of psychology

Let me first revisit Turing's initial version of the game, which featured a machine taking the place of A, a female B and interrogator C. Would this not have been quite an ordeal for the woman involved? Indeed, C could reach the following possible conclusions: X (the computer) is:

1 a woman.
2 a man posing as a woman.
3 a computer posing as a woman.

If in the first version of the game (with a male posing as a female) C would have wrongfully identified the man as a woman, then this would have turned the woman into a man, as she would have had to acknowledge that a man proved to be better at posing as a woman. However, in the case of a computer joining in, a woman would potentially then be confronted with the fact that a third party considered a machine to be more of a woman than she herself. At the risk of psychologising this again, would this not be the final and most bitter blow to her self-love? At the very least, once again, Turing's imitation game shows us that sexual difference is not so much about gender performativity, but, rather, about sexual difference as caught up in a symbolic opposition, whose logic hits upon an existential issue, namely, the enigma of what it is to be a woman or a man.

However, even though Turing left the initial set-up behind with a woman acting as the opponent of either a man or a machine, one could argue that the existential and sex issues hardly disappear. For example, existential problems clearly return in the various science fiction versions of the imitation game, with machines wanting to be humans, or falsely believing that they are humans. On the other hand, there are countless novels and movies where sexual difference and sexuality are most centrally related to AI. However, even in the so-called theatrical reconstructions of the Turing test (i.e. concrete attempts to play the imitation game), it is obvious that the machine or the programme must be assigned a sex as it has to play either a woman or a man in order to deceive the interrogator. But is it not evident that it is here that various clichés, psychologisms and naturalistic conceptions of womanhood and manhood come into play? That is to say, is this not the very point at which the programmers sat a psychology textbook on gender and identity on their laps whilst coding?

Hence, if Turing's imitation game wanted to sidestep the unresolvable questions (*what is thinking? what is it to be human?*), the elimination of sexual difference that was involved in this move ultimately led to essentialising and even psychologising versions of what it is to be human, which were then mimicked by the machine. Moreover, this is not only the case with respect to the science fiction genre and theatrical versions, but can, I would argue, already be discerned in Turing's seminal essay itself. Let me illustrate this, for starters, by referring to Turing's point that digital computers mimic the things that humans do:

> The idea behind digital computers may be explained by saying that these machines are intended to carry out any operations which could be done by a human computer. The human computer is supposed to be following fixed rules; he has no authority to deviate from them in any detail.
> *(Turing, 1950, p. 436)*

Turing's imitation of a computer mimicking the human boils down to a computer mimicking a human computer. Clearly, by opting for the question, *can machines successfully pose as a human?* the question thus becomes: which human, or better yet still, which model of the human should the machine mimic? The answer to this question is, to begin with, a simple one: the model would appear to be the clerk, or even the obedient clerk, who follows fixed rules. This might, in part, help us explain why digital technologies are so easily aligned in the service of what has been called 'communicative capitalism' (Dean, 2005). Moreover, Turing clearly sought to ground the model of the human that the machine would mimic in simplified psychologies. For example, when Turing engages with a range of counterarguments that defy that a computer could successfully be humanlike, he evokes the 'argument of consciousness' as follows:

> This argument is very, well expressed in Professor Jefferson's Lister Oration for 1949, from which I quote. "Not until a machine can write a sonnet or compose a concerto because of thoughts and emotions felt, and not by the chance fall of symbols, could we agree that machine equals brain-that is, not only write it but know that it had written it. No mechanism could feel (and not merely artificially signal, an easy contrivance) pleasure at its successes, grief when its valves fuse, be warmed by flattery, be made miserable by its mistakes, be charmed by sex, be angry or depressed when it cannot get what it wants."
> *(Turing, 1950, pp. 445–446)*

Ultimately, even though Turing countered this with the argument that the computer did not have to be humanlike, but, rather, only had to be successful in mimicking and thus deceiving the human, eventually, the initial models and psychologies (of what the human ostensibly is) come into focus and come to define what the computer should mimic. Hence, can we not oppose Geoffrey Jefferson's eulogy on the human with the more prosaic lessons of psychoanalysis about human beings who, for example, can be made miserable by sex, be angry, or depressed when they get what they want, and repeat the same mistakes time after time? At the very least, what is the computer expected to mimic here? Not the human itself, but the psychological models! The question here is whether Turing—and hence other AI-developers who followed in his footsteps—was not inclined to orient digital computers to simplified psychologies, rather than to other more sophisticated, or, at the very least, more twisted, conceptualisations of human beings?

To discern where Turing's reliance on unidimensional mainstream psychologies led to, consider how Turing, when countering 'the argument from various disabilities', discussed how you could never make machines 'enjoy strawberries and cream':

> The inability to enjoy strawberries and cream may have struck the reader as frivolous. Possibly a machine might be made to enjoy this delicious dish, but any attempt to make one do so would be idiotic. What is important about this disability is that it contributes to some of the other disabilities, e.g., to the difficulty of the same kind of friendliness occurring between man and machine as between white man and white man, or between black man and black man.
>
> *(Turing, 1950, p. 448)*

Is one not immediately struck by how Turing implicitly rejects the idea that white can go together with black. Are we to surmise racist motives here that are possibly even mixed in with sexual ones (see, e.g., Kevorkian, 2006; Leavitt, 2006)? However, is the key to this passage not, in fact, the issue of pairing? That is, the underlying question is whether strawberries and cream naturally fit with each other, or can men fit in with other men, and God forbid, can a white man fit in with a black man? Here, one could take recourse to a psychoanalytic and psycho-biographic interpretation and link this passage to Turing's own sexuality. However, perhaps we can restrict ourselves to the observation that what Turing is haunted by here is the Freudian 'beyond the pleasure principle' or Jacques Lacan's notion of 'jouissance'. In short, 'jouissance' is that dimension that only opens up as the human being becomes a speaking-being; it is jouissance which explains why humans are not merely driven by instincts, but, rather, by drives and desires which escape them and which he or she can never 'subjectify'. Jouissance, then, is that which lies on the other side for human beings. Consider in this respect the French term for orgasm, *la petite mort* (the little death), which according to Jacques Lacan, shows that the subject cannot coincide with enjoyment, as it is in enjoyment that the subject fades (see, e.g., Lacan, 2004, class given on May 29, 1963). As such, jouissance is that which lies outside the subject, the I who enjoys is always the other. Moreover, it is here that this other is often fleshed out into an external figure. Two well-known figures are traditionally situated here: the figure of the Woman and the figure of the Black, who are both attributed as possessing this strange jouissance that the subject itself is exempt from. In this respect, if Turing's main idea was to make a machine that would deceive us into thinking that it was human, is this not precisely the same issue which is at stake with the figures of the Woman and the Black? That is: are the Woman and the Black not also denied of their humanity, whilst, simultaneously, being denounced as deceivers. Hence, in Turing's essay a rather strange line-up presents itself behind the scenes of the imitation game: the computer, the Woman and the Black, all trying to convince (or deceive) us that they are human?

However, most clearly, the figure of the Black stays behind the scenes and the Woman only makes a short appearance on Turing's stage. When the machine is introduced, the complex, twisted, paradoxical subjective constellation of the sexualised human being who is confronted with their Otherness is discarded. Arguably, Turing needed to expel all of this in order to be able to devise of the machine. The questions of *what it is to be a woman? What is it to be a man? What is it to be a human?* All had to be repressed in order for Turing to get the development of AI moving. Perhaps it could be argued here that this is where the repressed cannot but return, and that it was simply inevitable that we end up with a 'racist, fascist, xenophobic, misogynistic, intelligent machine' as Kenneth Lim (2017) put it in his article in *The Business Times* which referred to computer programmes such as 'COMPAS' (predicting recidivism with convicted persons) and chatbots, such as Twitter's 'Tay', which turned out to be racist and fascist. However, the main argument voiced in this article is that all of this is ultimately down to human psychology. As the philosopher Abelard Podgorski exclaims:

> (…) it's very natural for people to identify in-groups and out-groups, and to treat them differently, and that stereotyping is part and parcel with very basic operations of the human mind. This is, I think, very relevant to the issue of algorithmic bias … We don't normally think of ourselves this way, but our thought processes are themselves basically algorithms responding to inputs and producing outputs, and they're subject to the very same failure modes as the ones we've seen in algorithms.
>
> *(cited in: Lim, 2017)*

I'm not a racist but… my algorithmic thought processes are?! It's the psychology, stupid!? In contrast to this, I would argue, no, it is the technology that is grounded in psychology! This can clearly be observed with Alan Turing, who after trading the question 'can a machine think'? for 'can a machine successfully pose as a human', then found himself confronted with the questions 'What is it to be a woman? What is it to be a man? What is it to be a human'?, which led to him discarding these and taking recourse to psychologising technology. Alan Turing can thus be said to become psychologistic at the very moment that he assumes that we know very well what humans are, and moreover, opts to use this knowledge in order to raise intelligent machines:

> Instead of trying to produce a programme to simulate the adult mind, why not rather try to produce one which simulates the child's? If this were then subjected to an appropriate course of education one would obtain the adult brain. Presumably the child brain is something like a notebook as one buys it from the stationer's. Rather little mechanism, and lots of blank sheets. (Mechanism and writing are from our point of view almost synonymous.)

> Our hope is that there is so little mechanism in the child brain that something like it can be easily programmed. The amount of work in the education we can assume, as a first approximation, to be much the same as for the human child.
>
> *(Turing, 1950, p. 456)*

Does this not evoke an image of Turing programming an AI machine with a psychology textbook placed on his lap, laid open on a chapter examining Piaget's theories on cognitive development? As is well-known, Turing assisted in the lectures Jean Piaget gave at the University of Manchester in 1952 (Wilson, 2011, p. 40). It is interesting to consider *which Piaget* Turing, or for that matter, any other AI developer, was reading about on his lap. For, as Erica Burman (2015) argued, British psychology, which was deeply involved in providing instruments for surveying and evaluating colonial populations, selectively used Piaget's genetic epistemological framework and interpreted child development as a general, uniform sequence of ages and stages, all the while negating Piaget's links with psychoanalysis (Burman, 2015, p. 70). With respect to the latter, while Piaget valued psychoanalysis, he nevertheless first and foremost rejected Sigmund Freud's interpretation that thinking and cognitive functions were directly related to sexuality (Morss, 1990, p. 140). All in all, then, the problems of race and sex(uality) that haunted Turing were already inherent to the psychological models that he chose to inform his technology. Further, it is clear that the choice for a particular kind model or theory of psychology ultimately decides which kind of technology and machines that one will construct. With Turing, this is abundantly clear from his choice of pedagogical model to educate the machines:

> It will not be possible to apply exactly the same teaching process to the machine as to a normal child. It will not, for instance, be provided with legs, so that it could not be asked to go out and fill the coal scuttle. Possibly it might not have eyes. But however well these deficiencies might be overcome by clever engineering, one could not send the creature to school without the other children making excessive fun of it.
>
> *(Turing, 1950, p. 456)*

Turing's quip in the above passage should be read literally: the computer child will receive a private and solitary education. In this formulation, group mechanisms and social mechanisms, which, according to the psychoanalytic pedagogue Hans Zulliger (whom we will deal with later in this book), form the basis of schooling, will not be covered. Rather, the education of digital machines would be modelled on a narrow positivist and cognitivist psychological model, which itself is based on a decontextualised model of the human being:

> The idea of a learning machine may appear paradoxical to some readers. How can the rules of operation of the machine change? They should describe completely how the machine will react whatever its history might

be, whatever changes it might undergo. The rules are thus quite time-invariant. This is quite true. The explanation of the paradox is that the rules which get changed in the learning process are of a rather less pretentious kind, claiming only an ephemeral validity. The reader may draw a parallel with the Constitution of the United States.

(Turing, 1950, p. 458)

Indeed, the laws of cognitive psychology have a lot in common with the Constitution of the United States, in as much as their universality and a-historicity can both be contested! It is clear that in matters of education and schooling there is no natural or normal way to proceed, and that this explains why different theories, models and ideological choices come into play. Hence, *tell me which psychological perspective you are setting out from and I will tell you how you will educate*. However, this is what Turing (had to) set aside when resorting to an ostensibly natural evolutionary teaching model, which, in turn, was based on a supposedly uncontested universal cognitive psychology. This cannot but lead us to conclude: *tell me which psychological perspective you are setting out from and I will tell you what kind of technologies you will devise*.

However, there remains a further issue to tackle, namely, the issue of faking and deception. For if the challenge that Turing set for the machine was to successfully deceive a human being, then he failed to question how *faking, mimicking*, and *deceiving* are always already central aspects of being human. Hence, is the true task not for the machine to deceive the deceiver? I turn to the intricacies of this paradoxical situation in the next section.

To feign or feigning to feign, that is the question

To begin, Turing introduced the issue of mimicry prior to discussing his imitation game. Turing's 'universal machine' was conceived as a *de facto* mimicking machine: the digital universal machine was a machine that could mimic any other machine. A so-called discrete-state or non-universal machine can be programmed to perform a specific task or set of tasks and will do only that. Turing's digital machine, however, was a universal machine which could do (and thus mimic) what other machines could do.[7] This leads to the following convoluted argument: Turing's universal machine mimicked other machines which were already mimicking humans, in that these discrete-states machines performed tasks that a 'human computer' was supposed to do. One could argue, then, that Turing quite adeptly manages all these levels, with the exception that what he is not willing to (or cannot) see is that the human at its core is involved in mimicking, and, therefore, is always already engaged in second-order mimicry.

Consider here how Turing responded to opponents of AI who argued that a machine will not pass '*viva voce*'. Viva voce involves checking whether someone has learned or studied something not only in a parrot-like fashion but instead has truly understood or integrated the information. Turing settles this issue quickly, arguing that it suffices that a computer can pose as if it has really appropriated the knowledge in a subjective way (Turing, 1950, pp. 446–447). However, Turing fails to take into account the fact that when you ask a person 'ok, now tell me the same thing in your own words', you only tend to get *the disguised parrot* to speak. Or, phrased otherwise, what each good and smart student is good at, or has prepared at very well, is making it sound to the teacher that they have really appropriated the subject matter. Hence, when the teacher concludes *this student really appropriated the theory and speaks in his/her own voice*, he or she is arguably describing a student who in a transferential way has appropriated the theory, via a transferential identification with the teacher. Can we not generalise this point and argue that humans are always feigning and mimicking their subjectivity? Or, fake it 'till you make it'? Hence, Turing went down an interesting path when arguing that a computer does not have to be humanlike, but only successfully pretend to be human. However, what Turing refrained from acknowledging (or simply chose not to) is that this scheme is always already operative at the human level.

To explore this in greater detail, let us now turn to consider how central mimicking was to Turing's imitation game. Evidently, the element of faking and deception is a primary condition of the game itself. Suppose, in the first version of the game, that there was only a man and a woman being asked questions by figure C that they had to answer straightforwardly; the game would be over in no time at all, even if you ruled out a number of questions that inquired directly about sex. It is only when the element of feigning comes in that the real game starts, and the interrogator 'C' must proceed as a detective, or as noted earlier, as a psychologist.

However, playing the psychologist might be unproductive here, in light of the fact that the psychologist is the naive believer who takes things at face value, or, above all, who tends to overlay preconceived theories and models upon reality? Alternatively, let us imagine a psychoanalyst in the role of C: a psychoanalyst is not supposed to seek the truth behind the lie, but, rather, to discern the truth of the lie itself. How, then, would a good psychoanalyst handle Turing's imitation game, specifically, the final version where a machine pretends to be human?

Of course, the psychoanalyst would ask his or her interlocutor about their history, love life, family, work, and so on. In this respect, would the machine then not be the one who responds with the most standard psychologising answers, reproducing mainstream psychological frameworks and discourses, and thus easily being discernible to the analyst as a fake? Of course, in the case that the interlocutor was a human subject, one would also receive the same standard psychologised discourse! However, a well-trained psychoanalyst would see through this, and perceive the true subject perspiring through the cracks of the neat and measured psychologised story. Or, to be more concise, the psychoanalyst would be able to discern not some underlying psychological truth of the subject, but rather the very absence of it, due to the fact that in psychoanalysis the subject only constitutes itself via discourse, and hence, is also always outside of it. As aforesaid, from this perspective, the 'psyche' of the human being is not a positive thing, it is a fissure, a negative issue. To quote Slavoj Žižek here:

> …the subject is correlative to its own limit, to the element which cannot be subjectified, it is the name of the void which cannot be filled out with subjectivization: the subject is the point of failure of subjectivization.
>
> (Žižek, 2006, p. 254)

Hence, I would argue that this absence of subjectivity (which nevertheless carries particular weight in that it structures presence as such) would paradoxically be lacking in the computer and that it would not be capable of mimicking it. Of course, I am not saying that AI is incapable of dealing with the non-calculable or the non-computable, it can, but what I am arguing is that the computer would never be the subject of the point of failure of computation. For, while a major failure in a digital system would lead to a crash, in contrast to a computer that would come to a halt, the human subject is that which can survive its own death, its own being a *caput mortuum*. Given this, can we thus not claim that the machine may well be able to mimic psychology, but can it mimic non-psychology? Certainly, the machine could pose as a deconstructed or even post-human subject (the post-truth subject, the multiple identity subject) but, arguably, it could never mimic a subject that is but itself a mimicry of a human being. Or to put it more concisely: it could mimic desubjectivation, but it could not mimic the subject being 'the subject of one's own desubjectivation', to borrow Giorgio Agamben's phrase (Agamben, 2002, p. 142).

At the very least, Turing's idea to devise an intelligent machine capable of mimicking humans bypasses the fact that the human subject is defined itself by its mimicking of what is human. I would argue that any human that would be subjected to the Turing test would have their reasons for being scared. Consider in this respect being halted in the street by a police officer or picked out of the row at an airport: even though one has nothing to hide, one nevertheless ponders the possibility that something incriminating might be found. In a similar vein, is being a human not always already about trying to convince the other that one is human. Must one not always conceal and silence the unhuman roar that burns like a ghost in one's breast?

At the origin of the attempts to create AI and cybernetics lies the aspiration to create a new kind of machine, as David Bates puts it, "a wholly new kind of machine technology, a flexible, adaptive one that would mimic the vital improvisation of the organism" (Bates, 2016, p. 207). But does this not point to the crux of the problem? In the end, the machine mimics *the vital organism* rather than the human subject. The latter testifies to a different logic than the former; that is, it testifies to the logic of Logos, which was what Turing started out from, the mortifying logic of Logos which places the subject in the place of the *caput mortuum*.

Hence, what the history of AI and cybernetics demonstrate is precisely the same fallacy that haunts psychology: as one is unable to rigorously consider the logic of the speaking-being (as I formulated it earlier, the human as a machine working according to the logic of Logos), then one inevitably succumbs to the temptation to think of the human (and the digital machine that is intended to mimic the human) along the lines of the vital organism and its physical organisation. Is this not why, as David Bates shows, cybernetic machines (such as self-guided missiles and other servomechanisms) in the end are still governed by the logic of automaticity, despite their ability to correct their behaviour through negative feedback circuits (Bates, 2016, p. 206)? At the very least, these cybernetic machines are not humanlike because they lack the vital logic per se, but, rather, because they lack the excess, the surplus, the negativity that characterises the logic of logos.

For example, intelligent drones will never get PTSD or ADHD, for the simple reason that, to put it plainly, these categories do not exist. That is to say, only humans can suffer from pathologies that do not exist. At the very least, drones will not be subversive or say, 'I'd prefer not to', nor will they secretly enjoy the duty of killing. So, when we read that "Google's New AI Has Learned to Become 'Highly Aggressive' in Stressful Situations" (Crew, 2018),[8] we should see this as a merely instrumental and mimicked aggression, which is deployed when it is needed or effective. Is this not in marked contrast to humans, who are capable of enjoying aggression, deploying it even when it is not needed, or to enjoy it even when it is needed (the torturer who enjoys his duty), which represents perhaps the pinnacle of human features?

Hence, my argument here is not that humans show and experience simple and non-feigned aggression. Rather, human aggression is always twisted: the Nazi executioner who displays aggression as a necessary duty and who precisely in this way experiences a surplus enjoyment is in fact also involved in a pretence. To understand the twisted structure of this, it is expedient to refer to the joke mentioned by Freud:

> Two Jews met in a railway carriage at a station in Galicia. "Where are you going?" asked one. "To Cracow," was the answer. "What a liar you are!" broke out the other. "If you say you're going to Cracow, you want me to believe you're going to Lemberg. But I know that in fact you're going to Cracow. So why are you lying to me?"
>
> *(Freud, [1905]1960, p. 115)*

So, concerning the Nazi executioner, one could ask him: why pretend to be aggressive when you do really enjoy it? Is this twist not always at play in human affairs? For example, when someone declares their love, is the addressee not always justified in asking: "why are you saying that you love me when you really mean it?"

At the very least, designing a machine that pretends to be a human being omits the fact that human beings are always already engaged in the business of pretending and in a twisted way. Indeed, is the human being above all not he or she who *pretend*s to be a human, and who hopes nobody notices? Is it only there that the dimension of something that can be considered to be human arises. In contrast, those who seem to be simply what they are, I would argue, are not to be trusted or even to be feared, as they are stuck in a mere simple, mono-dimensional form of acting and feigning. Here, one can refer to what Lacan considers to be the crucial difference between humans and animals: while animals can pretend, only human beings can pretend to pretend:

> (…) an animal does not feign feigning. It does not make tracks whose deceptiveness lies in getting them to be taken as false, when in fact they are true—that is, tracks that indicate the right trail. No more than it effaces its tracks, which would already be tantamount to making itself the subject of the signifier.
>
> *(Lacan, 2007, p. 683)*

We might understand Lacan's point as follows: when humans play a role, it is not to hide a true self, but, rather, to hide the fact that it is playing a role. Are we thus not driven to the conclusion that, in the same way, an animal cannot pretend to pretend, neither is a machine capable of doing so? Therefore, while pretending or simulating that it has 'a human self' might be within the reach of the digital machine, the redoubling of this is outside of its capability, that is, the pretending to pretend. Instead, the machine can only pretend to be something that it is not (feigning that it is human although it is a machine [simple negativity]), but it cannot pretend that it is human in order to hide the fact that it is not (absolute negativity). Or, phrased otherwise, being human is based on a core of un-humanness, which, I claim, is not within the grasp of a machine. Humans can thus tell the truth by pretending to lie, while machines cannot engage in this double pretence, or, at the very least, it would be without effect, that is to say, it would not engender a subject capable of this double pretence. The machine can pretend that it is a machine, but not with the express goal of convincing us to think that it is truly a machine, as this is precisely where some sort of subjectivity would arise. This is because in the simple pretence a veil is shown while removing it reveals another reality, the disguised reality: the fact of being an animal, the fact of being a machine. In the case of humans, in feigning to feign, removing the veil only shows an absence, thus testifying to the disturbing truth that it is in the veil itself that the truth resides.

Psychology and technology: a *folie à deux*

Are we not slowly, and finally, coming to the conclusion that AI and cybernetics have (and continue to) taken recourse to simplified schemes of the human from psychology, which depict a mono-dimensional human being, as they would not have been able to design their digital machines otherwise? Indeed, the twisted theory of psychoanalysis, which depicts humans as capable of feigning to feign, would be too paradoxical, if not impossible, to drive the development of digital technology. In contrast, the unidimensional model proffered by the psy-sciences, which depicts the human as a simple being whose feigning can easily be decoded, appears to offer easy entry points for AI and technology developers.

The fact that both spheres, the hegemonic mainstream psy-sciences and contemporary digital technologies, are so well aligned becomes especially poignant when one considers the remarkable digital turn within the psy-sciences themselves. Consider in this respect the European funded research project named the 'Human Brain Project', whose principal aim is to digitally model the human so as to 'gain fundamental insights into what it means to be human' (Walker, 2012, p. 25). The idea is to 'use data-mining techniques to derive an understanding of the way the human brain is constructed and then apply what is learned' (Paul M. Matthews in Kandel, Markram, Matthews, Yuste, & Koch, 2013, p. 659). This could even be understood as a reversed Turing test: it is the machine itself that will reveal to us the signature of human life. At the very least, does this not represent the outsourcing of attempts to understand humans to Big Data? As such, the basic assumption here is that computer simulations will allow scientists to allocate certain human issues and functions in the brain. Moreover, via this simulation, it is believed to be possible to discern which chemical substances or certain 'concrete' or 'symbolic' interventions (e.g. performed by another virtual person) would influence this. Hence, the argument goes that tampering with 'detailed computer reconstructed models and simulations of the brain'[9] will lead to knowledge, or at the very least, *in silico* knowledge, about human beings:

> Through this new in silico neuroscience, there will be nothing we cannot measure, no aspect of the model we cannot manipulate, there will be no question we cannot ask.[10]

In short, one simulates, one feigns, and expects that this will lead to the truth of 'what it means to be human'. The crucial question apropos this simple feigning (in contrast to the double feigning Lacan designated as being unique to human beings) pertains to which scripts are then mobilised? For is it not clear that the basic data out of which the digital brain is built, and which are used to set up the virtual scene, are not merely objectively given? For example, if one wants to model 'aggression', then the question that needs to be asked is what is aggression? So, to simplify things somewhat, the programmers of the Human Brain Project will have to make choices: will they use the theories and models of behaviourists, cognitivists, social psychologists, or for that matter, critical psychologists, or even psychoanalysts? Clearly, these models and theories are not wholly compatible with each other, so one will have to make choices. Even taking recourse to basic neuroscientific research on aggression to bypass these theory wars will solve little. For the same issue—that one must choose between different theoretical models—is always already at stake with, for example, fMRI-research: in the latter one cannot but rely on pre-suppositions and theorisations on the issue of aggression, while to devise the triggers that are used in fMRI research, one inevitably must fall back on psychological models of aggression. It is here, I argue, that the feigning begins, with the modelling of the human via theory. In the Human Brain Project, a fake human being is thus being constructed, on the basis of certain psychological theories and models, which, allegedly, lead to the truth about what humans are.

However, what one should not overlook here is that this charade and the ensuing pretence that we can know what the human is, ultimately engenders a (virtual) reality via which *homo psychologicus* gets 'materialised'. That is to say, if projects such as the Human Brain Project are most likely to be the proverbial mount that gives birth to a mouse (various critics doubt that this costly project will ever lead to a substantial outcome), there are nonetheless other digital settings where in a similar way mainstream theories and models of the human are being used to set up all sorts of virtual scenes that define our subjectivity and intersubjectivity. Of course, I am referring here to the general and all-encompassing digitalisation of our (inter)subjectivity, as the latter ever more takes place in virtual environments online. It is there, I argue, that we can see how the various fantasies and phantasms of the psy-sciences serve to define the scenes and preconceived roles in such a way that models and moulds the subjective and intersubjective domain.

So, when scientists claim that digital social media can teach us a lot about what it is to be human, they overlook the fact that these media are already filled to the brim with psychological models. Or, to use a Flemish expression: *only the cat that has been put in the sack can come out of the sack*. Thus, to the extent that digital platforms, algorithms, and software co-configure (inter)subjectivity, we must analyse which theories and psychological models are operating in the background. Today, more than ever, we need a psy-critique: in these digitised times, the human being, who can pretend to pretend, runs the risk of being locked up in the digital straitjacket of simple pretence.

It is precisely this issue of needing to feed the machine with psychological scripts which is initiated by Alan Turing's imitation game. Consider how he resorted to mainstream cognitive behaviourist theory at the very point that opines about the way that a machine as if it were a child, should be educated. Turing, for example, argued that one should 'start with an unorganised machine and to try to bring both discipline and initiative into it at once' (Turing, 2013, p. 515). From then on, one would 'try out new combinations of these routines, to make slight variations on them, and to apply them in new ways' (Turing, 2013, p. 509). As one can discern, he thus opted for mainstream developmental psychology and cognitive psychology, that is, a form of psychology that depicts the human being as a unidimensional and easily manipulated and steerable creature. Here, although Turing initially rejected simple answers to the questions of *what is thinking?* and *what is the human?* in order to model the openness of the human being, he eventually ended up drawing upon closed psy-models and their naturalising and essentialising answers about what the human is.

Conclusions: a Lacanian epilogue

Turing's imitation game cannot be viewed in isolation from Turing's other innovative conception of the 'universal machine' (which is also called the Turing machine). The universal machine basically reads a paper strip, which is devised in sections (as discrete states) with each carrying a symbol: the universal machine reads one case at a time. As such, this is quite a remarkable set-up, in that a digital machine is not a machine that works simultaneously with a whole array of data, but, rather, deals with one data-case at a time. One might be tempted here to compare this to Freud's idea of the 'Enge des Bewußtseins',[11] the narrow passage of consciousness:

> Only a single memory at a time can enter ego-consciousness. A patient who is occupied in working through such a memory sees nothing of what is pushing after it and forgets what has already pushed its way through.
> *(Freud, [1895]1955, p. 291)*[12]

Is this not precisely how Turing's universal machine is organised: it has a head, a kind of reader, or scanner that is 'conscious' so to speak of only a single square at a time; it reads the square, performs an action (rewriting, or not, the data in the square) depending on the given instructions, before then proceeding to move onto another square.

However, to indicate the true difference between a psychoanalytic understanding of consciousness and Turing's universal machine, we must refer to Lacan's conceptualisation of the chain of signifiers, more specifically, his formulation that 'a signifier represents the subject for another signifier' (Lacan, 1978, p. 207). For Lacan, the human being is a speaking-being, who constitutes itself via the chain of signifiers, which means that the split subject $\) (split between two signifiers) could be compared to Turing's reading head in a certain respect. However, the main difference is that in Turing's universal machine, Lacan's split subject is traded in for a full presence: the head simply reads the square it is dealing with, and it is on this level itself that a meaningful operation is performed. In contradistinction to this, Lacan situates in his chain of signifiers a 'caput mortuum' (which literally means 'deadhead' or 'worthless remains'), which is a kind of zero-level of the subject that is defined by neither S1 (signifier one) nor S2 (signifier 2), but instead only sees light in the gap between the two (see, e.g., Seminar on 'The Purloined Letter' in Lacan, 2007). Consequently, the subject is not the reader in this respect, but, rather, can be said to be the result of the reading. That is to say, split between two signifiers, the subject only exist vis-à-vis this excess, this surplus of operation in the chain of signifiers.[13] If one will allow me a further digression on Lacanian theory: the name for this excess and surplus is the '*objet a*', the object of desire, that which guides or steers the subject through its reality. In Turing's formulation, the reading head is not problematised, and thus it could be said to stand for the fiction of the psychological individual (literally, the non-divided person), who moves through the symbolic universe guided by a script (as opposed to desire), which can be understood as the programme that defines the actions of the reading head. Hence, is this not similar to the issue of the digitalisation of (inter)subjectivity? That is to say, the scripts that guide and steer us through the virtual worlds we inhabit derive from mainstream psy-theories and models. It is Turing who can be said to have initiated this: as he ended up referring to cheap cardboard psychologies grounded in a vulgar neuro-materialism. See, for example, how he seeks out simple models that can be straightforwardly implemented technologically:

> By "laws of behaviour" I mean laws of nature as applied to a man's body such as "if you pinch him, he will squeak."
>
> *(Turing, 1950, p. 452)*

Can this not be contrasted with the game we play as children: "pinch me and I'll either squeak or I won't", or perhaps in the more adult version: "I'll enjoy it?" At the very least, Turing opted for a non-problematised vision of the human in order to devise of a rather plain direct universal machine. The troublesome question that lurks in the background, *what is it to be human?* simply disappears. Indeed, Turing almost mockingly claims:

> I believe that at the end of the century the use of the words and general educated opinion will have altered so much that one will be able to speak of machines thinking without expecting to be contradicted.
>
> *(Turing, 1950, p. 442)*

Turing ultimately chooses to neutralise the question of *what it means to be human* from the notion that 'the human' is after all just a word, a historical-contingent conception. Hence, if one can succeed in convincing everybody that thinking is nothing more than the mere sequencing of symbols, that is, that existing and being alive is simply a matter of being present on virtual platforms and getting likes and other tokens that confirm one's existence, and, moreover, that social and political action must start with a hashtag, then this might be where human beings effectively become indistinguishable from machines.

Ultimately, then, this is the too much *of/within* the digital which I opposed at the beginning of this chapter to the common and unproductive claim that there is too much human/too much psychology to be subsumed within the digital realm (a *too muchness* that resists digitalisation). Rather, there is too much psychology within the digital realm; the machine is not imitating human psychology, it is scripted with psychological theories, which we are expected to not contradict or deviate from.

Notes

1 "What do I know of what I'll be, I who don't know what I am?" (Pessoa, 1972).
2 The reference to which I allude here is, of course, 'L'homme machine' ('Machine Man') by Julien Offray of La Mettrie ([1747]1996). Most interestingly, La Mettrie

does not have a merely mechanical idea of the human but conceives of the human as being defined, on the one hand, by its capacity to speak, and, on the other hand, by its search for pleasure and enjoyment. As for the latter, it can be said that La Mettrie already prefigures the Freudian idea of showing the difference between humans and animals, the latter of whom seek the mere satisfaction of their instincts. For a more extensive analysis, see (De Vos, 2011).
3 Hence, as I will address later, this does not merely concern 'performativity' (the issue of establishing what you are through a performance): performativity puts forward an agent able to freely choose how they act. The central element of 'deceit', at the very least, introduces a split subject, but only, as we shall see later, when the deceit is redoubled and thus becomes something else than merely an intentionally false performance.
4 Albeit, of course, that for psychoanalysis sexual difference is not a natural given as such, in that it passes through the subjectivation and symbolisation processes that Freud tried to grasp in his famous Oedipus complex.
5 I owe this concise formulation to David Gunkel (personal communication).
6 The fact that I introduce the figure of the psychologist here will likely come as no surprise, given that Joseph Weizenbaum's well-known chatbot ELIZA was designed to simulate a Rogerian therapist (Weizenbaum, 1967). We will return to the figure of the psychologist later in this chapter.
7 As David Bates summarises:

> As a simple machine with nothing more than the capacity to manipulate two symbols on a moving tape, this digital computer was defined as a radically open machine whose sole purpose was to take on the configurations of other discrete-state machines.
>
> (Bates, 2016, p. 206)

8 "The Google team ran 40 million turns of a simple 'fruit gathering' computer game that asks two DeepMind 'agents' to compete against each other to gather as many virtual apples as they could. They found that things went smoothly so long as there were enough apples to go around, but as soon as the apples began to dwindle, the two agents turned aggressive, using laser beams to knock each other out of the game to steal all the apples" (Crew, 2018).
9 As stated on: https://www.humanbrainproject.eu/nl_BE/discover/the-project/research-areas.
10 https://www.humanbrainproject.eu/nl_BE/discover/the-project/research-areas; https://www.youtube.com/watch?v=_UFOSHZ22q4.
11 Sometimes this is badly translated as the 'defiling of consciousness' or the narrowing of consciousness.
12 Given that Freud compares this to camels passing through the eye of a needle, one could imagine how they do this: as this would be a quite strenuous passage, they would have to pass one by one. Another Freudian reference here would be "A note upon the 'Mystic Writing-Pad,'" where he conceives of the system of consciousness as that which has to be wiped clean intermittently so as to allow for new perceptions and thoughts (Freud, [1925]1955).
13 The relation of $\mathcal{S}$ vis-à-vis the *objet a* is expressed in the Lacanian matheme of $\mathcal{S} \Diamond a$, which is also referred to as the basic phantasm, which defines the relation between the subject and the symbolic universe. I return to *objet a* in Chapter 8.

References

Agamben, G. (2002). *Remnants of Auschwitz*. New York: Zone books.
Asimov, I. (1965). Evidence. In W. F. Nolan (Ed.), *The pseudo-people: Androids in science fiction* (pp. 94–118). New York: Berkley Medallion Books.

Bates, D. (2016). Automaticity, plasticity, and the deviant origins of artificial intelligence. In D. Bates & N. Bassiri (Eds.), *Plasticity and pathology: On the formation of the neural subject* (pp. 194–218). New York: Fordham University Press.

Burman, E. (2015). Developmental psychology. The turn to deconstruction. In I. Parker (Ed.), *Handbook of critical psychology* (pp. 70–79). London: Routledge.

Crew, B. (2018). Google's AI has learned to become "highly aggressive" in stressful situations. *Science Alert*. Retrieved from https://www.sciencealert.com/google-deepmind-has-learned-to-become-highly-aggressive-in-stressful-situations

Danaylov, N. (Producer). (2013, January 2, 2020). Marvin Minsky on AI: The Turing test is a joke! (interview). Retrieved from https://www.singularityweblog.com/marvin-minsky/

De Vos, J. (2011). From La Mettrie's voluptuous man machine to the perverse core of psychology. *Theory & Psychology, 21*(1), 67–85.

Dean, J. (2005). Communicative capitalism: Circulation and the foreclosure of politics. *Cultural Politics, 1*(1), 51–74.

Evans, D. (2001). It's the thought that counts. *The Guardian*. Retrieved from https://www.theguardian.com/theguardian/2001/oct/06/weekend7.weekend6

Foley, M. (2014). "Prove You're Human": Fetishizing material embodiment and immaterial labor in information networks. *Critical Studies in Media Communication, 31*(5), 365–379.

Freud, S. ([1895]1955). The psychotherapy of hysteria (J. Strachey, Trans.). In J. Breuer & S. Freud (Eds.), *Studies on hysteria (in: The standard edition of the complete psychological works of Sigmund Freud: vol. II)* (pp. 253–306). London: Hogarth Press.

Freud, S. ([1905]1960). Jokes and their relation to the unconscious. In J. Strachey (Ed.), *The standard edition of the complete psychological works of Sigmund Freud: Vol. VIII* (pp. 3–249). London: Hogarth Press.

Freud, S. ([1925]1955). A note upon the "Mystic Writing-Pad". In J. Strachey (Ed.), *The standard edition of the complete psychological works of Sigmund Freud: vol. XIX* (pp. 227–232). London: Hogarth Press.

Goertzel, B. (2014). What does chatbot Eugene Goostman's success on the turing test mean? *Humanity + Magazine*. Retrieved from https://hplusmagazine.com/2014/06/09/what-does-chatbot-eugene-goostmans-success-on-the-turing-test-mean/

Jankélévitch, V. (2015). *Henri Bergson* (N. Schott, Trans.). Durham, NC: Duke University Press.

Kandel, E. R., Markram, H., Matthews, P. M., Yuste, R., & Koch, C. (2013). Neuroscience thinks big (and collaboratively). *Nature Reviews Neuroscience, 14*(9), 659–664.

Kevorkian, M. (2006). *Color monitors: The black face of technology in America*. Ithaca, NY: Cornell University Press.

La Mettrie, J. O. (1996[1747]). *Machine man and other writings* (A. Thomson, Trans.). Cambridge: Cambridge University Press.

Lacan, J. (1978). *The four fundamental concepts of psychoanalysis* (A. Sheridan, Trans.). New York: Norton.

Lacan, J. (2004). *Le séminaire, Livre X: L'angoisse, 1962–1963*. Paris: Seuil.

Lacan, J. (2007). *Ecrits: The first complete edition in English* (B. Fink, Trans.). New York: Norton.

Leavitt, D. (2006). *The man who knew too much: Alan Turing and the invention of the computer (great discoveries)*. New York: WW Norton & Company.

Levin, S. (2017). New AI can guess whether you're gay or straight from a photograph. *The Guardian*. Retrieved from https://www.theguardian.com/technology/2017/sep/07/new-artificial-intelligence-can-tell-whether-youre-gay-or-straight-from-a-photograph

Lim, K. (2017). The racist, fascist, xenophobic, misogynistic, intelligent machine. *The Business Times*. Retrieved from https://www.businesstimes.com.sg/brunch/the-racist-fascist-xenophobic-misogynistic-intelligent-machine

Morss, J. R. (1990). *The biologising of childhood: Developmental psychology and the Darwinian myth*. Hove: Erlbaum.

Pessoa, F. (1972). *Obra Poética*. Rio de Janeiro: Aguilar Editóra.

Snyder, T. (2019). And we dream as electric sheep. On humanity, sexuality and digitality. *Eurozine*. Retrieved from https://www.eurozine.com/dream-electric-sheep/

Turing, A. M. (1950). Computing machinery and intelligence. *Mind, 59*(236), 433–460.

Turing, A. M. (2013). Intelligent machinery (Report written by Alan Turing for the national physical laboratory, 1948). In S. B. Cooper & J. Van Leeuwen (Eds.), *Alan Turing: His work and impact*. Amsterdam: Elsevier.

Walker, R. (2012). *The human brain project: A report to the European commission*. Retrieved from Lausanne: https://www.humanbrainproject.eu/documents/10180/17648/TheHBPReport_LR.pdf/18e5747e-10af-4bec-9806-d03aead57655

Wang, Y., & Kosinski, M. (2018). Deep neural networks are more accurate than humans at detecting sexual orientation from facial images. *Journal of Personality and Social Psychology, 114*(2), 246–257.

Wilson, E. A. (2011). *Affect and artificial intelligence*. Seattle: University of Washington Press.

Weizenbaum, J. (1967). Contextual understanding by computers. *Communications of the ACM, 10*(8), 474–480.

Žižek, S. (2006). *Interrogating the real* (R. Butler & S. Stephens Eds.). London: Continuum.

3
CYBERNETICS AND THE WAR OF THE PSYCHOLOGIES

Introduction: why psy-critique?

Perhaps this book will make people frown, maybe even chuckle or, for that matter, deeply annoy them: a psychoanalytically grounded critique of digitality? Would that not be akin to critiquing quantum physics through recourse to alchemy? My retort to such critics is rather simple: even a cursory reading of the work of a seminal figure such as Alan Turing demonstrates the centrality of psychological matters within his work, which helped to bring into being digital technology as we know it, and, in turn, today's digital culture. This chapter examines another crucial historical antecedent of digitality, the field of cybernetics. Similar to Turing's work, one can find, perhaps unsurprisingly, direct references to Freud and psychoanalysis in the writings of early cyberneticists, which lends further support to critiquing digitality from a psychanalytic perspective. At the very least, if it can be shown that psychological models and theories are inherent to digital technology and our contemporary digital culture (and its discontents), then a critical questioning of this theoretical and methodological lineage is wholly justified, and, moreover, urgently needed. For, as I have argued elsewhere, the psy-sciences are fundamentally and structurally problematic (De Vos, 2012, 2016), and thus AI-theorists and developers of digital technologies reliance upon them is a deeply vexing issue.

To briefly sketch out the issues at stake vis-à-vis the problematic status of the psy-sciences, it is instructive to refer to Edmund Husserl's diagnosis of 'The Crisis of European Sciences' in the interbellum in the 20th century (Husserl, 1970). Simply put, Husserl argues that in the age of science, it became abundantly clear that science had to be grounded in something other than itself, with the primary candidate being logic. However, as one would expect, this did not necessarily solve anything, but rather only shifted the problem towards consideration of what logic would be grounded upon? This is where psychology was called upon, albeit with the very same problem that, according to Husserl, psychology itself lacked any grounds. Husserl argues that psychology attempts to circumvent its structural problem by adopting the methods of the objective sciences, which he refers to as the tragic failure of psychology, inasmuch as it can never address the issue of subjectivity in its own right.

It is at this precise point that Husserl proposes his phenomenological method as an alternative, and it is at this point that he and I depart from one another. In contradistinction to Husserl, I argue that if one wishes to perform a critique of the psy-sciences, and for that matter, of the neuropsy-sciences, then one must inevitably and necessarily engage with psychoanalysis. This is despite—and perhaps because of—the fact that psychoanalysis is at odds with the psy-sciences. This is based on the fact that while the latter have historically opted to objectify the issue of subjectivity, psychoanalysis, conversely, is a theory and praxis predicated on the very impossibility of objectifying subjectivity. Of course, this is not to say that psychoanalysis and the psy-sciences do not intersect; they do, and at various points. To begin with, one could argue that Freud's psychoanalysis became the main reference point for psychology, in the sense that every school and theory within the broader psy-sciences was forced to engage with psychoanalysis in some form or another (be it refuting, amending, previsioning, rejecting, neglecting, and so forth). Moreover, psychoanalysis itself was evidently a key driver in the process of psychologisation (consider, in this regard, Freud's 'The Psychopathology of Everyday Life' (Freud, 1960[1901])), by helping to plant seeds at the end of the 19th century that would only fully come to fruition at the end of the 20th century, which is why, as I have argued elsewhere, psychologisation must be seen as a central and inextricable component of the psy-sciences themselves. In this sense, it would be wrong to think of psychology as a science whose knowledge only spills over into culture, education, and other societal spheres in a secondary movement. Rather, the psy-sciences qua eternal would-be science should be understood as precisely that which establishes itself, both theoretically speaking and as a praxis, via the psychologisation of subjectivity. That is to say, it precisely grounds itself, unwittingly, by interpellating its subjects to look upon and understand themselves, others, and the world at large via the signifiers and theories of the psy-sciences. Here, the radical twist in this tale is that psychoanalysis, as aforesaid, is inherently at odds with psychology, if for nothing else than for the fact that it signals the impossibility of a theory and praxis of the psyche. Psychoanalysis can even be said to develop its own theory and praxis on the very basis of this impossibility. To put it both simply and dramatically: psychoanalysis accepts the paradox of being a Von Munchhausian discipline:[1] the human being who looks at oneself is always in trouble, in the sense of having to understand and look upon their own gaze that stares back at them, only partially recognising that gaze as their own. Here, psychoanalysis is in its very core a non-psychology, albeit that it continually has to resist the temptation of becoming a psychological theory, discourse, or praxis. Therefore, I argue, one must begin with both a critique of and from psychoanalysis in order to address these aforesaid processes of psychologisation, namely, the fact that psy-matters have proliferated into almost every facet of modern life.

The issue of psychologisation is precisely clear in matters of digitalisation: as aforementioned, one is immediately struck by the lineage of the psy-theories and models, both at the level of technology (see, as illustrated in Chapter 2, how Alan Turing could not but take recourse to psychological theories and models when devising his technology) and the level of digital culture and digital practises. Concerning the latter, it is interesting how the first major scandal in digital social media concerned the use of *psychological* profiling for commercial and political goals (for my discussion of the Cambridge Analytica scandal, see Chapter 4). I adopt a hard stance with respect to this specific point: any viable and rigorous critiques of the psy-sciences (and how they are deployed in other fields), and for that matter, of psychoanalysis itself, must either come from or engage with psychoanalytic thought. Indeed, the fact that psychoanalysis is a central exponent of modernity itself should make it unavoidable. As Lacan argued, psychoanalysis operates on the subject of the sciences, which is to say that the subject of the modern sciences *is* the subject of psychoanalysis. In other words, modernity and the scientific age spawned psychoanalysis as a key mode of thought and praxis through which to think of the subject. Hence, if one wants to think of or critique (which amounts to the same) modernity, then one not only has to deal with the fact that critique is a by-product of modernity itself, but rather one must also address the fact that one's own thinking is inevitably psychoanalytic (and, in turn, is always at risk of succumbing to the temptation to slip into becoming psychological, and believing that a complete, closed, unparadoxical theory and practice of human subjectivity is possible). However, that is enough for the preliminary justifications and caveats, it is time to get to work examining the debt to psychoanalysis in early cybernetic thought, before moving onto discuss the vicissitudes of this. I will discuss the work of Marvin Minsky, Norbert Wiener, Gregory Bateson, and Warren McCulloch, in turn.

Marvin Minsky: fleeing Freud's demons

Let us begin with Marvin Minsky, the person who considered Turing's imitation game to be no more than a joke (see Chapter 2). Minsky is considered to be a founding father of AI, along with collaborating with key figures in cybernetics, such as Warren McCulloch and John Von Neuman. Minsky is a prime example of how developers of digital technologies not only (cannot but) evoke and take recourse to the psy-sciences, but also of how they invariably are confronted with the Husserlian problem of the groundlessness of psychology and its tragic failure to obfuscate in its fixation on objectivity the precise issue of subjectivity itself. Minsky writes:

> When intelligent machines are constructed, we should not be surprised to find them as confused and as stubborn as men in their convictions about

mind-matter, consciousness, free will, and the like. For all such questions are pointed at explaining the complicated interactions between parts of the self-model. A man's or a machine's strength of conviction about such things tells us nothing about the man or about the machine except what it tells us about his model of himself.

(Minsky, 1965, p. 431)

Here, Minsky appears to be pointing towards something that, as a rule, psychologists generally skim over. This pertains to the fact that when psychology approaches the human being in order to theorise and model it, it finds a human being that already theorises and models itself. The temptation here is to simply define this self-modelling as 'folk psychology' and, hence, as something far removed from scientific psychology. It is on this basis that Minsky hastily rejects these self-models as being irrelevant to the truths of both 'man' (sic) and machine. However, by doing so, Minsky is too quick to write-off human beings' theories and models about themselves, by juxtaposing or opposing them to an underlying real reality that is unbeknownst to us, rather than understanding these theories and models as, at the very least, being co-constructive of human beings, up to the point that we could argue that there is no underlying reality whose essential logic and laws we could (or could not) discover. Therefore, what if the radical conclusion to be drawn from this is that, given that there is no underlying reality, no essential logic or laws, the subject is nothing more than the gap between these self-theories and the non-existing essential core.

As was demonstrated in Chapter 2, this non-psychology precisely formed the starting point for Turing, subsequently leading him to a rather prosaic approach: let us not try to make a machine that is humanlike, but, rather, as the signature of the human cannot be simply pinned down, let us devise a machine that could fool a human into thinking that it is a human. Upon closer examination, we also find an interesting non-psychological or even anti-psychological approach in Minsky's work on AI:

> What we never did do was to use a lot of statistical psychology to learn what some 'average' person does when solving these problems. For a long time, I had a rule in my laboratory that no psychological data were allowed. I had read a lot of such data when I was in college, and I felt that one couldn't learn very much by averaging a lot of people's responses. What you had to do was something like what Freud did. Tom Evans and I asked ourselves, in depth, what we did to solve problems like this, and that seemed to work pretty well.
>
> *(interviewed by Bernstein, 1981)*

Of course, the introspectiveness displayed here by Evans and Minsky is not psychoanalytic per se. Rather, in their rejection of mainstream psychological traditions that objectify the human being via statistical forms of capture, they are instead opting for an intuitive, if not, in fact, folk-psychological approach: in their respective attempts to circumvent the limitations or impossibilities of a 'scientific' psychology, they end up doing something Freudian-esque. At the very least, Minsky does not appear concerned with either the logical impossibility of this kind of introspective auto-analysis or its broader implications. From the perspective of psychoanalysis, even if psychoanalysis is based on a transferential relation with a psychoanalyst as opposed to being an introspective practice, the logical impossibility of analysis, the bedrock if you will and the point at which it inevitably falters, is still precisely related to Freud's auto-analysis. In other words, Freud's inevitable and structural blind spots can be said to have persisted throughout the whole subsequent genealogy of psychoanalysts who were trained by Freud.

However, my guess is that Minsky was not particularly interested with the intricacies of psychoanalysis. Even if his talk 'Why Freud was the first good AI theorist' sounds pretty promising, for the most part, he engages in a cognitivist and neurobiological reading of the early Freud. So, on the one hand, you have Minsky, for example, valuing how Freud in the 'Interpretation of Dreams' conceives of the mind in such a way that wholly rejects the idea of a singular homunculus or mastermind pulling the strings, while, on the other hand, Minsky sticks to a limited biological reading of Freud's unpublished manuscript 'A project for a scientific psychology', which he labels as the first attempt 'to consider that the mind is a big complicated kludge of different types of machinery which are specialized for different functions' (Minsky, 2013, p. 169). From here, Minsky does not hesitate to minimise the importance of the later Freud, who, as Minsky puts it, dealt primarily with emotions and neuroses.

Clearly, Minsky, like Turing, refrains from fully thinking through his initial non-psychological approach, which is how Freud's psychoanalysis ends up being psychologised precisely by resorting to an unquestioned and unproblematised (neuro) biological and naturalising gaze. For example, when in 'The Society of Mind' Minsky wants to account for how ethics and ideals develop in children's mind, he refers to Freud's Oedipus complex, albeit while stressing that he does not agree with all of Freud's theorising on the subject, instead asking 'what could be the biological and psychological functions of developing complicated self-ideals?' (Minsky, 1988, p. 181).[2] This is where, I argue, Minsky fails to remain true to his non-psychology and instead seeks a form of closure in biology.

What is it exactly that Minsky discards from Freud, however? In this respect, it is instructive to turn to yet another of his explicit references to Freud in one of his interviews:

> My view of mathematical thinking is like Freud's view of everyday thinking. We have in our subconscious a number of little demons, or little parasites, and each of them is afraid of something. Right now, I am working on the society-of-the-mind theory. I believe that the way to understand intelligence is to have some parts of the mind that know certain things, and other parts of the mind that know things about the first part. If you want to

learn something, the most important thing to know is which part of your mind is good at learning that kind of thing. I am not looking so much for a unified general theory. I am looking for an administrative theory of how the mind can have enough parts and know enough about each of them to solve all the problems it confronts. I am interested in developing a set of ideas about different kinds of simple learning machines, each one of which has as its main concern to learn what the others are good at. Eventually, I hope to close the circle, so that the whole thing can figure out how to make itself better. That, at least, is my fantasy.

(Bernstein, 1981)

In this lengthy passage, it is notable how Minsky, like so many other AI-theorists and cyberneticists, on the one hand, alludes to psychoanalysis' rejection of the homunculus (the idea that there is a central agent in the mind),[3] but, on the other hand, leaves out the fears, demons, and parasites, the very scandals of psychoanalysis one might say, and trades them for his bio-cognitivist constructions. Indeed, at the very end of the quotation, Minsky discusses the different parts of the intelligent system that watch over each other and eventually optimize the overall system, which would suggest that the demons and fears have seemingly left the building. Are these scandals and fears excluded because they cannot be mimicked by a machine, inasmuch as they are non-psychological and incapable of being scripted by a digital machine? Is this then not also the final upshot of Turings's endeavour? You cannot build a machine that is truly humanlike, as we are unable to concretely pin down what the defining characteristics of humans are, so, in the absence of this, let us build machines that can merely pose and pass as humans so to speak. It is precisely here that the psychological fantasies of the human come in and are used as the simplistic models for the machine to adopt when posing as a human, thus cutting out the logical impossibilities and paradoxes of being human, which, I would argue, correspond to the fears and demons that Minsky set out with. In an attempt to recover these fears and demons, let us now turn to discussing Norbert Wiener, the central figure in cybernetics, and the specific task he set himself to oppose the end of the world with information.

Nobert Wiener's end of the world

In light of the above discussion and the previous chapter, the reader will perhaps no longer be surprised to learn that Norbert Wiener also initially connected his cybernetic work to Freud. Given that, for Wiener, the informational domain comes in where objectivation and rationalisation falter, taking recourse to the Freudian understanding of how rationality intersects with irrationality was an obvious step. Orit Halpern argues that Wiener started from "the impossibility of describing a world in its totality, of ever rendering 'reality' legible": from here, he wanted to trade ontology, description and materiality with communication, prediction and virtuality (Halpern, 2015, p. 40). Moreover, Halpern continues,

Wiener affirmed 'an operative lack that cannot enter description but can produce something else—a self-referential and probabilistic form of thought' (Halpern, 2015, p. 40). It is here that Wiener explicitly refers to the Freudian conceptualisation of the unconscious:

> ... in a probabilistic world we no longer deal with quantities and statements which concern a specific, real universe as a whole but ask instead questions which may find their answers in a large number of similar universes. Thus chance has been admitted, not merely as a mathematical tool for physics, but as part of its warp and weft. This recognition of an element of incomplete determinism, almost an irrationality in the world, is in a certain way parallel to Freud's admission of a deep irrational component in human conduct and thought.
>
> *(Wiener, 1989, p. 11)*

One can discern above how a dark element already enters the fold, as Wiener connects this irrational component to 'a fundamental element of chance in the texture of the universe itself' (Wiener, 1989, p. 11). Wiener calls this random element, this organic incompleteness, evil—albeit the negative evil of St. Augustine, rather than the positive malicious evil of the Manichaeans. I return to this point later.

For the moment however, let us continue with the Freudian reference in Wiener's work and consider how, as Orit Halpern points out, he understood psychoanalysis as a process of mobilising information, rather than, say, digging up or unearthing meaning, which is why he considered it to be wholly compatible with cybernetics (Halpern, 2015, p. 68). In this respect, Wiener's approach is very interesting, in that it goes against the grain of the widely held misunderstanding that psychoanalysis is a 'depth psychology' in search of deeply hidden meanings. This was something that Freud himself was at pains to point out, stressing that psychoanalysis as a practice remains on the surface of what is said and that, if anything, psychoanalysis is a 'surface psychology' that concerns the superficial dimension of the spoken (Freud, [1916–1917]1963). However, the designation 'psychology' might be somewhat superfluous here, for, as Friedrich Kittler suggested, psychoanalysis led to the externalisation of the psyche and its incorporation into larger discursive networks.[4] Hence, one could argue that what Wiener was attempting to engage with above all was the *non-psychological* kernel of psychoanalysis. This is also precisely what Jacques Lacan valued in cybernetics: in the digital machine, there is no difference between what is treated and who or what is treated (see: Saint-Jevin, 2017); or, phrased otherwise, in the machine, the I, the undivided psychological Ego who ostensibly deals with the world of meaning, is radically deconstructed. However, as one may now expect, the question I will keep pursuing here pertains to whether Wiener remained faithful to his alliance with Freud, or, like Turing and Minsky, he ended up adopting a psychologised stance?

To begin this discussion, it is expedient to refer to Katherine Hayles' interesting point that Wiener's cybernetic approach was not an attempt to juxtapose 'men and machines' in order to bring 'two pre-existing objects into harmonious relation', but, rather, for Wiener 'the analogical relation constitutes both terms through the process of articulating their relationship' (Hayles, 2008, p. 92). Wiener's analogy between the human and the machine is thus not an essentialist position: at its centre is the relation between the human and the machine. Consequently, here, it is not the case that humans resemble machines for naturalist and essentialist reasons, as it is in contemporary doxa (the idea that the information processing brain's next natural and evolutionary step is to build a machine in its own image). Rather, Wiener was purporting that the analogy between the human and the machine concerns primarily the *relation* between the human and the machine. Hence, understanding the impact of technology is not so much a matter of the question, 'what does technology do with the human being (as a biological, psychological being)?', but, rather, pertains to how the two define and co-constitute each other. From this perspective, there is thus no such thing as an *a priori* neurobiological or psychological subject against which we could assess the vicissitudes of digitalisation; rather, there is only the technologised subject (in the same way that the neurological or psychological subject does not exist, but rather there only exists neurologised and psychologised subjects). Overall, then, the neurobiological sciences and the psy-sciences should be understood as the site of the technological, with which the human relates in an analogous relation.

Even though thinking of the human and machine as being within an analogous relation with one another would have allowed Wiener to envision the subject as a mere empty place, a mere excess or surplus that derives from the juxtaposition of the terms, 'man' and 'machine', this is precisely the conclusion that Wiener himself eventually shies away from. I would argue that Wiener subsequently moves away from such a strong conception of this analogy (co-constituting humans and machines) and regresses into the classical formulation of finding some form of common ground between the two, which, of course, is some overarching psychology spanning across these two terms. As Hayles notes, for Wiener, even emotions may be achievable for machines, if these are considered not as 'merely a useless epiphenomenon of nervous actions' (Wiener, 1989, p. 72), but, rather, as control mechanisms governing learning (see: Hayles, 2008, p. 104). Hence, it is no longer about a co-constitutive relation between humans and machines, but rather about them having a common psychology, a psychology of emotions, the latter of which is understood within an informational or cognitive-evolutionary rationale: emotions serve the adaption of an evolving and learning human/machine.

How can we begin to understand this move, one which I would argue also signals a shift away from the non-psychology of psychoanalysis—which would posit that there are no such things as emotions—towards psychology? Is it, as I discussed apropos Turing, a mandatory step in order to be able to devise of a new technology? At the very least, as Hayles has already observed, Wiener finally refused the conclusion that cybernetics itself led to, namely, that personal identity and autonomous will are merely illusions (Hayles, 2008, p. 110). Backing away from the original analogous relation between man and machine—in which there is no room for a real, positive Self—Wiener resurrected the psychological Self and its attendant notions of emotions, identity, and free will. Hayles describes this shift as follows: Wiener needed to reconcile cybernetics with the liberal humanistic subject:

> The danger of cybernetics, from his point of view, is that it can potentially annihilate the liberal subject as the locus of control. On the microscale, the individual is merely the container for still smaller units within, who dictate its actions and desires; on the macroscale, these desires make one into a fool to be manipulated by knaves.
> *(Hayles, 2008, p. 110)*

I would add to this that in his attempt to ward off this image of the human, Wiener succumbs to a psychologising perspective.

Having said this, perhaps this turn from Freud to psychology can be understood in another way. That is to say, Wiener's horror at the end of the liberal humanistic subject could be related to his other central preoccupation: the idea of entropy. This idea, which derives from thermodynamics, concerns the tendency within a closed system to direct itself towards the loss of order and the homogenisation of differences, which, in the long-term, means the end of the world. As Wiener himself writes:

> We are swimming upstream against a great torrent of disorganization, which tends to reduce everything to the heat death of equilibrium and sameness described in the second law of thermodynamics. What Maxwell, Bolzmann and Gibbs meant by this heat death in physics has a counterpart in the ethic of Kierkegaard, who pointed out that we live in a chaotic moral universe.
> *(Wiener, 1989, p. xiii)*

Wiener's obsession, if one will forgive me putting it in such a psychologising way, can, on the one hand, be tied to Wiener's biography—Hayles, for example, connects it to Wiener's childhood's experiences—and, on the other hand, to history: Céline Lafontaine, for example, situates the birth of cybernetics within the prevailing political pessimism during the devastating Second World War (Lafontaine, 2007). Let us take a closer look at how Wiener deals with this issue of entropy, which he referred to as the arch-enemy of the scientist.[5] This is what drives Wiener to return to the aforementioned opposing world views of St. Augustine and the Manicheans: is nature equivalent to the Manichaean devil (a wicked devil) or an Augustinian devil (not wicked per se)? Wiener opts for the latter, based on the rationale that while nature is extremely complicated, it cannot be ascribed with the intentionality to deceive or outsmart us. By rejecting the Manichaean world view, Wiener is thus able to assign a positive role to science, contending that science is not a chess game in which time pressures play a factor:

> The research physicist has all the time in the world to carry out his experiments, and he need not fear that nature will in time discover his tricks and method and change her policy.
>
> *(Wiener, 1989, p. 36)*

However, is the very notion that we have time on our side not the epitome of the denial of entropy? For if we must swim 'upstream against a great torrent of disorganization, which tends to reduce everything to the heat death of equilibrium and sameness', then are we not thus justified in saying that taking it slow or taking a pause might not be the best idea? Consequently, how can we understand the fact that Wiener repeatedly in his book rejects the idea that nature is a wicked devil, who wishes to deceive and, ultimately, trump human beings? His reference to von Neumann may be crucial in this regard:

> The Manichaean devil is playing a game of poker against us and will resort readily to bluffing; which, as von Neumann explains in his Theory of Games, is intended not merely to enable us to win on a bluff, but to prevent the other side from winning on the basis of a certainty that we will not bluff.
>
> *(Wiener, 1989, p. 35)*

Wiener's adoption of the element of chance, the 'element of incomplete determinism, almost an irrationality in the world' (which he first coupled with Freud's unconsciousness) is, on the one hand, that which he wants to incorporate and bring into the economy of technology, while, on the other hand, it must also be silenced and mastered. In the end, Wiener encountered the same horror as von Neuman did vis-à-vis uncertainty. As aforementioned, Wiener considered it to be an evil that ultimately leads to entropy. This is where we stumble upon a central paradox within cybernetics, which is that its aim is to make use of the element of chance, but in an attempt to control it, to domesticate it, and, henceforth, neutralize it and bring it to order. Given this, are we then not justified in reversing Wiener's proposition: it is order which is evil, precisely because in the end that is what entropy is about? Or, to put it in terms of thermodynamic entropy, does the fact that differences in temperature within a system tend to equalize over time not represent the ultimate expression of order and organisation?

Hence, chance and randomness are ultimately what both von Neumann and Wiener were trying to confront in their respective work. As Andrew Glikman argues, von Neumann's game theory sought to find a deterministic solution to Heisenberg's Uncertainty Principle, and from finding a way to eliminate the element of randomness from the quantum world, he then proceeded to further model human motives and actions in an effort to map all possible actions by all potential actors (Glikman, n.d.). Wiener can be said to be following von Neumann's footsteps here, by resolutely dismissing the element of deception in an attempt to paint a clearer picture: nature and its randomness are thus not sheer evil, but, rather, can be dealt with.[6] It is in this respect that Wiener posits the human and the machine as being on one and the same plane: they share the same essential nature; they are both informational and, hence, share the same psychology. This allows humans and machines to unitedly withstand entropy, that is, by producing information that enables them to mount, albeit only temporarily, pockets of negentropy.

> The machine, like the living organism, is, as I have said, a device which locally and temporarily seems to resist the general tendency for the increase of entropy. By its ability to make decisions, it can produce around it a local zone of organization in a world whose general tendency is to run down.
> *(Wiener, 1989, p. 34)*

However, is the malicious agency rejected by Wiener, or at the very least, an entity who seeks to deceive, not wholly congruent with the basic assumption of Turing's test, in which the whole construction hinges on the possibility of deceiving, that is, of a human being deceived by the informational machine? One way to think of this may be as the return of the repressed of Turing showing the truth behind the cyberneticist idea. In other words, was Wiener, in his rejection of a Manichean deceiving devil, not desperately attempting to keep entropy within the site of the material and the natural? As he himself firmly stated: "The view that nature reveals an entropic tendency is Augustinian, not Manichaean". In short, Wiener chooses to define entropy as a cosmological and metaphysical truth,[7] which he does, I argue, in order to ward off the conclusion of a malicious, non-natural, non-cosmological, non-metaphysical entropy *within the computable and informational itself*. That is to say, what if entropy and the end of the world has nothing to do with the world or with nature, but, rather, is intimately connected to the fact that we are children of Logos? Perhaps Wiener himself understood what the true defiance was towards, as one can discern in the following statement:

> It seems almost as if progress itself and our fight against the increase of entropy intrinsically must end in the downhill path from which we are trying to escape.
> *(Wiener, 1989, pp. 46–47)*

Apropos this above point, is this not the principal lesson of Freudian theory and certain currents within critical theory, which is that the tools with which one tries to cure the wound, are ultimately the very same weapons that caused the wound in the first place?[8] So, if for Wiener information represented a way through which to counter entropy, perhaps in the first instance, we must consider the point that perhaps it is information itself that brings entropy. Resultantly, entropy was never external or cosmological (ostensibly slowly but surely encroaching on the human being), but, rather, was always already internal, that is, on the side of the human, on the side of information itself (that which was supposed to counter entropy). Or, phrased otherwise, entropy was never natural, but was always on the side of the symbolic order, on the side of the logic of Logos. Consider Freud's famous 'discontents' of culture here: it is via culture that one attempts to face up to the rupture that is itself caused by culture (its discomfort, its division) (Freud, [1930a]1955).

The radical conclusion to be drawn here, then, is that the symbolic system, Logos as such (that which cybernetics try to control in the form of information), is not just a vestige against entropy, but, rather, contains entropy within its very bosom: entropy is its eventual end goal. If we can be said to be speaking beings, as Lacan refers to us, then we speak in order to not disappear in language, or, to put this more concisely, to mark our very disappearance within language. This is perhaps what Wiener shies away from, and what leads him to ultimately regress into psychologisation:

> In a very real sense we are shipwrecked passengers on a doomed planet. Yet even in a shipwreck, human decencies and human values do not necessarily vanish, and we must make the most of them. We shall go down, but let it be in a manner to which we may look forward as worthy of our dignity.
> *(Wiener, 1989, p. 40)*

This is Wiener's cosmological myth, which serves to frame the scene of our poor ship rocking back and forth in the maelstrom of cosmological tides. The only thing we can cling onto is human decency and dignity, as if this essentialist psychological or neuropsychological make-up of the human being is our lifeboat and temporary safeguard against oblivion. Having said this, what if there is a problem with the vessel of 'human decency and dignity'? Here, one should oppose Wiener's appeal to dignity with the words of a Nobel Prize winner: "Dignity [has] never been photographed".[9] Or, perhaps even better, let us oppose Wiener's humble quietism with Dylan Thomas's poem, which violently lays waste to any claim to dignity:

> Do not go gentle into that good night, Old age should burn and rave at close of day; Rage, rage against the dying of the light.
> *(Thomas, 1953)*

However, Wiener's psychologising turn can also be understood in an economico-political way. That is, immediately following the passage on dignity, Wiener engages in a long discussion about the history of humanity and its economic expansion. Whilst humans always pushed ever further the boundaries so as to be able to exploit new resources, Wiener argued that the 20th century signalled a turning point: as we reached the end of the age of discoveries, we instead were forced to consider the limits of this expansion and our ever faster advancement towards exhaustion. It is in this context that Wiener writes:

> We have modified our environment so radically that we must now modify ourselves in order to exist in this new environment.
>
> *(Wiener, 1989, p. 46)*

Does this not signal that the informational and cybernetic turn is, in fact, a turn towards ourselves, and, in so doing, is directly related to the commodification of ourselves that is so central to contemporary digitalised forms of capitalism? Indeed, it was precisely at the point at which capitalism had to seek out new resources or else risk coming to a screeching halt, or should I say, risked reaching a certain level of entropy, that cybernetics offered capitalism new terrain for colonisation: digitalised and psychologised (inter) subjectivity.

The central question here concerns whether this signifies a decisive shift in capitalism or not. Consider in this respect that subjectivity, for Lacan, was something that lay outside of both the machine and the workings of the symbolic (Lacan places the symbolic and the machine on the same level here):

> The world of signs functions, and it has no signification whatsoever. What gives it its signification is the moment when we stop the machine. These are the temporal breaks which we make in it. If they are faulty, we will see ambiguities emerge, which are sometimes difficult to resolve, but which one will always end up giving a signification to.
>
> *(Lacan, 1988, p. 284)*

The subject is thus nothing more than the external cut or fault that thwarts the meaningless of the informational machine, and, hence, is the precondition for meaning itself to arise. But what Lacan perhaps did not envision was that technology was well on its way to eventually drawing this external point into the workings of the machine itself. Consider how, especially since the emergence of the so-called Web 2.0, digital machinery requires the subject to be on the inside and to participate: we are not only supposed to deliver our content (to feed the machine) but also must be present in the machine (via, for example, social media). For, if the new digital business model can be said to be about anything at all, then it is about the exploitation of the surplus of subjectivity. In other words, if, in the early days of the Internet, we were still able to be outside of it and, indeed, had to 'go on' the Internet so to speak, today the virtual is ever more where (inter)subjectivities are permanently housed or hosted, so that they can operate within the digital economy. In response to the potential criticism that information is, in fact, the ultimate commodity, that is, the universal commodity that money used to be,[10] I would proclaim that information in and of itself is worthless, and that it ultimately requires the subject qua necessary cut to imbue it with surplus value. It is for this reason that the digital economy needs us inside the machine. This is why we should understand the various avatars and smart environments as operating as placeholders for (inter)subjectivity, and why we need to critically inquire into the kinds of psychological theories and models that are used to design and preconfigure (inter)subjectivity, as well as considering how these models provide algorithms through which to extract surplus value.

However, is this a sustainable model? Can we be sure that the cybernetic turn to ourselves and our 'psychologies' will stall the political-economical entropy of capitalism? That is to say, what if capitalism simply reaches yet another boundary, maybe even its final one? Let me move onto refer once again to Ray Kurzweil's fantasy that in the not-so-distant future, it will be possible to digitally upload a human being onto a computer (Kurzweil, 2000). At first glance, Kurzweil appears to be seeking a way out of the twin-ordeal of personal and cosmological entropy that inevitably awaits us. The next logical question, then, would surely concern what would become of this uploaded subject? What will it become once it is digitalised? Would it not, as a result of entering cyberspace, assimilate the entire history of human knowledge, all information, and, in so doing, become everything, become the Internet itself and, as a consequence of this, come to a halt? From this perspective, the subject would thus not be erased like a face drawn in the sand on the shoreline, but, rather, would disappear like a drop of water dissolving into the ocean. Is digitality thus the final frontier for human beings, where subjectivity encounters its final entropy? Here, the destiny of humanity within the Logos would be none other than its own erasure. Logos, as it becomes unbound and unleashed via digital technology, would thus only lead to the final and full realisation of the zero level of subjectivity, inasmuch as it would be the point where subjectivity disappears as such.

However, one should stress that for this truth or dark destiny of the logic of Logos to be realised, the illusory myth or the foundational lie of a naturalised psychology must first be put in place. That is to say, my argument is that psychological theories and models are utilised to design avatars and digital environments, or, in Kurzweil's fantasy, psychology is required to upload or digitise subjectivity. Let me explain the latter through a way of an anecdote. Once when I was giving a class to psychology students at an American university, I talked about Kurzweil's idea of converting a person's mind into digital data and asked the students: what models or algorithms would be used here, psychoanalytic or behaviourist ones? I continued: how would you prefer to be uploaded, in a Freudian or a Pavlovian way? In response to this, one student exclaimed spontaneously and animatedly: 'Oh, surely, not in a Freudian way!' And, of course, he was absolutely right: who would want to be uploaded into the caricatured cardboard psychological schemes of pseudo-Freudianism that are taught to students worldwide! Perhaps my final argument on this point is as follows: if you would wish to use psychoanalysis in an algorithmic way, then you would first need to betray it and psychologise it (I return to this argument in the ensuing chapters).

Therefore, when confronted by the dark Telos and entropy of the Logos, my contention is that we should fight against bad psychology, or, to say the same thing in a different way, we should fight psychology because it is evil, not in Wiener's preferred Augustinian sense, but in its Manichaean meaning. While, one day, far in the future, the sun will reach its final destiny and the earth shall perish along with it, capitalism (eventually it exploits the energy of the sun) dramatically hastens this process. Given that psychology constitutes one of the central technological components of today's digital capitalism, our duty in the time that we have left (the in-between-time or the chiaroscuro of entropy) is to fight both capitalism and psychology.

However, before engaging in this fight, should it not be crystal clear what we are fighting for? Indeed, failure to do so culminates in the paradoxical, but nevertheless routine, trap of critique unwittingly reinforcing that which it claims to fight. So, if Wiener can be said to lead us to the conclusion, that what awaits us is full digitalisation and the end of our world as we know it, then should we thus be defending or safeguarding the analogue? Indeed, one could easily think of psychoanalysis as the discipline best equipped to touch upon the analogue. However, I would strenuously warn against this, for what if the analogue is that which only sees light from within the digital perspective, and is thus the necessary other of digitality? This is what would be overlooked in such a naïve crusade to rescue the mythical pre-digital analogue. Consequently, let us stay a little bit longer within cybernetics and consider how the analogue is considered there.

Gregory Bateson's dream of the analogic

Before unpacking Bateson's work, let us first return to Marvin Minsky and his argument that the first common step of AI-theorists and cyberneticists is to put forward the informational and communicational levels as distinct from the biological and neurological levels. In the end, then, the analogue is, ostensibly, the meaty stuff, the brain, neuronal matter. As Minsky writes:

> Many scientists look on chemistry and physics as ideal models of what psychology should be like. After all, the atoms in the brain are subject to the same all-inclusive physical laws that govern every other form of matter. Then can we also explain what our brains actually do entirely in terms of those same basic principles? The answer is no, simply because even if we understood how each of our billions of brain cells work separately, this would not tell us how the brain works as an agency. The "laws of thought" depend not only upon the properties of those brain cells but also on how they are connected. And these connections are established not by the basic, "general" laws of physics (…).
>
> *(Minsky, 1988, p. 26)*

So, in contradistinction to the neurobiological level, there is the informational level, which can be considered to operate at the digital level. However, Minsky's contention should be amended with the observation that AI theorists and cyberneticists also attempt to bring precisely this other neurobiological level into the digital and technological levels. As aforementioned in Chapter 2, David Bates argues that AI theorists and cyberneticists wanted to construct 'a wholly new kind of machine technology, a flexible, adaptive one that would mimic the vital improvisation of the organism' (Bates, 2016, p. 207). So, yes, there is this tendency to see the digital as relying on the informational and as being distinct from the biological level (see my discussion in the previous chapter about how Turing considers the physical substrate of the machine to be irrelevant to its logical operation). However, there is also the other and equally basic rationale exemplified by Turing and Wiener, which attempts to ground the digital and the technological precisely in the supposedly analogue neurobiological realm itself.

Let us explore this 'double bind' further through recourse to Gregory Bateson, another seminal figure within cybernetics. Bateson was a British scholar who was one of the founding members of the Macy Conferences (held in New York between 1946 and 1953), which are widely considered to be the breeding ground for cybernetics and systems theory. In his book 'Steps to an ecology of mind', an anthology of his major works, Bateson interestingly tries to grapple with the juxtaposition of the analogue and the digital. He starts with depicting an isomorphous relation between the use of symbols and language and the neurobiological. For example, Bateson argues that if one writes the word 'many', then this entails restraints at different levels, such as not using the letter 'K', as well as, at a higher level, not using the words 'few', 'several', or 'frequent'. Bateson continues that this implies that the unused alternatives must be conceivable to the person, and thus 'must exist as distinguishable and possibly labelled or coded patterns in my neural processes' (Bateson, 1972, p. 413). In this way, one could argue that, for Bateson, language is ultimately fully neurologically traceable. However, Bateson argued that in the world of communication, even though perceptions of sound waves or printer ink constitutes neurophysiological messages, the only relevant realities are messages themselves: 'including in this term parts of messages, relations between messages, significant gaps in messages, and so on' (Bateson, 1972, p. 255). It is here that Bateson proceeds to make a dialectical move: the communicational and informational principles can eventually be discerned at the neuronal level itself:

> A priori it can be argued that all perception and all response, all behavior and all classes of behavior, all learning and all genetics, all neurophysiology and endocrinology, all organization and all evolution—one entire subject matter must be regarded as communicational in nature, and therefore subject to the great generalizations or "laws" which apply to communicative phenomena. We therefore are warned to expect to find in our data those

principles of order which fundamental communication theory would propose. The Theory of Logical Types, Information Theory, and so forth, are expectably to be our guides.

(Bateson, 1972, p. 287)

At first glance, this may lead us to conclude that everything is communicational and informational, and that there is thus no analogical level as such; rather, everything is from the very beginning digital? At the very least, as W.J.T. Mitchells nicely put it, the difference between the digital and analogue representation is far from a 'rigid binary opposition' (Mitchell, 2015, p. 57). However, this is not what Bateson started out from, as he believed that there is a very clear differentiation between the analogical and the digital: Bateson argued, from an evolutionary perspective, that there has been a transition from the analogical to the digital. Most notably, for Bateson the digital can first be discerned at the neuronal level:

> It seems also that while much of the behavioral communication of even higher mammals remains ostensive or analogic, the internal mechanism of these creatures has become digitalized at least at the neuronal level. It would seem that analogic communication is in some sense more primitive than digital and that there is a broad evolutionary trend toward the substitution of digital for analogic mechanisms. This trend seems to operate faster in the evolution of internal mechanisms than in the evolution of external behavior.
>
> *(Bateson, 1972, p. 296)*

Here, for Bateson, it is first the neurobiological level which gets digitalised, whereas external behaviour is seen as having atavistic tendencies. One might have not expected this, as the typical way of framing this is to say that there was first the messy analogical meaty level of the body out of which then evolved our symbolic and digital forms of communication. The dialectical move to make here is to reject the evolutionary rationale, in both its traditional form (of digital communicative behaviour evolving from analogue neurobiology) as well as Bateson's alternative version (of digitalisation starting primarily alongside neurobiology, with the external behavioural lagging behind in terms of evolution), on the basis of the biblical dictum: In the beginning, there was the word. Simply put: the domain of the non-verbal only sees light in the domain of the verbal. Or, to rephrase this in terms of digitality: it is the digital itself that opens up to the analogical dimension, the analogical promise, that is, the supposedly primordial domain of behaviour and psychology. Given that we are the first children of Logos, we cannot but see the world in terms of pairs of opposites, binaries, and, thus, in digital terms. Hence, the domain of the analogue is not only inaccessible to us, rather, and above all, the analogue is nothing more than the dream or the fantasy of the digital itself: it is its imaginary other! Consequently, androids do not dream of electric sheep, but, rather, of the analogue kind.[11]

It is here that I argue Bateson takes a psychologising turn. By setting out from the digital communicational and informational level and subsequently even finding the digital within the neurobiological level, he began to conceive of there being a field of analogical behaviour, which, in turn, leads him to posit the existence of a psychological realm. Let us, for example, consider how Bateson, apropos a discussion about dolphins, wolves, and cats, argues that their analogical communication is relational and positions the individual in relation to others. It is this *psychological* realm, as I would classify it as being, that Bateson argued remains active and manifests itself through our digital and informational communication:

> What was extraordinary—the great new thing—in the evolution of human language was not the discovery of abstraction or generalization, but the discovery of how to be specific about something other than relationship. Indeed, this discovery, though it has been achieved, has scarcely affected the behavior even of human beings. If A says to B, "The plane is scheduled to leave at 6.30," B rarely accepts this remark as simply and solely a statement of fact about the plane. More often he devotes a few neurons to the question, "What does A's telling me this indicate for my relationship to A?" Our mammalian ancestry is very near the surface, despite recently acquired linguistic tricks.
>
> *(Bateson, 1972, p. 371)*

For Bateson, then, digital language allows for a non-relational, purely informational level, which is not about abstraction or generalisation, but, rather, about the specificity of information. However, the analogue and relational level, the particular beyond the information, he claimed, will always manifest itself, and it was precisely in this psychological level that Bateson situated (inter)subjectivity.

From a psychoanalytic perspective, I would argue that Bateson is wrong about where he locates the subject in the pre-digital realm, in the non-verbal and the particular. For psychoanalysis, in contrast, the subject only sees light in the symbolic, albeit in a very specific way. Let me clarify what I mean here: psychoanalytically speaking, human language transcends the relation between the individual and the other and instead opens up to a relation between the subject and the Lacanian Big Other. To put it plainly, language means that I no longer merely relate to specific others, but, rather, also to an abstract and generalised Other that lays beyond the imminent situation and concrete circumstance. In so doing, this entails that the subject itself also transcends its specific and particular situation, and can thus be said to also be abstracted and generalised. Hence, the statement 'the plane is scheduled to leave at 6.30', ultimately opens up space for a *zero-level of subjectivity*, a place from where specific, factual, non-relational, objectifying statements are made. This is arguably the perspective from where the speaking subject, and in a still yet more structural way, the modern subject, has come to look upon itself, others, and the world. The speaking subject is, in the end, a subjectless subject, an acephalous subject, that which adopts the point of view of nowhere; it is only in its claim to objectivity, and only there, that it becomes a singular subject, whilst speaking, whilst being represented by a signifier for another signifier, that is, in relation to the Big Other. Arguably, this is not the level of the analogue (the imaginary psychological realm) as such, but, rather, the level of the non-psychological qua the very foundation of subjectivity and sociality. While this is eventually where the surplus or excess would be identified, in the interim Bateson remained within the traditional confines of situating the excess in the too muchness of the analogical psychology of the human. Hence, he imagined a psychological reality which was simply too big to grasp with words:

> We humans become very uncomfortable when somebody starts to interpret our postures and gestures by translating them into words about relationship. We much prefer that our messages on this subject remain analogic, unconscious, and involuntary.
> *(Bateson, 1972, p. 379)*

With respect to the digitalisation of (inter)subjectivity, then, perhaps Bateson puts our worries to rest: the analogue will never be digitalized, so we can relax? However, when turning to consider communication between dolphins, Bateson argues that as a result of evolutionary mechanisms, dolphins traded their analogical channels for relational communication and thus turned fully to digital language (Bateson, 1972, p. 376). Are they, thus, the first species to use digital language to express their psychology, to be followed soon by man; or, to paraphrase Freud, where the analogical was, the digital shall be?

However, if, in contrast, psychoanalysis proffers a different kind of relationality that is associated with human language—not something old or atavistic such as aggression and domination as we imagine it to be with animals, but something new, concerning, if one will allow me to get a little ahead of myself here, sexuality and jouissance—is then not the central question: will this relationality, which is itself the excess of Logos, ever be digitalisable?

Hence, is this the fight we should be engaging in: to safeguard the precious human agalma from digitalisation? Should we be pleading to keep open non-digital spaces? Or should we be preserving it by securing for it a place within digitalisation itself? Should we, critical theorists, critical psychoanalysts, work together with digital theorists and digital engineers, to, at the very least, attenuate the anti-subjectivising, anti-humanising tendencies of today's mode of digitalisation? It should be clear by now that my answer to all these aforesaid questions is 'no', which I shall explain by way of an anecdote. Some time ago, while finishing my post-doc at the university, I was offered a job with an NGO to do critical (even perhaps subversive) work on the digitalisation of social care. I really considered accepting the job—one has to earn a living after all—but I did wonder at that moment: is this the margin we are condemned to, to try to save a bit of our privacy, secure a certain level of our subjectivity vis-à-vis the roaring and seemingly unstoppable digital monster? However, what if this attempt to smooth out the sharp edges of digitalisation only serves to pave the way for the machine? As it happens, I ended up accepting another job, in a relatively speaking more academic position, working on a research project on the issue of burnout in education. A good friend wrote to me at the time: perhaps you can give it a psychoanalytic touch? But I wondered, should I do that? Should I not let the project run according to its own logic and follow its own disastrous trajectory? When I reflect upon (higher) education I see how often well-meaning policies, covertly or openly inspired by neoliberal agendas, contribute to the further decline of education. Hence, similarly, I find myself currently, on the one hand, along with many other enthusiastic people in education zealously implementing disastrous strategies, while, on the other hand, critical people try their best to slow things down and preserve certain aspects. Now, I am inclined to think that perhaps me and my critically-minded colleagues should not try to stall the system, but instead let it run its course, so that it will crush under its own weight as soon as possible. Resistance? Not on my watch!

Of course, sitting back, relaxing, and watching melancholically from my little temporary backroom in Hotel Academia/Hotel Abgrund while the digital ship heads into its entropic storm is no solution either. For having examined the psychoanalytic inspiration behind Turing, Minsky, Wiener, and Bateson's work (who also has a history of being connected to psychoanalysis), even though I argued that all of them betrayed the Freudian heritage and engaged in a psychologising perspective, a more unsettling question looms in the dark background: what if this psychoanalytic inspiration, despite its subsequent abandonment, remains the key to understanding the current digitalisation of (inter)subjectivity and its inherently apocalyptic core? Here, allow me to approach this question, which I will return to at various points in this book, through recourse to Warren McCulloch, who in contrast to the aforementioned central figures in the history of AI and cybernetics, is well-known for his outright rejection of Freud. In his pamphlet 'The Past of a Delusion', McCulloch wanted to make it abundantly clear to his fellow cyberneticists that Freud had to be dropped.

Warren McCulloch: control of our chaotic dreams

I would designate McCulloch's text 'The Past of a Delusion' as a pamphlet as one would be hard pressed to call it an essay. To begin with, it is replete with rather gratuitous ad hominem attacks on Freud, while the tone is unscholarly disdainful up to and including the use of foul language. In fact, it would be more appropriate in our own Trumpian era where this kind of style appears to have become the new standard in public discourse. To illustrate my point, see McCulloch's critique of psychoanalysts:

> (...) incompetence is not the worst reason for becoming a psychiatrist, nor are these civil servants the men who sold short psychiatry. The worst

> reason is the desire for filthy lucre. Psychoanalysts say that they discovered that gold is a symbol for feces, but they formed a sect in psychiatry where there should be none.
>
> (McCulloch, 2016, p. 311)

McCulloch's rant here is not that different from contemporary populist rants on the incompetence of the political elites and monetary greed. Indeed, his 'arguments' even have an anti-migrant flavour to them, referring to 'refugee physicians' from Europe to the point of anti-Semitism: McCulloch recounts the birth of Sigmund Freud as follows: the "new young wife of an unsuccessful aging Jewish miller gave birth to a son covered with pitch-black hair". One can only speculate as to the reasons for McCulloch's diatribe.[12]

It is in vain that the reader waits for a logical, or, at the very least, coherent argument against psychoanalysis. Of course, one could side with McCulloch purely on the basis that there are manifold critiques to be made about Americanised forms of psychoanalysis. Despite this point, the main problem with McCulloch's rant is that, apart from its unscientific tone and style, it evidently adopts various elements from psychoanalysis itself. Consider, for example, his diagnosis that followers of Freud must suffer from some 'strange defect to think one knows God's will, or Matter's dialectical determination, or how his own brain works to fool him!' If one initially thinks that McCulloch was engaging in some kind of parody of psychoanalysis, then it patently becomes clear over the course of the text that this is not the case. For, when he for some reason or another thinks it is useful to engage in a biographical sketch of Freud, it is clear, not only that he means it, but also that he cannot but utilise psychoanalytic paradigms in order to criticize Freud. For example, he writes concerning the Freudian theme of infantile sexuality:

> I do not for one moment believe his story of sexual advances made by him, an infant, to his mother, nor of her turning him over to old Jacob for castration, nor that a baby of that age has such a notion. These are ideas Freud had in later life, after he had extended sex to mean all pleasure and affection, and then projected them upon his past of which he had no recollections clear enough to stop him from confabulating.
>
> (McCulloch, 2016, p. 319)

Is this not the typical psychoanalytic reasoning associated with 'Nagträglichkeit' ('deferred action'), where infantile memories get reworked and re-inscribed a second time? This is the crux of Freud's shift away from his pre-psychoanalytic period with Breuer and his abandonment of seduction theory towards instead laying the emphasis on fantasies and the intricate timelines of 'psycho-sexual' maturation. Interestingly, as if McCulloch himself realises that he has been overtaken by psychoanalytic reasoning, he attempts to both correct and distance himself from what he considers to be the typical Freudian psycho-biographical explanations:

> What's most important here is that Freud's early life, with or without his fancied past, cannot account for his delusion. For Freud did not invent the ideas of which it is composed. It is not likely we will ever learn just why or how these ideas came together in his brain rather than in some other, but the ideas were rampant in his world. Sex, the Unconscious, and Materialism were matters of discussion among physicians and the public generally.
> (McCulloch, 2016, p. 319)

Here, McCulloch appears to reproach Freud for not only having confabulated his 'sexual' memories, but for the fact that his fantasies are not even his own. Once again, however, is this not a very psychoanalytic point to make: that the core of what you think and your subjectivity always necessarily comes from others and from outside of you? This is what Lacan explicates via the Big Other: a subject subjectivises itself through signifiers and discourses that are in the end alien to itself, which means that there is a radical alterity at the very core of subjectivity.

Perhaps the one 'real' argument that McCulloch develops in his pamphlet is the fact that the 'Dependence of the data on the theory separates psychoanalysis from all true sciences' (McCulloch, 2016, p. 313). The point being made here is that psychoanalysis shapes and constructs its data according to its own theories as he proceeds to argue that "Interpretations of chaotic dreams are still controlled by theory, and that theory was in the head of Freud" (McCulloch, 2016, p. 313). However, if one will permit me to quickly and freely associate to McCulloch, is this not precisely what we now know to be the case in the era of digitalisation, where our reality (and/or our dreams) are controlled digitally precisely via the psychological theories and models that form the basis of the algorithms? Let me make this point more clearly yet still. McCulloch's argument, then, is that real science, in contrast to psychoanalysis, locates its findings in time and space:

> All our hypotheses are of a kind that do require, if they be right, that we shall find this going on now, here; and that, then, there: whereas Freud's notions fail to locate in space and time his hypothetical Id, Unconscious, Ego, Super-Ego, or to predict what they will look like in the brain.
> (McCulloch, 2016, p. 318)

McCulloch thus rejects Freud's (meta)theory as nothing more than the imprecise reconstruction and representation of reality, demanding in its place, a precise location in time and space. But the paradox, here, is that he does so precisely in order to ground the discipline of cybernetics, whose modelling of reality via informational schemes ultimately defies time and space![13] For Wiener, at the very least social systems were, in contrast to neurobiological systems, characterised by shifting relations in space and time (Wiener, 1948).[14] Does this not constitute the very ground for our contemporary virtualised lifeworld in which time and space have fundamentally become volatile issues?

Consider, in this respect, how McCulloch opposes Freudian heuristics to a cybernetic approach: building and modelling humanlike machines from which we are then able to infer what humans actually are:

> We even have some notions of the many disparate processes that we call glibly "Memory," and as we build our engines that can have ideas, lay plans, elaborate their purposes and forecast the outcome of their acts to make them match the probable events around them, we begin to make a better guess as to the ways our brains can do these things that we call mental.
>
> *(McCulloch, 2016, p. 318)*

Hence, in rejecting Freud's allegedly theoretically controlled interpretations of dreams, McCulloch himself promotes the construction of a human model in the technological realm—which, of course, is nothing but the realisation of a theory, if not a fantasy, within the machine—and from there makes inferences about concrete human beings. Or, phrased otherwise, McCulloch controls the virtual with theory to then argue that this allows us to say something about real human beings, the latter of whom are situated in concrete space and time. This move is particularly egregious in light of the commonly known story that McCulloch modelled the artificial after the organic. In his famous paper 'A Logical Calculus of the Ideas Immanent in Nervous Activity' (McCulloch & Pitts, 1943), operations of mind (memory, perception, consciousness, problem-solving) are understood as all-or-none events, thus, arguably, providing the model for the digital computer itself. As Norbert Wiener wrote:

> The all-or-none character of the discharge of the neuron is precisely analogous to the single choice made in determining a digit on the binary scale, which more than one of us had already contemplated as the most satisfactory basis of computing-machine design.
>
> *(Wiener, 1948, p. 14)*

This is the official story about technology mimicking nature. However, what I am instead arguing here is that McCulloch did not start from nature or neurology but, rather, from a *psychologising* model of *what the human is* to model the artificial, from which he then claimed to be able to make inferences about the nature of man. I have demonstrated that these moves not only rest on a virulent rejection of psychoanalysis but also function as a 'Verneinung' (negation): that is, McCulloch bows to the explanatory schemes of Freud. However, while Freud has been (unjustifiably) accused of pan-sexualism, and Lacanians (unjustifiably) castigated for pan-symbolism, McCulloch could be accused of pan-digitalism or pan-binarisation.

Overall, then, this chapter has demonstrated references to psychoanalysis, be it positive (e.g. Turing, Minsky, Wiener, Bateson) or negative (e.g. McCulloch) is the decisive recurring factor in the history of AI and digital technologies. Moreover, from here, all references, whether positive or negative, end up being used to psychologise human nature, with the latter then informing the designing of digital models and technologies. Hence, the task that awaits any of us seeking to conduct a critique of the digital sphere and digital technologies is to fully investigate the non-psychological core that psychoanalysis situates in the children of Logos.

At the very least, in an attempt to return to the earlier discussion about the analogue versus the digital, the pitfall to be avoided is to reject McCulloch's digital interpretation of the neurobiological via a reclaiming of the analogical domain. Doing so, I argue, leads one to fall right back into a psychologising perspective. Is this not the case with Elisabeth Wilson's work, for example, who, when discussing McCulloch's privileging of the digital (on/off) character of the neuron in his 1943 paper, argues with Katherine Hayles about analogical factors operating at the neuronal level (chemical, electrical) (Wilson, 2008)? In contradistinction to McCulloch and Pitts' argument that the fundamental relations are between two-valued logics (McCulloch & Pitts, 1943, p. 131), she purports that 'psychological events' such as affects are in the first place 'non-digital' (Wilson, 2008, p. 24).[15] From 'affect's analogic character', Wilson then proceeds to classify McCulloch's reduction of psychology to digital events as being pointedly unknowing (Wilson, 2008, p. 25).

There is something fundamentally problematic with Wilson's attempt to rescue the analogue as the true psychological dimension of the human. Wilson argues that other AI theorists did factor in issues such as affect,[16] referring specifically to Turing's 'enthusiasm and a discernible interest in coassembling the affective and the artificial' (Wilson, 2002). One could also discuss Wiener here, but as I have argued in my readings of both these seminal authors, this is precisely where both authors regress into promoting mainstream psychologising models, essentialising and neurobiologising the human being to the extent that any level of subjectivity and even of humanity eventually disappears from their thinking. Based on this, I would oppose this search for the analogical psychological core of the human being, perhaps surprisingly, through recourse to McCulloch and other's privileging of the binary, simply because it directly speaks to the psychoanalytic conception of the split subject. Indeed, the closer one looks at this, the clearer it becomes that psychoanalysis has always operated with oppositional pairs (albeit dialectically): conscious/unconscious, Eros/Thanatos, neurosis/psychosis, male/female… However, from a psychoanalytic perspective, of course, McCulloch's attempt to ground the informational in the alleged objective and material reality of the neuronal misses the true issue at stake. Conversely, for psychoanalysis, the informational, or Logos as such, points towards a *subject*: remember here how Lacan situates the subject between two signifiers, rather than in the materiality of neurons. At the neuronal level, one can only search for and find the phantasmatic psychological individual, with their respective affects and so forth.[17]

Moreover, it is precisely there where psychological fantasies stuff the human subject to the brim with affects and other signatures of life, that opponents of McCulloch inevitably find themselves coming close to his project of constructing 'engines that can have ideas, lay plans, elaborate their purposes, and forecast the outcome of their acts' (McCulloch, 2016, p. 318). In other words, both can be said to claim to know what the human is or should be. And here, if one will permit me to make yet another step in my argument, is where the domain of ideology becomes most apparent. Consider, for example, the following passage of McCulloch's, in which he, without mentioning Karl Marx, clearly also targets the latter during his rant against Freud:

> I will not rehearse the sad story of the industrial revolution. It is enough to note that from the village craftsman, whose life made sense to him, whose ideals were practical affairs of neighborly affection, whose God, although inscrutable, was worthy of all trust, it had made the proletariat, struggling for necessities in city slums, or owners, to whom wealth brought power without that tradition of responsibility which is the birthright of hereditary rulers.
>
> *(McCulloch, 2016, p. 322)*

Is this not the personification of the typical corporatist fantasy of the village craftsman living in peace with his trustworthy God and responsible King? From here the question becomes: what are the effects of these fantasies that are smuggled into our current technologies like one enormous Trojan Horse? In the next chapter, I discuss two concrete examples of how psychological fantasies and ideology in tandem drive the development of AI and digital technologies.

Notes

1 Recall the story of Baron Von Munchhausen who saved himself from drowning by pulling himself out of the swamp by his own hair.
2 Minsky's answer to this is eventually 'attachment mechanisms' through which he eventually reinterprets the 'sexual jealousy' detailed in Freud's Oedipus complex (Minsky, 1988, p. 181). One is also reminded of Turing here, who too needed to expel sex and sexuality and trade it for evolutionist and neurobiological thinking.
3 I owe this formulation to Carlos Gómez Camerena.
4 See Orit Halpern (2015, pp. 68–69). In this respect, perhaps Kittler's most famous phrase, "Nur was schaltbar ist, ist überhaupt" ("Only that which can be switched, can be") (Kittler, 1993, p. 182) can be read as a designation of the psychoanalytic dialectical conceptualisation of the subject as split and divided (I owe this point to Cindy Zeiher).
5 "The scientist is always working to discover the order and organization, and is thus playing a game against the arch-enemy, disorganization". (Wiener, 1989, p. 34).
6 This might be, as Cindy Zeiher remarks, precisely the suturing position proffered by contemporary environmentalism (personal communication).

7 Céline Lafontaine "As sociologist Philippe Breton (1995) has demonstrated, Wiener elevated entropy to the rank of metaphysical truth". (Lafontaine, 2007, p. 31).
8 I am, of course, once again subverting the classic idea that one has to cure the wound with the same spear that caused it (see Chapter 1).
9 https://bobdylan.com/songs/dignity/
10 One could argue that Wiener's cybernetics puts forward information as the ultimate commodity, that is, as the universal commodity, as money. Lafontaine writes: "Equally as abstract as the concept of energy, the notion of information then becomes a principle of statistical quantification whose universal scope is equaled only by its indifference toward the specific nature of signals (physical, biological, technical, or human)" (Lafontaine, 2007, p. 31). Hence, information as money, the universal trading currency, to ward of entropy, to pay it off.
11 Or: in the beginning, there was the word *and the word made flesh*.
12 Lawrence Kubie (a psychoanalyst who was part of the Macy group) wrote, in this respect, that this vitriolic tone might be due to McCulloch's own personal frustrations (Hayles, 2008, p. 72).
13 Defying time and space is precisely also what the Freudian unconscious is about (I owe this remark to Cindy Zeiher) and, moreover, could be said to be integral to both the endeavour of modern science and its outcomes (think of quantum theory here).
14 "The degree of integration of the life of the community may very well approach the level shown in the conduct of a single individual, yet the individual will probably have a fixed nervous system, with permanent topographic relations between the elements and permanent connections, while the community consists of individuals with shifting relations in space and time and no permanent unbreakable physical connections" (Wiener, 1948, p. 156).
15 Wilson writes: "Accurate measurement of the affects typically requires continuous rather than discrete calibration" (Wilson, 2008, p. 25).
16 Wilson writes:

> AI researchers were getting interested in how affective constraints could be factored into artificial systems. They showed that programming affective states into artificial agents makes them more resilient, better able to respond in real time, and more engaged with the vicissitudes of human use.
>
> (Wilson, 2008, p. 23)

17 However, to be absolutely clear, at the subjective level, psychoanalysis too thinks in terms of materiality: this is Lacan's materiality of the signifiers, which as I have argued elsewhere, in the end refers back to a different kind of object: *objet a* (De Vos, 2011).

References

Bates, D. (2016). Automaticity, plasticity, and the deviant origins of artificial intelligence. In D. Bates & N. Bassiri (Eds.), *Plasticity and pathology: On the formation of the neural subject* (pp. 194–218). New York: Fordham University Press.

Bateson, G. (1972). *Steps to an ecology of mind: Collected essays in anthropology, psychiatry, evolution, and epistemology*. Chicago, IL: University of Chicago Press.

Bernstein, J. (1981). A.I. *The New Yorker*. Retrieved from https://www.newyorker.com/magazine/1981/12/14/a-i

De Vos, J. (2011). From La Mettrie's voluptuous man machine to the perverse core of psychology. *Theory & Psychology, 21*(1), 67–85.

De Vos, J. (2012). *Psychologisation in times of globalisation*. London: Routledge.

De Vos, J. (2016). *The metamorphoses of the brain. Neurologization and its discontents*. New York: Palgrave Macmillan.

Freud, S. ([1901]1960). The psychopathology of everyday life. In J. Strachey (Ed.), *The standard edition of the complete psychological works of Sigmund Freud: Vol. VI* (pp. 1–291). London: Hogarth Press.

Freud, S. ([1916–1917]1963). Resistance and repression. In J. Strachey (Ed.), *The standard edition of the complete psychological works of Sigmund Freud: Vol. XVI* (pp. 286–303). London: Hogarth Press.

Freud, S. ([1930a]1955). Civilization and its discontents. In J. Strachey (Ed.), *The standard edition of the complete psychological works of Sigmund Freud: Vol. XXI* (pp. 57–146). London: Hogarth Press.

Glikman, A. (n.d.). Cyb+org = (cold) war machine. *Frame 2*. Retrieved from http://elo-repository.org/trace/frame/frame2/glikman.htm

Halpern, O. (2015). *Beautiful data: A history of vision and reason since 1945*. Durham, NC and London: Duke University Press.

Hayles, N. K. (2008). *How we became posthuman: Virtual bodies in cybernetics, literature, and informatics*. Chicago, IL: University of Chicago Press.

Husserl, E. (1970). *The crisis of European sciences and transcendental phenomenology: An introduction to phenomenological philosophy* (D. Carr, Trans.). Evanston: Northwestern University Press.

Kittler, F. (1993). Real time analysis, time axis manipulation. In F. Kittler (Ed.), *Draculas Vermächtnis* (pp. 182–206). Leipzig: Reclam.

Kurzweil, R. (2000). Live forever—uploading the human brain… Closer than you think. *Psychology Today*. Retrieved from http://www.psychologytoday.com/articles/200001/live-forever

Lacan, J. (1988). *The ego in freud's theory and in the technique of psychoanalysis, 1954–55* (S. Tomaselli, Trans.). New York: Norton.

Lafontaine, C. (2007). The cybernetic matrix of french theory. *Theory, Culture & Society, 24*(5), 27–46.

McCulloch, W. S. (2016). *Embodiments of mind*. Cambridge, MA: MIT Press.

McCulloch, W. S., & Pitts, W. (1943). A logical calculus of the ideas immanent in nervous activity. *The Bulletin of Mathematical Biophysics, 5*(4), 115–133.

Minsky, M. (1965). Matter, mind and models. In M. Minsky (Ed.), *Semantic Information Processing* (pp. 425–432). Cambridge, MA: MIT Press.

Minsky, M. (1988). *Society of mind*. New York: Simon and Schuster.

Minsky, M. (2013). Why Freud was the first good AI theorist. In M. More & N. Vita-More (Eds.), *The transhumanist reader: Classical and contemporary essays on the science, technology, and philosophy of the human future* (pp. 167–176). Chichester: Wiley-Blackwell.

Mitchell, W. J. T. (2015). *Image science: Iconology, visual culture, and media aesthetics*. Chicago, IL: University of Chicago Press.

Saint-Jevin, A. (2017). La "machine électronique" de Lacan: Alan Turing chez les psychanalystes. *L'Évolution Psychiatrique, 82*(4), 761–773.

Thomas, D. (1953). Do not go gentle into that good night (1952). *The collected poems of Dylan Thomas* (p. 128). New York: New Directions.

Wiener, N. (1948). *Cybernetics: Or control and communication in the animal and the machine*. Cambridge, MA: MIT Press.

Wiener, N. (1989). *The human use of human beings. Cybernetics and society*. London: Free Association Books.

Wilson, E. A. (2008). Affect, artificial intelligence, and internal space. *Emotion, Space and Society, 1*(1), 22–27.

4

TOWARDS A PSY-CRITIQUE OF THE DIGITALISATION OF INTERSUBJECTIVITY

Two case-studies

Introduction: it's the psychology, stupid, or is it?

Andrew Hodges recounts in his biography of Alan Turing that Turing at some point asked his lover "Can you think what I feel? Can you feel what I think?" (Hodges, 2014, p. 570). The scenario in which this utterance occurred was a complicated one, insofar as Turing was lying on the floor with his lover, both slightly intoxicated after having wine with dinner, while the latter described a recurrent childhood nightmare of being suspended in an absolute empty space and being subjected to a strange noise that grew ever louder. Turing, who himself had been in Jungian analysis and was deeply interested in the interpretation of dreams (Wilson, 2005), began to associate to this and invented a story in which he himself was locked up in a big empty space, and in order to escape had to defeat a machine in a game of chess. Turing imagined that the machine would be so fast that the only way he would be able to defeat it would be to pretend to be so stupid so that the machine would commit suicide in despair. It is when explaining this scenario to his lover that Turing is said to have uttered the words: "Can you think what I feel? Can you feel what I think?"

Is this aforesaid scenario not reminiscent of what one would imagine a bad therapist to be like, answering your dreams with their own associations, desperately trying to get you onboard: *do you understand what I am trying to tell you?* More than this, however, what it represents is Turing's desire to *fully connect* with his lover, to which we can refer to the psychoanalytic idea that communication always relies upon a successful misunderstanding of each other (see for example, Žižek, 1991, p. 30), as well as oneself. Be that as it may, what I am interested in here is the extent to which such intricacies are lost on social media and in other Big Data applications, which would invariably answer Turing's questions *can you think what I feel? can you feel what I think?* with a resounding: *yes, on both counts!*

Before we get into this discussion, however, it is first worthwhile to highlight how Turing's associative story represents a kind of reversal of his own imitation game. Namely, here it is about the machine having to discern whether Turing can truly think? Hence, the question then becomes, in light of Big Data probing and psychologically profiling us in all of our online and offline activities, can machines truly grasp the sense of doubt involved in a human asking him or herself, *can I think?* or, *do I truly think?* Or, phrased otherwise, could a machine grasp the precise subjective deadlock involved in such questions, if one will permit me to twist Turing's terms, *can I think what I feel? can I feel what I think?* Indeed, such questions can be said to be constitutive of human thinking and human feeling. Moreover, the crucial issue at stake here is not some kind of inherent antagonism between *thinking* and *feeling*, that is, between Logos and the affective, whereby the latter would be neurobiologically accessible via scanning or other technologies. Rather, one could argue that for the human speaking being, the entire realm of feelings and affects only arises as a result of the antagonism inherent to thinking itself. In other words, rather than *"I feel so much that I can't put into words,"* the true human stance is, *"I say so much that I cannot contain the effects and affects of my utterances"*.[1]

It should be evident by this point that this book is not about understanding the effects of the digital or digital culture on (inter)subjectivity through recourse to (neuro)psychology, albeit the temptation to (neuro)psychologise digitalisation is omnipresent. This should not come as a surprise given the profound effects that digitalisation has on (inter)subjectivity. Bernard Stiegler and David Berry explain the exigent problem in the following way: it is not just that the progressive digitalisation of our lifeworld fundamentally transforms *social life;* it also transforms *psychical life* (in: Berry & Beer, 2014; Stiegler, 2012). Hence, public discourse is in an alliance with neuropsychologising approaches to the digital. For example, at the 2018 World Economic Forum at Davos, George Soros grounded his attack on Facebook and Google (who he referred to as 'a menace to society') in psychologising terms, underscoring the engineering of addiction and its harmful effects on adolescents in particular (Soros, 2018). Alternatively, consider the comments of Facebook's co-founder, Sean Parker, who described the operational principle of Facebook as 'hacking people's psychology to hook them', to which he added, 'God only knows what it's doing to our children's brains' (Ulanoff, 2017). Similarly, academic research readily takes recourse to the neuropsy-sciences in order to understand the digitalisation of (inter)subjectivity, either in a direct way (e.g. Turkle, 2011, who examined the 'psychological power' of digital devices to change us, see also Aboujaoude 2011; Carr, 2010), or more covertly (e.g. Cover, 2015, whose study of online performative identities can be said to rely heavily on psy-theories of identity, see also Hansen, 2004; Massumi, 2002; Thrift & French, 2002). Stiegler (2014) explicitly promotes the use of neuroscience to understand the digitalisation of (inter)subjectivity, based on the fact that the digital sphere ostensibly has profound effects on the brain.

However, rather than examining how digitality shapes or alters our brains and psychology, should the task not be instead to critically investigate how neuro-psychological models themselves are always already shaping digitality?

Indeed, my close examination of some of the key antecedents of digital technologies (AI theories and cybernetics) in the previous chapters showed the centrality of psychological theories and models in its development. Given this genealogy, one should not be surprised that contemporary developments in the digital and virtual spheres are still intimately connected to the neuropsy-realms. This is critically important because it is only from this position of acknowledging how the digital is entangled with the psychological, I claim that one can truly begin to discern its impact on (inter)subjectivity. This point is completely overlooked in simple and straightforward accounts that utilise neuropsychology to understand the digital. Simply put, to claim, for example, that Facebook posts or Google searches tell us a lot about human psychology foregoes the fact that Facebook, Google, and other platforms are always already informed by psychological theories and models. Indeed, the architecture of social media, in terms of how it both pre-positions its users and pre-configures the digital social space itself, unquestionably relies on psychological models. In this respect, the algorithms upon which search engines are built can also be said to tap into the same vein, in that Google Search's main rationale relies upon adapting search results to fit their 'user's intent'. Such an assessment of users' intentions, or even their desires, places us squarely within the psychological domain. Or, as I read somewhere: 'search engine optimization has far less to do with content, coding, or site architecture than with psychology'.[2]

Based on this, can we therefore not conclude that many contemporary assessments of the digitalisation of (inter)subjectivity—and also critiques of digitalisation—inevitably reach an impasse, due to the fact that they use the same neuropsychological models that are already deeply embedded in the very thing that they are researching? To repeat the old Flemish expression that I cited in the previous chapter: *only the cat that has been put in the sack comes out of the sack*. Consequently, utilising social media data to study something like 'empathy' completely overlooks the fact that social media already uses psy-models and theories on empathy to set-up their platforms in the first place, as well as to subsequently exploit and commodify this data for profit.

To explore both how this problematic circular logic is overlooked and the ways in which this denial constitutes the backbone of certain widespread (mal) practice within the digital and virtual sphere, I will examine two case studies: first, the well-known Cambridge Analytica scandal that centred around the use of users' personal data for political advertising purposes, and, second, the well-known Facebook AI experiment in which it was claimed that so-called bots automatically evolved so as to showcase human behaviour.

Cambridge Analytica or psychology as a dangerous fantasy

We love to know you digitally

Cambridge Analytica became a huge news story when it went public that the consulting firm (a private corporation who had links to academia) had used the psychological profiles of Facebook users to target them in a customised and individualised way. More specifically, Cambridge Analytica is said to have been involved in the manipulation of voters in the US presidential elections to vote for Donald Trump, as well as in the Brexit referendum in the UK.

The whistle-blower Christopher Wylie immediately gets to the heart of the matter, when describing himself as the digital whizz kid who created 'Steve Bannon's *psychological* warfare tool' based on Cambridge Analytica's 'sophisticated *psychological* and political profiles' (Cadwalladr, 2018, my italics). Does this example testify to how psychology comprises a dangerous mode of knowledge when used for nefarious purposes? We should not be completely surprised by this, of course, as psychologists are deeply embroiled in other key contemporary biopolitical practices, ranging from reality TV (see: De Vos, 2009), humanitarian camps (see: De Vos, 2011b), up to and including the torture chambers at Guantánamo Bay (see: De Vos, 2011a). Hence, as one may have expected, psychologists acted as the central figures in the Cambridge Analytica scandal, by designing the algorithms that were used to mine social media data and exploit them for deceptive ends.

To both understand and problematise the claim that psychological data mining is a potential tool of warfare, it is expedient to turn to the work of psychologists Michal Kosinski and David Stillwell, whose work has been linked to Cambridge Analytica, albeit they themselves have denied any direct involvement with the firm. I will return to both the allegations against Kosinski and Stillwell and their denials, but for now, let me state clearly that their involvement or lack thereof with Cambridge Analytica is irrelevant to my argument. What does appear to be clear is that either their data or their 'myPersonality' app was used by Cambridge Analytica, with or without their consent (Venturini & Rogers, 2019). However, what is of interest for our purposes here is how Kosinski and Stillwell describe the basic rationale of their 'myPersonality project':

> In recent years there has been a remarkable shift towards more social and less anonymous Internet use. Interactions between people using anonymous nicknames, email addresses, or avatars are increasingly replaced by interactions within Online Social Networks (OSN) that are based on real identities and connections that largely mirror offline social links (…).
> *(Stillwell & Kosinski, 2004, p. 93)*

As one can discern from the above quote, the central idea here is that we no longer deceive or play a role on the internet, and even if we do, the internet can see through this. This is because Big Data knows who we are due to the desires that we express while surfing on the internet. In this account, is the internet not reminiscent of a psychologist or a psychoanalyst, while the act of surfing the internet is akin to free association with psychoanalysis? Remember, in this respect, the title of Stephens-Davidowitz's book (2017): "Everybody Lies. Big data, new data, and what the Internet can tell us about who we really are". Hence, must we answer in the affirmative the question I posed earlier about whether psychology constitutes a dangerous form of knowledge? For, it would appear that with the manifold advances brought about by digital technology, psychologists now have truly unprecedented and direct access into human psychology.

However, does this claim of there being a direct link between the psychological and the digital—and here I connect to discussions I engaged with in previous chapters—not raise the question of whether it is truly possible that our 'psychology' is quantifiable in this way, that is, that our 'psychology' is fully digitalisable? Alternatively, is life not precisely that which resists quantification, and, as such, digitalisation? Indeed, this is what Antoinette Rouvroy purports: for her, the truly important aspects of life are not quantifiable, and, hence, life is that which resists calculation and digitalisation (Rouvroy, 2018). Does such a view of life not lead us to conclude that data mining techniques like myPersonality are thus doomed to miss out on the real agalma of our psychology? However, nobody besides Slavoj Žižek appears to contradict this point: referring to the alleged technological advances associated with so-called 'wired brains' through which computers can now capture our thoughts, Žižek notes apropos the prospect of a post-human era:

> We as human beings are precisely what we are, free individuals as far as we can be sure that you do not know what I am thinking. I think what I think, I am free in my mind. What happens if I cannot be sure even of this?
> *(Žižek, 2019b)*

Žižek would have benefitted from being a little more precise here, given that he would undoubtedly acknowledge how, from a psychoanalytic perspective, we are not exactly free, and certainly not in our minds. Above all, psychoanalysis tells us that we do not just think what we think, which is precisely where the unconscious comes in to play: I am never sure of what I actually think, which is perhaps why I keep thinking and reformulating my thoughts.[3] Hence, when Žižek proffers that 'lying' will become more complicated and more privileged—making the interesting point that only the elite will be able to exclude themselves from the network—as a consequence of the new technologies, it would be perhaps more interesting to delve deeper into the prior lies (made by those privileged persons who created data mining and data control) that gave birth to the illusion of technology being able to access our true thoughts.

The first and most important move to make here is to reject both Žižek's seeming belief that the digital can truly access what 'I think' (or uncover the truth behind my lies) and the stance adopted by Rouvroy and others, according to which human truth would resist quantification and digitalisation. In fact, the very idea that there is a true positive human core (a psychological one or otherwise) that is reachable or otherwise through technology is precisely what we should be rejecting from the outset. Hence, that which would succumb to Žižek's ostensible position or, alternatively, resist (Rouvroy) digitalisation is not something external or primordial to it, something vitalistic shall we say, but, rather, digitalisation is ultimately thwarted by the internal antagonism (something inherently problematic) within psychology and, hence, the digital itself! Let me refer here to the Lacanian concept of the Real. Jacques Lacan distinguished between three registers that structured human life: Symbolic, Imaginary, and the Real. The most common understanding of the Real is of that which resists symbolisation, which remains outside of our conceptual grasp of reality. This puts forward an idea of reality as something which is too expansive for our limited representations, which, I would argue, is a misunderstanding of Lacan's concept of the Real. To make my argument more tangible here, let us return to the naïve, common understanding that I mentioned in the introduction of this chapter: *I feel so much that I can't put into words*. This reproduces the idea of reality exceeding our representations. However, in a true psychoanalytic conceptualisation of the Real, the former colloquial utterance must be reversed: *I say so much that I cannot contain the effects and affects of my utterances*. Consider, in this respect, the notion of the Freudian 'slip of the tongue': when we speak, an excess arises that we as subjects cannot fully master or control. This is a true psychoanalytic understanding of the unconscious, which, in turn, helps us understand the Lacanian Real. Or, phrased otherwise, the Real is on the side of the *too much* of the Symbolic qua a monstrous excess, which only sees light precisely because of the fact that human beings speak. The Freudian unconscious is thus not that which exceeds symbolisation, but that which is the result of the excess of symbolisation itself. At the very least, this emphasises why psychoanalysis is a non-psychology, insofar as it situates the very core of subjectivity in a non-psychological surplus. The central questions guiding this book are what happens to this non-psychological excess in the contemporary digital era? Is it this that, in the end, prevents the digital from achieving full closure, or, conversely, will it come to be fully contained within the digital? And, if not, how then do psychological theories and models, and psychologists who are themselves involved, proceed to disavow (the Freudian Verleugnung) this non-psychological kernel in order to set up their digital technologies and deal with both their ostensibly accidental un-emancipatory side effects and explicit abuses?

To explore the latter question, it is expedient to examine more closely the work of the aforementioned psychologists Kosinski and Stillwell who, while having denied any direct link to Cambridge Analytica, nevertheless provided the latter with the basic rationale for their practices, which is that social media now provides us with so much personal data that our personalities have finally become wholly quantifiable (Stillwell & Kosinski, 2004). How do Kosinski and Stillwell operationalise their rationale? They devised an app 'myPersonality' and disseminated it via Facebook where it proliferated like wildfire. To be absolutely clear from the outset, myPersonality is nothing more than a simple psychological questionnaire, which was commonplace in popular magazines in pre-digital times. Kosinski and Stillwell claimed that their quiz app allowed them to 'chart personalities' and subsequently link and match this data—and this was the specific novel move that they made—to what people did on Facebook. Hence, data on Facebook activity is believed to be utilisable for psychological profiling.

I argue that this entire idea is problematic for two reasons. First, what remains unquestioned is the previously noted popularity of the app. Indeed, on Stillwell's personal website this is proudly stated as follows: "Soon, thousands of people were participating every day for fun, self-insight, and to donate their data to psychological research".[4] Hence, it is both fun and charitable to donate data to science! However, notwithstanding Stillwell's sloganesque pitch, what is never questioned is why the app went viral. That is to say, why do people love being tested and profiled, and why are they so gratified with the verdict 'this is what you are'? It is precisely here that the 'we love to know you' from the researcher meets the 'I love to know myself', which is the first thing that the two researchers failed to take into account. As I have described elsewhere, this is the very essence of the phenomena of psychologisation and neurologisation: psychology and the neurosciences not only constitute their object (the neuropsychological object) but also their subject: the psychologised and neurologised subject. This is the situation with the colourful brain scan that engenders the 'oh-my-god-is-this-what-I-am' subject: science creates a new subject, who contemplates itself, others, and the world from a scientific perspective (De Vos, 2016c). Hence, the modern neuropsychologised subject can itself be understood as the surplus or excess of psychology and the neurosciences (recall here the Lacanian logic of the Real as that which is the excess of the symbolic). Psychologists and neuroscientists, as a rule, disregard this point; rather, they think they can directly research *real subjects* and, in so doing, are fooled by the mirages that are a product of the meeting of, on the one hand, science's desire to know the human, and, on the other hand, the desire of the human subject to know itself.

It is here that we can formulate the second problematic aspect of Kosinski and Stillwell's rationale. For it is precisely where the (neuro)psy gets lost in the aforementioned hall of mirrors that Kosinski and Stillwell take recourse to digitality. This pertains to the fact that they believe that social media opens up a window through which to view human beings as they allegedly really are, which is to say that digital data provides psychology with the closure and grounding that it has hitherto lacked. More specifically, their primary methodology was to cross-check the psy-profiles from their psychological questionnaires with data on what people liked, did, or posted on Facebook. This Facebook data supposedly provided neutral parameters that could be correlated with the psychological data. However, the problem is that Facebook likes and other Facebook activity can by no means be viewed as genuine, unconditioned, spontaneous, or natural expressions of human behaviour. First and foremost, Facebook and other social media platforms are founded on a business model and are designed to generate profits from steering and shaping behaviour. This means, at the very least, that commodifiability colours and underpins all the data deriving from Facebook. Moreover, it is evident that the architecture of Facebook and other social media platforms is built upon mainstream psychological insights into human beings and social behaviour? Consider here how Mark Zuckerberg once proclaimed that Facebook is all about psychology:

> I think that that's one of the core insights that we try to apply to developing Facebook. What [people are] really interested in is what's going on with the people they care about. It's all about giving people the tools and controls that they need to be comfortable sharing the information that they want. If you do that, you create a very valuable service. It's as much psychology and sociology as it is technology.
>
> *(Larson, 2011)*

We should read this statement literally: Facebook is developed, constructed, and set up using social-psychological theories and models, which are used to create 'a valuable service' qua profitable commodity. So, at the very least, Kosinski and Stillwell's move to correlate their psychological profiles, obtained via their personality app (whose validity could be contested as it is arguably a superficial questionnaire), and cross-check this with Facebook data is deeply problematic. Simply put, it correlates data obtained through psychological models and theories with behaviour or data that is already informed and shaped by the same psychological theories and models. Or, phrased otherwise, what 'we love to know you digitally' is in fact about is pulling the cat out of the sack that was put in the sack.

Therefore, we should argue against the idea that Big Data is able to hack into our psychology. The internet is not a psychologist as it were, but, rather, the internet is structured *as a psychologist*. In other words, the web is not able to reveal our real psychology so to speak, our deep psychological desires, but, rather, it is set up in such a way that ultimately shapes, guides, and moulds our 'psychology'. Hence, psychology is used as a circular rationale for the business model of social media, which, in turn, constitutes the tautological base of digital capitalism.

What works in digitalisation

However, the question still remains that, even if it is lost in digital mirrors and structurally fraudulent, does digital psychological profiling still work? Does the role played by Cambridge Analytica in the US elections and the UK Brexit campaign not testify to how psychological profiling allows individuals to target and augment people's political positions? Before proceeding any further, it is important to note that the effectiveness of this has already been called into question, insofar as Cambridge Analytica's influence on the American presidential elections and the Brexit campaign cannot truly be proven, and, in fact, might be a promotional pitch developed by Cambridge Analytica itself (Wright, 2018).

Furthermore, the public appears to love such stories and is endlessly fascinated by these kinds of accounts of being manipulated and brainwashed. Note again the redoubling at play here, as these stories create a surplus subject capable of self-contemplation: *look how easily we, or our brain, are tricked!* As this paradoxical ground of human subjectivity is an excess that is structurally overlooked by the psy-sciences, is the conclusion to be drawn, then, not that psychology, rather than being a dangerous knowledge that can be misused by people or corporations with bad intentions, is instead *a dangerous fantasy* in and of itself? That is to say, although the pretention to be able to digitally chart the real of the human being is, as aforementioned, nothing but a myth based on a tautology, it is a dangerous fantasy, insofar as it shapes and drives deceptive and manipulative methods and technologies. Hence, does Cambridge Analytica ultimately not represent old school propaganda that uses new digital methods for which the psy-rationale is not an explanation, but, rather, only a script which sets up the virtual scene in which the manipulation takes place?

At the very least, we should be wary about reports and outcries about the dangers of Big Data being able to hack into our psychology. The latter is the very message that Michal Kosinski—after having left Cambridge University and having taken up a professorship in psychometrics at Stanford University—himself is trying to drum home and warn us about. Kosinski denies having been directly involved with Cambridge Analytica and actually claims to be 'one of the first scholars to point out the privacy threats posed by the predictive algorithms already widely employed by companies and governments at that time'.[5] In an article in 'Das Magazin', Kosinski placed all the blame upon a younger erstwhile Cambridge professor Aleksandr Kogan, whilst denying any contact with Cambridge Analytica or any of the companies associated with it (Grassegger & Krogerus, 2016). Kosinski proposed that his team's research on the data might have been stolen or, at the very least, reused without their permission. However, in an article in Medium, it is argued that Kosinski's timeline on these issues did not make a whole lot of sense (Textifire, 2017). Be that as it may,[6] what is of greater interest for our argument is the way in which Kosinski adopted the Pilate position, by literally saying: "This is not my fault. I did not build the bomb. I only showed that it exists" (Grassegger & Krogerus, 2016).

This is the myth Kosinski wants to keep reproducing: psychology is an explosive science, especially when it is connected to contemporary digital technologies. One might hear echoes here of the discussions on the role of psychology and psychologists in US torture practices in Guantánamo Bay and Abu Ghraib. Both the psychologists involved in the 'enhanced interrogation techniques' (see the erstwhile official APA policy that psychologists must ensure that interrogations are 'safe, legal, ethical, and effective' (Moorehead-Slaughter, 2006)) and those psychologists who opposed it all referred to the same body of knowledge of psychology. The position of the opponents was, above all, that psychology can be used for either good or bad purposes, that is, its knowledge is so powerful that it can both heal and wound. However, one should pose a simple question in response to such accounts: did psychologists 'improve' torture through designing new and more effective forms of torture? I claim that the simple answer to this question is no (see: De Vos, 2011a): at most, torture has become a bit less bloody as the focus has shifted to leaving no marks, which is perhaps the most concise way to describe psychological torture. However, what can definitely be attributed to the input of psychologists is their role in systematising torture, as indicated by a Red Cross report on Guantánamo Bay that stressed the formalisation and systematisation of interrogation techniques used there (Lewis, 2004). Of course, the psychologisation of torture, above all, served as the legalistic *coup de théâtre* of the Bush administration. Torture was redefined as any practice that leads to organ failure or death, which, in turn, opened the gates for 'enhanced interrogation techniques' to enter (McCoy, 2006, p. 123). Psychology, here, was an ideal partner in this newspeak operation, as was evident from the aforementioned APA policy about psychologists ensuring that interrogations were kept *'safe, legal, ethical, and effective'*. To conclude: psychology has not provided a new theoretical framework or modern innovative techniques for torture, but it has provided the rationale for contemporary forms of torture, or, to put it more bluntly, the fantasies associated with torture.

I argue that this is also the case with the alleged effectiveness of Cambridge Analytica. The answer to the question of whether *psychologists* have *'improved' propaganda by designing new and more effective forms of propaganda techniques?* should also be no. At most, psychologists have covered up the explicitness of propaganda via applying the pseudo-scientific gloss of psychology. Or, phrased otherwise, behind propaganda you will not find the truth of psychology (pointing to an essentialist and naturalist core of the human being), but rather, one will merely encounter yet more propaganda and lies. The latter of these pertains to the lie that the psy-sciences claim to have direct, unmediated, and objective access to subjectivity. Hence, while psychology did not provide the theoretical framework or modern techniques for propaganda, it did provide its rationale qua a phantasmatic framework that allowed for propaganda to be used in a more direct and 'individualising' way, the latter of which was facilitated via digital communicational technologies.

Of course, here the burning question becomes: what about the truth of psychoanalysis? Is psychoanalysis an expedient theoretical framework through which to set up a truly innovative propagandic technology (or, for that matter, to connect with the previous issue, to devise truly novel torture techniques)? Indeed, considering the manifold analyses of fascism, authoritarian leadership and propaganda that utilised Freudian mass psychology, imagine what *Vienna Analytica* could do? However, the argument I am advancing vis-à-vis the truths of psychoanalysis is that they would be useless for devising new forms of propaganda or torture unless psychoanalysis was first turned (and betrayed) into a psychology. This is because psychoanalysis is ultimately not a theory about what works in or with (inter)subjectivity, but, rather, precisely about that which does not work in or with (inter)subjectivity. At most, it can say something meaningful about the ways in which this aporia of intersubjectivity is covered up or muffled, which is to say that psychoanalysis is expedient for providing an understanding, analysis, and, hence, a critique of the various vicissitudes of human subjectivity. Moreover, such a critique cannot claim to be *objective* in the commonly held understanding of objectivity, but, rather, is only objective in a partisan and partial way, which is to say, in a political and ethical way. One may discern at this point how, for me, the political concerns a distinctly emancipatory and leftist project.

At most, considering today's digital and communicative technologies and how fundamental they are to contemporary digital capitalism, one should perhaps not be afraid, in the way that Žižek appears to imply that technology will rob and expropriate our thoughts from us; rather, what we should dread above all is that these technologies will take away our un-thoughts, that is, they will not expropriate from us 'I think what I think', but, rather, expropriate from us 'I don't know what I'm thinking'. Of course, this is the point where Big Data would fill in the gaps, the fissures of subjectivity as it were, which it would do via recourse to the fantasies of mainstream psychology, precisely for the purposes of commodifying my being. It is here, specifically concerning intersubjectivity and the social, where digital technologies seek to rob from us the (productive) misunderstandings that ground and drive the social, in order to turn it into something containable, steerable, and once again, commodifiable. Žižek hints toward precisely this: commenting on Elon Musk's idea to capture one's thoughts and emotions directly (and broadcasting this to other people), thus bypassing the reductive and mediating dimension of language, Žižek's critique is that it is precisely in this very symbolic reduction that the actual wealth of thoughts and, hence, of the social itself arises (Žižek, 2019a). My argument is that the rationale for the illusion to bypass symbolic mediation is grounded in the psy-sciences.

Based on this, I must restate my argument: the psy-sciences do not harbour a dangerous knowledge per se, but rather, they contain a dangerous fantasy that is currently guiding the development of digital technologies and digital applications in specific directions. The fantasy of the psy-sciences of delivering the final truth about human beings is now believed to be fully realisable due to the support from the digital sphere and Big Data. Hence, the first thing to be contested is this fantasy of the 'first reality', that is, a basic, natural psychology that one can finally fully encounter via new Big Data technologies. This idea that *there is a psychology out there*, independent of the scientific psychological gaze, constitutes the core tenet of the dangerous fantasy that fuels this datafication and subsequent commodification of subjectivity.[7] What is missed, or more accurately, *obscured*, in these concrete practices of data gathering and psychological profiling, is that the whole operation is based on the prior psychologised pre-fabrication of the digital environment itself. What works in digitalisation is precisely this: the pre-structuring of (inter)subjectivity via the chimeras of psychology. In this way, our avatars and smart, virtual environments represent the digital straitjackets of (inter)subjectivity.

Another technology for another world?

The next logical question to ask here is whether we can think of the digital outside of the hegemonic economico-political constellation? Christian Fuchs, for example, advocates for non-commercial digital media (Flisfeder, 2016), albeit without explicitly outlining what this would look like. Alternatively, Geert Lovink called for the nationalisation of social media platforms such as Facebook (Lovink, 2012). Irrespective of these alternative ways of organising social media, the question remains about how these public, non-commercial social media platforms would be designed? For example, would they retain emoticons? Would they still prompt users to express their feelings? Would they ask for 'likes'? Would they remind you to post something, or remind you of interesting stories you missed when you were offline for a while?

One could also refer back to Bernard Stiegler here, who could be said to advance the proposition that another world is possible because other forms of technology are possible (see, e.g., Stiegler, 2015). This is a fascinating idea insofar as it suggests that today's technology could have taken on a completely different form than its current one, thus emphasising that technological development does not follow a natural Telos, and, hence, that other outcomes qua the basic structuring or functioning of technology were once possible, or are even still possible. Despite this, once again, one would immediately ask which kind of theory or model of the subject would then be, overtly or covertly, mobilised?

Hence, must we not conclude that there will always be some kind of psychology informing both the setup and architecture of digital social media and, on a more fundamental level, the basic structure of digital technology itself? Perhaps one could argue that an alternative to this would be to stick to purely neuroscientific insights, or better yet still, neurology itself. Perhaps neuroscience could be cleansed from all its contaminations with psychological theories and models. However, as I have claimed elsewhere (De Vos, 2016b), the latter is structurally impossible. Neuroscience cannot be considered as a *first science*, due to the fact that what it lays under the scanner does not come out of the blue; for example, neurological research on aggression cannot but draw upon a specific theory of aggression, which is where, I claim, psychology enters the scene. There is no such thing as first, natural, theory-free data of human nature to put under the scanner,[8] and thus the idea of constructing digital communication technologies based purely on neurology is compromised from the outset.

Resultantly, could a more radical option be to opt for a digital technology that is cleansed of whatever theory or model of the human? Hence, instead of demanding *less automaticity and more subjectivity*, should we not be crying out for *less subjectivity and more automaticity*? That is to say, let us keep out the psychologists and neuroscientists from the digital labs? Imagine new smartphones, or a new version of Facebook, launched with the motto: no psychology guaranteed! potentially with the attached disclaimer: 'may contain traces of critical psychoanalysis'. All jokes aside, would it really be possible to stick to the pragmatic and the functional? Would doing so mean that, when designing digital technologies, one would restrict themselves purely to the functioning of the symbolic, that is, to the rules and structures of language?[9] This would perhaps allow one to stay away from (neuro)psychological waters when designing digital technologies.

However, the following question would once again rear its head: how would we construct our avatars and our digital environments, which constitute the placeholders of (inter)subjectivity? Could we really keep these empty? Perhaps I am calling here for a type of AI that is modelled on psychoanalysis, albeit a slightly psychologised version of psychoanalysis. In so doing, I would have to accept that this minor sin cannot be avoided, as it would only be from this basis that a viable alternative technology, codes and algorithms could be built, whose modes of (inter)subjectivity could not be expropriated by digital capitalism? When stated in this way, it should already be clear that such a minor sin would constitute a major concession to capitalism itself.

In order to explore whether more radical options are possible, it is instructive to consider another case study, specifically Facebook's experiment with AI that sought to train bots who were ostensibly capable of spontaneously developing protohuman behaviour.

Facebook's training of bots

Filling the machine with psychology

'An Artificial Intelligence Developed Its Own Non-Human Language', ran the title of an article on the Atlantic.com site discussing an experiment conducted by Facebook's Artificial Intelligence Research lab. In the experiment, Facebook's researchers trained so-called 'bots' to negotiate with other opponents in a game (whether they were human or other bots). The commentary on Atlantic.com highlighted the finding that, when the bots had to negotiate with one another, they 'made up their own way of communicating' (Lafrance, 2017). Evidently, this greatly excited the commentator, who noted:

> If this doesn't fill you with a sense of wonder and awe about the future of machines and humanity then, I don't know, go watch Blade Runner or something.
>
> *(Lafrance, 2017)*

One should not miss the aforementioned 'oh-my-god' dynamic at play here, that jubilatory enthusiasm with which we approach revelations about the world or human nature itself. While it positions the human being in an Archimedean vantage point removed from the world where the human contemplates the sublunary, here one can also discern an underlying super-egoic injunction: everyone is enjoined to take this step back and enjoy the view. Moreover, if you are not filled with wonder in response to this information, then something must be wrong with you. Never mind that the commanded astonishment appears to be wholly out of place: one would be forgiven for already expecting that machines would behave like machines and communicate in an artificial and non-human fashion, no? Moreover, given that one of the principal aims of AI has always been for a computer to think in a humanlike way—or convincingly imitate the human, as per Alan Turing—why then all this fuss and astonishment if machines end up being merely machinic? Perhaps we must conclude that this fascination, above all, testifies to our own relief that machines are reassuringly different from us after all? This perhaps also explains the super-egoic injunction: if you are not fascinated by this, then maybe you are not completely human yourself.

Interestingly, however, in the very next line the author marvels at the exact opposite:

> The larger point of the report is that bots can be pretty decent negotiators— they even use strategies like feigning interest in something valueless, so that it can later appear to "compromise" by conceding it.
> *(Lafrance, 2017)*

Here, the author notes that in the negotiation game, the bots were able to pretend that they granted their opponent something, whereas, in fact, it had no value for them. This, once again, left the commentator in an exalted state. How can we understand this not easily discernible shift from fascination with the non-human character of machines to fascination with the supposedly *more human than human* aspect of the technology? Is this a case of 'tremendum et fascinans': in being fascinated by the non-human aspect of machines, we are also scared by their mechanical artificiality, which, in turn, incites us to look for reassuring humanlike characteristics in the machine so that we can conclude that machines are not that dissimilar to us? After all, it is humans who built them, right? Or, conversely, should we consider it from yet another perspective, namely that the 'tremendum' evoked in the commentary refers to our horror towards our *own* artificiality, our own mechanistic nature, our own *more inhuman than inhuman* condition that resurfaces via the machine? Consider in this respect Freud's notion of 'das Unheimliche' (the uncanny): what causes the peculiar effect of the unsettling strangeness is precisely what we are unconsciously most familiar with (Freud, [1919]1955). Hence, in the brute mechanical logic of the machine, we come to recognise ourselves as brute symbolic machines that are caught in the logic of the death drive.

But, before we prematurely get lost in psychologisation, let us proceed with our argument and ask, from where does the (in)humanity of the bots derive, how does this realise itself, or to be more precise, how is this realised? Indeed, rather than merely accepting that the bots began to display protohuman behaviour spontaneously and naturally, we must instead examine how precisely this scenario was realised. To do so, we must consider the original report from Facebook's Artificial Intelligence Research lab. It advances the following argument about human negotiation:

> Negotiations require complex communication and reasoning skills, but success is easy to measure, making this an interesting task for AI.
> *(Lewis, Yarats, Dauphin, Parikh, & Batra, 2017, p. 2443)*

Is the above quotation not blatantly grounded in a rather simplistic psychological conceptualisation of success, according to which one succeeds when one gets what one wants? Whether success is about skills and something measurable is highly debatable. According to psychoanalysis, for example, one's symptoms can be highly successful, while, conversely, success itself can be highly symptomatic. Consider here the words of the same Nobel Prize Literature winner mentioned in the previous Chapter, who states: "there is no success like failure." Or, alternatively, consider Lacan's argument that when you refuse the very thing you want, you maintain your desire as unsatisfied (see for example, Lacan, 2007, p. 622). At the very least, the Facebook experiment is predicated on a rather simplistic human model, in that it features a human who knows what it wants and pursues this directly. This meagre cardboard form of psychology apparently suffices as the basic script for the bots. Let us scrutinise how this turned out in the experiment by following it from the beginning. The basis of the experiment was a game in which two opponents must negotiate over several different items.

> Users were shown a set of items with a value for each, and asked to agree how to divide the items with another user who has a different, unseen, value function.
> *(Lewis et al., 2017, p. 2443)*

The opponents thus did not know each other's value attributions of certain items and had to reach an agreement through dialogue. Only humans participated in the first iteration of the experiment, and it was their actions that subsequently informed the protocols for the AI models (the so-called 'neural networks'). This produced the following result, which was wholly unexpected to the researchers, and apparently something they did not desire:

> We first train recurrent neural networks to imitate human actions. We find that models trained to maximise the likelihood of human utterances can generate fluent language, but make comparatively poor negotiators, which are overly willing to compromise.
> *(Lewis et al., 2017, p. 2443)*

Here, the AI models that were instructed to imitate human subjects apparently turned out to be all too human: while they generated relatively well humanlike utterances, they turned out to be bad negotiators. Hence, can we not say that the bots came to resemble too closely maladapted humans, who were not good business (wo)men and thus had to be re-educated or required therapy? The latter constituted the next step in the experiment, as the bots were re-educated through 'reinforced learning' to maximize their business rewards. Simply put: the bots were fed ideology via psychological methods, which enshrined in them the capitalist maxim of pursuing profit via techniques from behaviourism. It was only then that the bots truly began to exhibit the appropriate protohuman behaviour, that is, the desired behaviour.

> Analysing the performance of our agents, we find evidence of sophisticated negotiation strategies. For example, we find instances of the model feigning interest in a valueless issue, so that it can later 'compromise' by conceding it. Deceit is a complex skill that requires hypothesising the other agent's beliefs, and is learnt relatively late in child development (Talwar and Lee, 2002). Our agents have learnt to deceive without any explicit human design, simply by trying to achieve their goals.
>
> *(Lewis et al., 2017, p. 2444)*

The authors take quite a surprising leap here: although they initially suggested that the intervention was needed to re-educate the bots (with, as I have argued, behavioural psychology and capitalist ideology), at this point they present it as if things had evolved spontaneously towards this situation, in accordance with the established body of knowledge in psychology. Notwithstanding their own machinations, they unabashedly claim here that the bots began to trick their opponents completely spontaneously. It is precise with this claim that they obscure how they themselves steered the bots towards the right (ideological) direction, by appealing to developmental psychology. Indeed, they claimed that the bots, from the moment they could imagine what another person would think or desire (which, as we read, is allegedly learnt relatively late in child development), they developed into perfect little cheating capitalists. By proposing this, the authors appear to be implying that maximisation of profit is itself a developmental milestone in child psychology.

From this perspective, does the amazement and fascination shown by the commentator from Atalantic.com not produce exactly the same effect here? That is to say, it masks the manipulations and staging (driven by the psychological and ideological models), and instead presents the outcome of the experiment as being in accordance with human nature. Once again, then, it is the cat that is put into the sack that eventually emerges from it. Moreover, and this is perhaps the most crucial point that is overlooked by both the Facebook researchers and this specific commentator, perhaps the fascination testifies to the actual position held by the modern human, that is, a spectator position far removed from the scene from whence someone gazes at 'the comedies that are played out there'.[10] Hence, the modern human being is not just that which he or she is said to be, but, rather, he or she is first and foremost situated at the precise point from whence he or she looks back at the image that is sketched of him or herself. In other words, the modern human being is above all to be found where he or she takes a step back to exclaim with surprise and fascination: '*look at how human the machines are!*' Does this not mean that our actual position cannot but be one that is located in a place that lies beyond both machines and humans, a perspective from whence we can contemplate both? This is where the statement '*look at how human the machines are!'* can easily be redoubled into its variant: *'look at how machinelike humans are!'* And, of course, all this is based on the meta-position underlying the utterance: *'look at how human humans are!'*, which paradoxically corresponds to human beings being fascinated by the human dimension.

Traditionally, all these niceties and subtleties of humanity are pretty much wasted on mainstream neuropsy-sciences, which restrict themselves to pointing out to everyone with great fervour: *look, this what you are!* So, returning to the question raised earlier, what is it then that makes the psy-sciences work in the manifold fields that they are engaged in, including education, culture, politics, the public sphere, and, arguably, technology, and especially digital communication technologies? The answer is as follows: the psy-sciences do not set out to understand or cure human beings, rather, their aim is to show human beings how to be human beings. This is abundantly clear in Facebook's AI experiment: the experimenters used psychology to train the bots to exhibit the ideologically desired behaviour. In so doing, the experiment highlights the socio-political role played by the psy-sciences, who instruct or train people on how to be human. This is why children with 'attention deficit hyperactivity disorder (ADHD)' receive forms of psycho-education, which teaches them in the very first lesson that ADHD is not a psychological issue, but, rather, a brain disorder. At the very least, the layperson today is enjoined to share the perspective of experts, to the extent that we could say that the phrase 'look at how human humans are!' constitutes the baseline of the psy-sciences. The psy-sciences proceed by educating and training their subjects into what they ought to be and how they should behave. One of the primary ways this occurs is via the reproduction of theoretical discourses. To the traumatized we say: 'You have a posttraumatic stress disorder, these are the causes, these are the symptoms, this is what you have to do or think'. To depressed people, we explain the biochemical conditions of their disorder. In contemporary societies, all of our children are taught psy-theories about the four emotions—happiness, sadness, fear, anger—upon which, for example, during a practice known as Circle Time, they are asked to express their 'personal' feelings by using four cardboard masks that portray the aforementioned standard emotions. Recently, I overheard a young woman on the tram conclude a story with the words: 'and I really felt so sad, scared and angry...'. Does this not testify to the pervasiveness and hegemony of psy-discourses? These discourses function as a straitjacket that restricts us to a highly limited and infantile repertoire of feelings. Of course, one could adopt an optimistic perspective here and argue that people are always creative with imposed signifiers and use them in new and unexpected ways. However, if psychologisation already possesses such a compelling discursive power capable of shaping certain forms of being, then what about digitalisation? Do digital communication technologies that pre-format modes of (inter)subjectivity precisely via the use of scripts developed from cardboard forms of psychology, not have an even stronger effect on (inter)subjectivity, narrowing evermore any potential leeway or elbow room?

Here, one could argue that the Facebook experiment signals a decisive shift in contemporary biopolitics. Indeed, as Bernard Stiegler argues, today sees a transition from the *psycho-techniques* described in the historical analyses of Michel Foucault (Foucault, 1985) to *psycho-technologies*. According to Stiegler, the latter refers to how all kinds of digital media and platforms shape contemporary (inter) subjectivity via algorithms, which is more totalising than ever as it makes any form of escape or alternative forms of subjectivation impossible (Stiegler, 2010). I would add to Stiegler's argument that, first, it is mainstream psy-models that inform these psycho-technologies, and, hence, we can speak of a psychologisation by means of algorithms. Second, it seems that this is a form of psychologisation that does not require the accompanying classical interpellative call: the subject is no longer called upon to view himself from the psy-perspective and shape and steer himself accordingly, but, rather, the algorithmic psychologisation gives direct form to the subject and directly controls it via digital nudging. Consider here how social media not only extracts data from us but also, and most importantly, pre-configures our 'innermost individual' expressions in order to lead us to certain behaviours or certain services or products. In this regard, the Facebook experiment can perhaps be viewed as a blueprint of how human subjects themselves will be (or are already) instructed: while the experiment claimed to have brought to the fore the natural protohuman behaviour of the bots, I have demonstrated that this behaviour is actually no more than a result of the experimental design and the underlying psychologising and ideological scripts and models that were used to educate the bots.

As a side note, if the field of education has always been a key domain for the hegemonic grip of the neuropsy-sciences (De Vos, 2015, 2016a), then it is also a crucial domain in which to examine the aforementioned redundancy of the interpellative call,[11] that is, the disappearance of the call to the layperson to adopt the scientific and expert position when reflecting upon themselves, others, and the world. We will explore this further in the second part of this book, but suffice to say here that the crucial question appears to be in this respect, will education and schooling not become themselves redundant once it becomes possible to directly connect the brain of our pupils and students to digital machines and the internet? Who would need teachers or schools even once students are able to directly download the requisite knowledge and skills themselves? Perhaps this is why educational and schooling levels are already dropping, while teachers and lecturers appear to no longer know what exactly teaching is (resorting to paper assignments, group work, abolishing exams…). In the future, the only entities that will still receive education and training may be the bots themselves.[12]

Given this radical shift in the prevailing *episteme*, to use Foucault's term, should we not once again return to the question over which we have pondered at several points in this book: could a psychoanalytic perspective offer a base for a more ethical or humane form of digital technology? Perhaps revisiting the Facebook experiment will help us to look at this afresh.

Psychoanalysis can be used to paint the veil

Apropos the Facebook bots, rather than using behavioural psychology and capitalist ideology, would it instead be possible to educate them in the more sophisticated models offered by psychoanalysis in conjunction with an emancipatory leftist project? In other words, let us trade Pavlov, Thorndike, and Ayn Rand with Freud, Lacan, and Marx? The starting point could be the jubilatory claim made by the Facebook researchers that their bots 'naturally' learned to feign and resort to deception. As psychoanalysts, could we not instruct the bots *to pretend to pretend, to feign to feign*. Here, I am once again referring to Lacan, more specifically his statement that what distinguishes humans from animals is that while the latter can feign, only human beings can feign feigning (Lacan, 1966, p. 807).[13] An instructive example of this is Žižek's example of politeness: I behave politely with regard to my superiors so that it seems that I respect and value them. But the twist is that 'I only pretend to be polite' is ultimately the standard way through which to show respect. That is to say, it is precisely by pretending that I am only pretending that I finally show my respect (Žižek, 2014).

Would this sophisticated *double entendre* not be compromised when technology makes it possible to read another person's mind directly? Suppose that I see you and consider addressing you in the standard way 'nice to see you, how are you doing'? A mind-reading technology, which would be based on a simple psychologised understanding of communication, would only broadcast that I do not care how you feel, thus overlooking that my polite inquiring actually testified to a minimal level of respect and interest. Of course, one could counter this point by arguing that such mind-reading technology would also be able to register these underlying thoughts and affects. However, in response to this argument, one must answer firmly: there is no underlying register, no subconscious where one's true feelings are situated and waiting for the scanners to pick them up. According to psychoanalysis, the unconscious level operates on the surface of speaking,[14] and, hence, it is only in the twists of speaking itself, in the cracks within discourse itself, that the truth is articulated. Consequently, in feigning to feign, one does not simply show one's 'true desire' (a desire which you could pin down, categorise and thus datafy), rather, it is in this redoubling of pretending itself that a desire is articulated, albeit not a straightforward desire. In other words, if the simple act of pretending (or lying) can be said to refer to an underlying and preceding truth, in *pretending to pretend* an additional and new truth sees light, which is inextricably linked to this redoubling itself.

From here, the question becomes whether psychoanalysis could provide the digital mind reading and broadcasting technologies of the future with more sophisticated algorithms, in turn, allowing for both more subtle and twisted modes of human communication? While the long answer to this question is no, let me nevertheless try to clarify this answer here by starting from Lacan's discussion of the famous competition in classical antiquity between Zeuxis and Parrhasios, before proceeding to connect this to the Facebook AI experiment. The two Greek painters wanted to determine which of them could paint the most convincing optical illusion. Zeuxis painted a grapevine so accurately that birds came to pick the grapes. When Parrhasios showed his painting, Zeuxis urged Parrhasios to pull back the curtain, only to then be ashamed to acknowledge that Parrhasios' curtain was so realistic that it had misled him. Lacan argued that if you want to deceive a person, then you have to show them a veil: that which makes them wonder what is behind the veil (Lacan, 1977, pp. 111–112). For Lacan, the optical illusion is not about the illusory object that is being evoked, but, rather, derives from it pretending to be something that it is not. While Zeuxis's grape vine referred to something specific, something it wanted to make present in an illusory way, Parrhasios' curtain ultimately only referred to something that was not there.

So, as a preliminary remark, can we not say that the bots in the Facebook experiment, by trying to deceive their opponents (be it another bot or a human opponent), ultimately remained a *simple act of* pretending where it was clear what each party desired? Indeed, the bots' pretence was driven by a singular desire: to make a profit. Of course, this one-dimensional desire is far removed from what constitutes the typical human desire in psychoanalysis: a redoubled pretending where desire only articulates itself *as desire*. At the very least, apropos desire, from a psychoanalytic perspective, there is no clear line of demarcation between loss and profit, in fact, they can become interchangeable. Remember here the aforementioned lyric: 'there is no success like failure'. It is here that we come to the crux of the matter: is it not clear that the whole scene that the Facebook researchers set up was only made possible by a simple psychological framework on pretending, that is, a psychology of deception underpinned by the idea that we all know very well what we want and desire? When considered in this light, it is obvious that psychoanalysis and its non-psychological conceptualisation of desire would have been completely useless for Facebook's researchers, inasmuch as they started out from the paradigm 'success is easy to measure', which is wholly antithetical to psychoanalysis.

Therefore, is the radical conclusion to be drawn not once again that psychoanalysis would be useless for designing AI or the algorithms that underpin digital communication technology? This is because both the former and the latter require simple knowledge and psychological scripts to set up their scenes. The enigmas of psychoanalysis, its double meanings, do nothing but deconstruct such scenes, or, at the very least, radically call such scenes into question. If I may formulate it in the following way: psychology paints the grapes and turns us into deceived birds. The theory of psychoanalysis presents a painting of a veil, which serves to illustrate that human beings are constituted from this double enigma. Psychology serves psychologisation by filling up human beings with psychological models and fantasies. Psychology serves neurologisation by filling up our brains with psychological models and fantasies. In contemporary societies, psychology now also serves digitalisation by filling up our avatars and virtual environments with psychological models and fantasies. Hence, it would only be by turning psychoanalysis into psychology that it could become usable as a psy-praxis, as a base for neuroscientific research, and, finally, a base for digital technology. Psychoanalysis only paints the canvas; it is useless at setting up and designing the digital scene itself.

However, as I argued earlier, when these machines are filled with psychological models, the latter should be understood as a Trojan Horse that carries a neoliberal capitalistic model, and, hence, there are still some options that we must address. That is to say, if we cannot replace the *bad psychologies* with *good psychoanalysis*, then at the very least can we not cleanse the psychological models of their political ideology, or replace them with alternative ones?

Towards a psy-political critique

Let us return once again to the Facebook experiment and examine how the initial data on the human beings who played the negotiation game were collected:

> We collected a set of human-human dialogues using Amazon Mechanical Turk. Workers were paid $0.15 per dialogue, with a $0.05 bonus for maximal scores.
>
> (Lewis et al., 2017, p. 2444)

Note here how the conventional concept of 'test subjects' is exchanged with 'workers'. Does this not make it immediately clear that the experiment, although presented at an academic conference and following the format of a scientific paper, can be framed above all in terms of Facebook's business plan? At the very least, it is striking how success ('success is easy to measure') is operationalised into working conditions. Moreover, the latter were strictly structured and codified, as was the whole context of the negotiating game. Hence, one could claim that this was not exactly a setting where 'natural language' could occur, although this is what the authors claim. The basic setup of the experiment thus appears to be as follows: first humans were reduced into simple and quantifiable schemes, in order to obtain data that could subsequently be used to devise the AI algorithms. Hence, if the experimenters eventually discovered that the bots ended up using a language that diverged from human language, then this should not have come as a surprise, given the initial setup of an artificial and strictly codified scene. Or, phrased otherwise, with the non-human language of the bots, the researchers ultimately only got back their own artificiality.

But, more importantly, we should not overlook the fact that the prior devised strict scripts in the entire experimental situation actually blocked any form of deviation, or for that matter, any resistance from the outset. As aforementioned, the negotiation game was based on opposing two agents with different value systems that were unknown to each other. Therefore, what the scripts made impossible from the outset was that the agents would communicate or share their value systems. For example, the agent could not simply say: "Well, let's divide the benefits equally" – or even beyond that, "these are not my values!" In short, by turning subjects into 'workers', the latter became trapped within a capitalist scene from which they could not escape.

So, the question becomes: is it possible to design the scene of AI, and digital technologies more generally, in such a way that makes it possible to achieve more egalitarian outcomes, or if you are so inclined, even a communist or revolutionary one? Hence, concerning the Facebook experiment, we could retain the behaviourist background (as psychoanalysis turned out to be useless) but draw upon a leftist emancipatory agenda to generate bots that have other objectives and desires than the mere pursuit of profit? However, I claim that such a scenario would only be possible within the basic constellation in which the Facebook researchers themselves occupied the central role, by covertly steering the entire scene. After all, what we should not lose sight of is precisely that the researchers themselves determined the a priori settings of the experiment. Is it not precisely here that class difference rears its head, with one class group designing the basic codes and algorithms and the other class group being determined by these very codes and algorithms? From this perspective, we should not fail to notice precisely where the first, primary deception is situated in the experiment:

> Humans were told that they were interacting with other humans, as they had been during the collection of our dataset (and few appeared to realize they were in conversation with machines).
> *(Lewis et al., 2017, p. 2448)*

In other words, rather than thinking that deception was the natural outcome of the experiment, one should situate deception as being the basic condition of the experiment. At this point, we ourselves should not be deceived to think that this experiment represents an example of the Turing test being passed. That is, when the experimenters claim that human agents were often not aware that they were competing with artificial agents, this should not surprise us: the scene was coded and controlled, completely artificial, and thus it was to be expected that humans would not realise that their adversary was a machine.

So, are we not justified in calling upon the bots and humans to unite and oppose the Facebook researchers with their hidden codes and silent algorithms? After all, as I have tried to argue in this chapter, the bots did not naturally come to display the ostensibly protohuman behaviour of using deceit to achieve 'their' goals; rather, both the goals (pursuing profit) and the means to achieve them (the requested behaviour) were pre-scripted into the basic settings of the experiment.

Hence, what I am rejecting here is the scheme of having a priori neutral technology, which is subsequently given form or filled out by ideology and psychology. Conversely, what the Facebook experiment shows is that both ideology (capitalist pursuit of profit) and psychology (shaping subjects in such a way that makes them compliant with the hegemonic ideology) were present from the outset. Ultimately, even the Facebook researchers themselves admitted that the bots did not simply come to imitate concrete people and that it was only re-educating the bots that did the trick, as it was only then that the bots became *more human than human*.

> This result confirms that attempting to maximise reward can outperform simply imitating humans.
>
> *(Lewis et al., 2017, p. 2449)*

Hence, the bots were not introduced in a neutral environment, but, rather, were set in motion in a setting that had already been designed in accordance with the fantasy of humans being good merchants. Hence, the psychological models and their ideological bias formed the basis of the experiment. Therefore, the idea of combining a leftist project with behaviourism ultimately boils down to accepting the neoliberal coordinates, that is, accepting that the situation is formulated in both mainstream psychologistic and capitalist terms. The primary battle is the battle against psychology, more specifically, its various fantasies of the human, as it is these that can be said to be the carriers of ideology.

Conclusions

Here, in the conclusion to Part I of this book, I can now briefly delineate the task of conducting a psy-critique of the digitalisation of (inter)subjectivity. The previous chapters have elucidated how technology requires the simple, straightforward (ideological) models of psychology to set up its scenes. In this sense, the enigmas of psychoanalysis have been shown to be useless for designing digital scenes, given that these enigmas actually deconstruct and problematise the scenes. I have shown that it is only by converting psychoanalysis into a psychology that psychoanalysis can be used as the basis for designing digital technology.

Robert Pfaller, a philosopher of art, argued that theory cannot tell art what to think, it can only tell art what not to think (Pfaller, 2017, p. 92). In the same way, a psy-critique, based, as it has to be, on psychoanalysis, cannot provide the base of technology, but, rather, can only show what should *not* constitute the base of technology. In the next two parts of this book, I aim to give a sense of the urgency for such a psy-critique.

Notes

1 Here, I am arguing against Elisabeth Wilson's interpretation of Turing's utterance "Can you think what I feel? can you feel what I think?", specifically as Wilson contends that Turing understood the psychological not in its mere cognitivist perspective associated with McCulloch and Pitts, but, rather, in terms of its "inter-implication of affect and cognition" (E. A. Wilson, 2011, p. 21).
2 https://www.quicksprout.com/the-psychology-of-search-engine-optimization/. See also: https://searchengineland.com/how-to-devise-a-psychology-based-seo-strategy-97390.
3 As far as I can surmise, the quote stems from an interview and might thus not truly reflect Žižek's position on this issue. Indeed, elsewhere, Žižek is more accurate when

he asks: "can the machine to which our brain is wired capture this virtual moment which belongs neither to the order of being nor to the order of non-being?" (Žižek, 2019a, p. 13).
4 https://sites.google.com/michalkosinski.com/mypersonality.
5 https://drive.google.com/file/d/1zRaTAx0mpRC0m7-3wQRaDPYTOGMdvNBt/edit.
6 For the sake of the anecdote, I wrote some preliminary thoughts on Cambridge Analytica in a Turkish academic journal, referencing Kosinski and his alleged involvement in Cambridge Analytica, which apparently triggered Kosinski to send me an e-mail demanding that I correct my "defamatory allegations". However, my intention was not to accuse Kosinski or others of direct involvement, nor was it to clear their names; rather, I only reported that he and others were named as being involved in Cambridge Analytica, which I also reported that Kosinski denied this. What does concern me in both this chapter and the paper in the Turkish journal is the problematic methodological and ethical aspects of this kind of research.
7 Here, I thus disagree with Antoinette Rouvroy, who argued that one could also use algorithms to both create diversity and let people discover ideas that they are habitually not confronted with (Rouvroy, 2018). Would this idea of using Big Data to achieve laudable goals not boil down to the manipulation of people for a good cause? Of course, the first problem with Rouvroy however, is that she accepts the premise that an algorithmic-based politics could truly address people at a pre-conscious reflex-level, thus short-circuiting their conscious and subjective engagement with politics. In contradistinction to this, I would argue that the first critical (and thus political) move needed here is to reject any essentialising and naturalising accounts of the human being and denounce them as being a priori political and ideological.
8 Hence, Stiegler's flirtation with the neurosciences, which was based on the notion that the neurosciences could objectify the effects of digital technologies on humans at the level of the brain, is equally problematic.
9 This would perhaps both boil down to and leave out the function played by what Lacan refers to as "the language", that is, the language in which enjoyment is involved (see for example: Lacan, 1975).
10 I am referring here, of course, to Descartes's reference to theatre (Descartes, 1996[1637], p. 16), for a more extensive discussion see Chapter 6.
11 See also Chapters 1 and 3, but also Chapter, 8 where I discuss this in relation to Louis Althusser's conceptualisation of interpellation.
12 As already noted in Chapter 3, for those of us who are involved in colleges and universities, the key issue is whether we should try to keep some spaces open for subjectivity (where something other than pragmatic, neoliberal, instrumental education can occur), or, alternatively, whether we should refrain from smoothing things out so that the hegemonic ideological machine can proceed to its own grave? Hence, if education and schooling are headed for disaster, then so be it; let us perhaps simply applaud the fastest version of its decline.
13 See my discussion of this in relation to Alan Turing's imitation game in Chapter 2.
14 See my argument in Chapter 3 that psychoanalysis is not a depth psychology.

References

Aboujaoude, E. (2011). *Virtually you: The dangerous powers of the e-personality*. New York: WW Norton & Company.

Berry, D. M., & Beer, D. (2014, May 1). Interview with David Berry on digital power and critical theory. *Theory, Culture & Society*. Retrieved from http://www.theoryculturesociety.org/interview-with-david-berry-on-digital-power-and-critical-theory/

Cadwalladr, C. (2018). The Cambridge analytica files. 'I made Steve Bannon's psychological warfare tool': meet the data war whistleblower. *The Guardian*. Retrieved from https://www.theguardian.com/news/2018/mar/17/data-war-whistleblower-christopher-wylie-faceook-nix-bannon-trump

Carr, N. (2010). *The shallows: How the internet is changing the way we think, read and remember*. New York: Norton.

Cover, R. (2015). *Digital identities: Creating and communicating the online self*. San Diego, CA: Academic Press.

De Vos, J. (2009). On cerebral celebrity and reality TV. Subjectivity in times of brainscans and psychotainment. *Configurations, 17*(3), 259–293.

De Vos, J. (2011a). Depsychologizing torture. *Critical Inquiry, 37*(2), 286–314. doi:10.1086/657294

De Vos, J. (2011b). The psychologization of humanitarian aid: Skimming the battlefield and the disaster zone. *History of the Human Sciences, 24*(3), 103–122. doi:10.1177/0952695111398572

De Vos, J. (2015). Deneurologizing education? From psychologisation to neurologisation and back. *Studies in Philosophy and Education, 34*(3), 279–295 doi: 10.1007/s11217-014-9440-5

De Vos, J. (2016a). The death and the resurrection of (psy)critique. The case of neuroeducation. *Foundations of Science, 21*(1), 129–145.

De Vos, J. (2016b). *The metamorphoses of the brain. Neurologization and its discontents*. New York: Palgrave Macmillan.

De Vos, J. (2016c). What is critique in the era of the neurosciences? In J. De Vos & E. Pluth (Eds.), *Neuroscience and critique. Exploring the limits of the neurological turn* (pp. 22–40). London: Routledge.

Descartes, R. (1996[1637]). *Discourse on the method and meditations on first philosophy* (D. Weissman & W. Bluhm, Trans.). New Haven, CT: Yale University Press.

Flisfeder, M. (2016). Digital labour and the internet prosumer commodity: In conversation with Christian Fuchs. *Alternate Routes: A Journal of Critical Social Research, 27*, 267–278.

Foucault, M. (1985). *De wil tot weten: Geschiedenis van de seksualiteit, Volume 1* (P. Klinkenberg, Trans.). Nijmegen: Socialistische Uitgeverij.

Freud, S. ([1919]1955). The uncanny. In J. Strachey (Ed.), *The standard edition of the complete psychological works of Sigmund Freud: Vol. XVII* (pp. 217–252). London: Hogarth Press.

Grassegger, V. H., & Krogerus, M. (2016). Ich habe nur gezeigt, dass es die Bombe gibt. *Das Magazin*. Retrieved from https://web.archive.org/web/20170127181034/https://www.dasmagazin.ch/2016/12/03/ich-habe-nur-gezeigt-dass-es-die-bombe-gibt/

Hansen, M. B. N. (2004). *New philosophy for new media*. Cambridge, MA: MIT Press.

Hodges, A. (2014). *Alan Turing: The Enigma*. London: Random House.

Lacan, J. (1966). *Ecrits*. Paris: Editions du Seuil.

Lacan, J. (1975). *Le séminaire de Jacques Lacan, livre XX: Encore 1972–1973*. Paris: Seuil.

Lacan, J. (1977). *The four fundamental concepts of psychoanalysis* (A. Sheridan, Trans.). London: Hogarth Press.

Lacan, J. (2007). *Ecrits: The first complete edition in English* (B. Fink, Trans.). New York: Norton.

Lafrance, A. (2017, June 15). An artificial intelligence developed its own non-human language. *The Atlantic*. Retrieved from https://www.theatlantic.com/technology/archive/2017/06/artificial-intelligence-develops-its-own-non-human-language/530436/

Larson, C. (2011). Mark Zuckerberg speaks at BYU. *Deseret News*. Retrieved from http://www.deseretnews.com/article/print/700121651/Mark-Zuckerberg-speaks-at-BYU-calls-Facebook-as-much-psychology-and-sociology-as-it-is-technology.html

Lewis, M., Yarats, D., Dauphin, Y., Parikh, D., & Batra, D. (2017). *Deal or no deal? End-to-end learning of negotiation dialogues*. Paper presented at the Proceedings of the 2017 Conference on Empirical Methods in Natural Language Processing.

Lewis, N. A. (2004, November 30). Red Cross finds detainee abuse in Guantánamo. *The New York Times*. Retrieved from http://www.nytimes.com/2004/11/30/politics/30gitmo.html?_r=2

Lovink, G. (2012). What is the social in social media? *e-flux Journal, 40*(12), 2012.

Massumi, B. (2002). *Parables for the virtual: Movement, affect, sensation*. Durham, NC: Duke University Press Books.

McCoy, A. W. (2006). *A question of torture: CIA interrogation, from the cold war to the war on terror*. New York: Metropolitan Books.

Moorehead-Slaughter, O. (2006). Ethics and national security. *Monitor on Psychology, 37*(4), 20.

Pfaller, R. (2017). *Interpassivity. The aesthetics of delegated enjoyment*. Edinburgh: University Press.

Rouvroy, A. (2018). À mon sens, Zuckerberg est dépassé. Interview. *L'echo*. Retrieved from https://www.lecho.be/opinions/general/antoinette-rouvroy-a-mon-sens-zuckerberg-est-depasse/9995228.html

Soros, G. (2018). Remarks delivered at the world economic forum. Retrieved from https://www.georgesoros.com/2018/01/25/remarks-delivered-at-the-world-economic-forum/

Stephens-Davidowitz, S. (2017). *Everybody lies: Big data, new data, and what the Internet can tell us about who we really are*. New York: HarperCollins.

Stiegler, B. (2010). *Taking care of youth and the generations*. Stanford, CA: Stanford University Press.

Stiegler, B. (2012). Die Aufklärung in the age of philosophical engineering. *Computational Culture, 2*. Retrieved from http://computationalculture.net/comment/die-aufklarung-in-the-age-of-philosophical-engineering

Stiegler, B. (2014). Les big data, c'est la fin de la pensée. Retrieved from http://www.ventscontraires.net/article.cfm/13444_bernard_stiegler__les_big_data_c_est_la_fin_de_la_pensee_.html

Stiegler, B. (2015). *La Société automatique: 1. L'avenir du travail*. Paris: Fayard.

Stillwell, D. J., & Kosinski, M. (2004). myPersonality project: Example of successful utilization of online social networks for large-scale social research. *American Psychologist, 59*(2), 93–104.

Textifire. (2017). A special relationship & the birth of Cambridge Analytica. *Medium*. Retrieved from https://medium.com/textifire/a-special-relationship-the-birth-of-cambridge-analytica-97633129cb06

Thrift, N., & French, S. (2002). The automatic production of space. *Transactions of the Institute of British Geographers, 27*(3), 309–335.

Turkle, S. (1995). *Life on the screen: Identity in the age of the Internet*. New York: Simon and Schuster.

Ulanoff, L. (2017). Sean Parker made billions off of Facebook. Today he basically called it evil. *Mashable*. Retrieved from https://mashable.com/2017/11/09/sean-parker-slams-facebook/#gVnUWCGJ1mqc

Venturini, T., & Rogers, R. (2019). "API-based research" or how can digital sociology and journalism studies learn from the Facebook and Cambridge Analytica data breach. *Digital Journalism,* 7(4), 532–540. doi:10.1080/21670811.2019.1591927

Wilson, E. A. (2005). "Can you think what I feel? Can you feel what I think?": Notes on affect, embodiment, and intersubjectivity in AI. *Scan: Journal of Media Arts Culture,* 2. Retrieved from http://scan.net.au/scan/journal/display.php?journal_id=54

Wilson, E. A. (2011). *Affect and artificial intelligence.* Seattle: University of Washington Press.

Wright, M. (2018). 'No evidence' Brexit was influenced by Cambridge Analytica scandal, Facebook says. *The Telegraph.* Retrieved from https://www.telegraph.co.uk/news/2018/11/21/no-evidence-brexit-influenced-cambridge-analytica-scandal-facebook/

Žižek, S. (1991). *Looking awry: An introduction to Jacques Lacan Through popular culture.* Cambridge, MA: MIT Press.

Žižek, S. (2014). *Žižek's Jokes:(Did you hear the one about Hegel and negation?).* Cambridge, MA: MIT University Press.

Žižek, S. (2019a). The digital police state: Fichte's revenge on Hegel. *Journal of Philosophical Investigations,* 13(28), 1–19.

Žižek, S. (2019b). Mind-reading AI may spell end to humanity as we know it, but not because it will enslave us. *RT.* Retrieved from https://www.rt.com/news/468228-mind-reading-computer-humanity-zizek/

PART 3
Educating the people
Digital deadlocks

5
DIGITALISING EDUCATION AND PARENTING

The end of interpellation?

Introduction: educating the digital and back

As elucidated in Chapter 2, Alan Turing (1950) argued that if one wants to construct an intelligent machine, the best way to do this is to construct a machine that is capable of learning. The basic idea here, which is now widespread, is that if one wants to build a machine with multiple capacities (to be humanlike, to supersede humans, or even have completely different skills than humans have), then programming this would be extremely difficult and demanding. The more convenient option is to build machines that can learn—either on their own or aided by education—so that they can perform the required (or even another) job or adapt to new work demands. Those with experience in the parenting, educating, or schooling of humans will attest to the demanding and gruelling aspects of education, whereas artificial intelligence (AI) technologists, conversely, appear to be less worried by this proposition. Consider here Turing's contention that 'there is so little mechanism in the child brain…it can be easily programmed' (Turing, 1950, p. 456), from which he argued that when attempting to simulate an adult's mind, one should begin by simulating a child's mind.

At this juncture, we are all aware of several convincing examples. For example, there is the robot that taught itself to walk: through a process of trial and error it learned what movements to make in order to maintain its balance and, above all, to get from point A to B.[1] The programmers set a limited range of parameters and goals (principal among which, the goal of getting from A to B) and the machine taught itself to walk. Alternatively, there is a more cognitive example of machines learning to recognise cats in photographs. You heard right: after presenting an AI system with 10 million digital images deriving from YouTube videos, AI learned to distinguish between *cats*.[2]

But, of course, the primary challenge is to understand and problematise the bidirectional exchange that is transpiring here. First, there is the exportation of educational theories and models from the educational sphere into the technological sphere. Turing, for his part, opted for the model of the child as a *tabula rasa*, albeit while also inscribing some innate capacities when speaking of 'the structure of the child machine' as if it were equivalent to the hereditary material of the human child (Turing, 1950, p. 456). The key question pertains to what models and theories of learning are either utilised or considered to be usable in AI technology, and which are not? Second, and this concerns the reverse issue or the notion of feedback, which digital technologies then insert themselves within the field of human education, and what is the effect of this? That is to say, how do these educational technologies influence and shape theoretical doxa and practices within the field of education?

A first quick critical remark apropos the export and import of educational models and technologies is that the learning that machines undertake appears to be far removed from educating human beings. For example, one could contend that neither learning to walk nor discerning between cats fall within the remit of what education and schooling institutions were designed for across the cultural history of humankind. Hence, should we argue that the rationale for machines learning to walk or recognising certain visual patterns has more to do with simple, mechanistic skills, which are wholly unconnected to the cultural project of education and schooling? Indeed, if in these aforesaid scenarios 'reinforcement learning algorithms' (RLA) are used (with 'digital rewards' to reinforce the desired behaviour and 'digital penalising' of unwanted behaviour) (Simon, 2019), then these may well be appropriate for dealing with the more basic and practical functions of machine learning, but one could contend that they should not be fed back into human education, which is characterised by higher levels of functioning. Simply put, should our argument, thus, be that the pedagogic principles involved in learning to walk and learning to recognise cats are fine for those who are learning to walk and recognize cats, such as children and computers, but that education proper is (or at least should be) about something else altogether?

However, this might be too straightforward an argument insofar as it overlooks that, for humans, even walking and visual recognition are things that may already supersede mere mechanistic, biological, evolutionary, or *natural* conditions. For example, the process of a child learning to walk is something that arguably takes place in a specific human relational context, and, as such, passes through the symbolic dimension. Just think of the manifold expectations and preoccupations held by parents, which, in turn, colour all of the child's endeavours and achievements, as well as the accompanying stories. Indeed, one could even go as far as to say that it is words and stories that support a child's first steps. Similarly, with respect to recognising cats, we could say that first and foremost children symbolically get to know cats, as a consequence of being interpellated as follows: *look there, a cat!* Or, alternatively, we show them pictures or images of cats and ask them *what does the cat say?* (*Dog goes 'woof'. Cat goes 'meow'*). At the very least, I would argue that children do not get to know a cat as a consequence of throwing massive amounts of data at them. As aforementioned, this is the situation, at least for the time being, with AI education. Resultantly, if it subsequently turns out that AI teaches itself what a cat is by recognising patterns and textures, while humans allegedly primarily scan shapes (Cepelewicz, 2019), then perhaps this could be understood as a consequence of humans' relation to the world being mediated by words and language. Moreover, arguably, it is only by considering the symbolic dimension that one can begin to fully appreciate the historical, cultural, and even political reasons for the well-known cat hype in the digital sphere.

With all of this in mind, are we not in danger of approaching machine learning from a basic reductionist (and thus deeply flawed) view of children's education and schooling? Of course, one could argue that if simple behaviouristic models suffice to teach robots to walk and machines to recognise cats, then why utilise more sophisticated theories and models? Indeed, is this not the ultimate upshot of Turing's conceptualisation of children as comprising 'a rather little mechanism, and lots of blank sheets' (Turing, 1950, p. 456)? To address this, it is expedient to ask two questions. First, what does it mean that we surround ourselves with machines and technologies, which are based on simplified, reductionist, and scaled-down models of subjectivity? To be clear, what I am arguing here is not just let us use *RLA for our dogs and robots, but not for our children*, as this would mean that I would concede that there are lower forms of learning (those described by cognitive behaviourists) that are suitable for animals and machines (and sometimes for humans?), which are to be contrasted to more sophisticated symbolic and humane forms of learning (for some humans?). I wish to firmly reject such a position on the grounds that, primarily, behaviourist techniques are pre-eminently symbolic, insofar as it represents a form of exerting power and producing obedience that is firmly situated within Logos. That is to say, it is through formulas such as S-R (stimulus-response) that the symbolic human being seeks to control animals, robots, and, for that matter, children and adults alike. Hence, notwithstanding the classic Watsonian rejection of the symbolic and, above all, of the imaginary, of 'spirit' and 'conscience', of 'content' and 'thought', of 'imagery' and 'mental states' (Watson, 1913),[3] behaviourism and its derivates are, thus, discursive practices to the core. Consider here how the binary structure of positive and negative reinforcement eventually ends up in the practices of the 'token economy' through its use of symbolic rewards, such as fake money, buttons, poker chips, and stickers. Conversely, notwithstanding behaviourism's fundamental rejection of internal physiological events, ultimately the main rationale of various behaviourist models today is that their practices work as a consequence of the neurobiological organisation of human beings. In other words, the famous behaviourist black box is not to be opened because it is assumed that we all know what is inside: the brainy matter that fully determines the human as we know it, and which can be fully explained by neurobiology. It is precisely here in relation to the fantasies about the signature of human life that the imaginary and ideological dimensions come to the fore: first, we imagine that we know what human life is, and second, how human life should be (suffice to recall here the manifold critiques of B.F. Skinner's psycho-politics) (Harré, 1979; Shotter, 1975).[4] Therefore, we must reject the idea that there is something like a natural, biological, and evolutionary base of learning (allegedly charted and mastered by cognitive behaviourism), and that we should, thus, strive towards a more humane form of education (if not for our dog or robot, then at least for our children). In contradistinction to this position, I argue that the very idea of a natural, biological base for learning is always necessarily symbolically structured, and, moreover, masks an ideological rationale based on control and power. Therefore, I will restate my first question as follows: what does it mean that we surround ourselves with machines and technologies, which are grounded in a problematic naturalising fantasy of human beings?

From here, our second question emerges: what does it mean that this reductionist technology is subsequently transplanted back into the educational system via for example digital learning platforms? As Ksenia Federova observed, a basic assumption in machine learning is the comparison between 'machines and organizations…to reveal the capabilities for learning and self-management'. 'Learning' is thus framed as something that is individualised and related to how a machine manages itself. As Federova notes:

> These systems were interpreted in terms of the epistemic autonomy of their behavior, i.e., ability to develop qualitatively new functions without external guidance. It is epistemic because it reflects decision-making, or "thought" processes that occur during feedback loops.
> *(Fedorova, 2016, p. 51)*

Would this not be precisely how many pedagogues would describe schooling today? This is the definition Wikipedia provides: "Learning is the process of acquiring new or modifying existing, knowledge, behaviors, skills, values, or preferences."[5] Or, phrased otherwise, both in the sphere of machine learning and human education, education today appears to serve highly pragmatic and functional goals, as well as taking the individual as its basic unit. Of course, in the sphere of human education, many other definitions pay greater attention to the social aspect of learning:

> Our research shows that young people learn best when actively engaged, creating and solving problems they care about, and when they are supported by peers who appreciate and recognize their accomplishments.
> *(Brandt, 2019)*

However, once again, is the social not extremely narrowly defined here, in terms of that which helps further the problem-solving process, with the function of 'peers' being reduced to strengthening the self-confidence of the person managing the problems? Teaching and schooling appear to be almost dehumanised here, as well as being instrumental and quasi-mechanical. One is tempted to ask: what will become of us if we choose to raise our children in this way? What are we subjecting future generations of children and students to? At the very least, we would have to reverse the myth that we merely model our machines on humans, because the opposite now appears to be the case: we model humans on machines, with, as argued in the previous chapters, the latter being constructed on the basis of ideological fantasies from psychology about what humans are or ought to be.

At the very least, would it not be interesting to inform machine learning with other, alternative models of learning? This raises the first problem: what other models? Are there any models that are of relevance in contemporary society? Here, we may need to restate and redouble Saramago's dictum that I evoked in Chapter 1, "we will know less and less what the human being is" to *we will know less and less what education or schooling is*. Indeed, arguably, no one seems to know anymore how to educate and school our children and youth. For example, university schooling ever more resembles high school teaching: university professors even plead to assess their students via weekly or bi-weekly tests. Moreover, a kind of infantilisation can be discerned in modern university textbooks: 'information' becomes a mode of entertainment presented via teasers and fun-to-know items, while 'key issues' are routinely repeated at least three times: in the text, as an illustration, and in the recap-section. This obligatory 'recap' section almost invariably contains 'fill in the gap-questions', as if the students were still in primary school.[6] Education has become *education-lite*, or, like coffee without coffee, beer without alcohol, we now appear to have education without education.

However, to be absolutely clear, the point here is not to oppose the *end of education as we knew it* with some kind of vision of what education would be, or, indeed, was in certain historical epochs in which education allegedly was at its best. Simply put: given that Freud considered education to be one of the three impossible professions (along with governing and practicing psychoanalysis) (Freud, [1925]1955), arguably, the most important issue is to examine how this impossibility is given form, how it is negotiated with, or, perhaps even more appropriately, how this impossibility is negated or covered up. At the very least, what education is or should be cannot be ascertained from an essentialist or natural perspective, but, rather, must be related to how people view themselves and the world, which makes education, above all, a cultural, ethical, and political issue.

The fact that the educational sphere cannot achieve full closure and is, as such, an antagonistic field, has over the course of last century been covered up by the educational sphere taking refuge in the psy-sciences, and, more recently, the neuro-sciences. Let me provide a brief sketch of this history, beginning with the events of May 68: as a protest movement predominantly initiated by high school and university students, it demonstrated, amongst other things, that the older models of education, based on discipline and the transfer of knowledge, had reached a deadlock. It is precisely here that the neuropsy-sciences entered the scene. Post-May 68, it was scientific experts, such as pedagogues and psychologists, who took the lead in informing us what education should be in modern societies. This, arguably, is what led to the psychologisation, and, subsequently, neurologisation of education. Simply put, education and schooling came to be reframed in terms of well-being, mental health, and taking care of one's brain.[7]

Consequently, at this historical juncture, should we understand the digitalisation of education in the same vein? Indeed, digital technologies today appear to be mobilised to rescue the yet again stranded discourses and practices of education and schooling. At the very least, the digital appears to entail yet another reframing of education, in which education is considered to be an informational process to be realised via digital technologies. Or, adopting a more minimalist perspective, we could say that one of the prime goals of education today is said to be guiding and steering young people in the informational highway (i.e. providing them with the tools to effectively navigate, circumvent, or confront the various dangers they encounter along their virtual routes). But, of course, the first thing to note here is that this is where, perhaps unsurprisingly, the neuro-psychologising perspective rears its head once again. Discussions about screen-time, for example, are invariably framed in psychological and, above all, neurological terms. Researchers claim, among other things, that more than 2 h of screen-time a day can damage children's brain development (see, e.g., Donnelly, 2018). Conversely, even those studies that argue that parents should not worry about the use of social media and or digital screens, more often than not also take recourse to neuropsy-terms, such as, for example, claiming that texting and engaging in other online activities do not lead to deleterious effects on mental health (see, e.g., Rizzi, 2019).

So, in this second part of the book, let us turn to examine the digitalisation of education. First, in this chapter, I attempt to disentangle in greater detail the interconnections between psychologisation, neurologisation, and digitalisation. Second, in Chapter 6, I aim to use the digitalisation of education as a means through which to further scrutinise the digitalisation of (inter)subjectivity. Third, in Chapter 7, we confront these discussions with a psychoanalytic perspective, specifically by returning to the figure of Hans Zulliger, one of the main propagators of the interbellum movement that brought psychoanalysis and pedagogy together. This movement, which withered away with the onset of the Second World War, arguably, comprises an interesting and radical perspective from which to conduct a novel reading of both digital technologies qua learning technologies and the digitalisation of education itself. But let us first, in this chapter, explore the vicissitudes of educational interpellation in order to question whether digitalisation alters anything in this process of educators or teachers hailing, summoning, engaging, calling upon their subjects.

Digitalisation and the vicissitudes of interpellation

Historically, education and schooling are practices that have involved symbolic interpellation, whereby its subjects are enjoined to take upon themselves certain signifiers within specific discursive schemes. Parents, for example, direct the attention of their toddlers in various ways: '*Look there, what's that? You see that cute little kitty?*' after which the little one is supposed to repeat the words. Similarly, in school pupils are also interpellated: '*Hey you, pay attention please, this is what the scientific expert says about this or that. Please repeat after me*'.

However, from the moment that the school's central vocation of knowledge transfer (combined with a disciplinary rationale) lost its hegemonic position and the neuropsy-sciences came in, engendering the aforementioned psychologisation and neurologisation of education, something profoundly changed with respect to interpellation. To explain precisely what changed, let me begin by arguing that the phenomena of psychologisation and neurologisation were preceded by yet another '-isation', that is, the medicalisation of education and parenting. Indeed, it was originally doctors and medical assistants who had key roles in educational institutional settings, by, for example, instructing mothers how to raise their children in accordance with medical knowledge. What perhaps constitutes the major shift from medicalisation to psychologisation and neurologisation, specifically with respect to education, is that the layperson him/herself came to be hailed to adopt the academic knowledge of psychology and neuroscience when reflecting upon themselves, others, and the world at large. From this moment on, expert knowledge incited laypersons to subjectivise themselves through the scientific gaze. Whereas in the old, pre-modern school the knowledge of the master (and his voice) above all envisioned a direct disciplining of its subjects, from modernity onwards, and especially in the era of psychologisation and neurologisation, knowledge came to produce a form of auto-discipline or self-governance. The crucial issue here is that, while the baseline of the neuropsy-sciences is arguably '*look, this is what you are*',[8] this invites the layperson not to identify with the thing (the psychological persona or the brain) that they are said to be per se, but, rather, to adopt the scientific view and respond as follows: *oh, really, can I have a look? Is this what I am?*

Of course, medical discourse is partly based on the same scheme. Hence, whilst one could argue that at fundamental-level medical procedures do not require the layperson to know—paracetamol lowers pain and fever irrespective of whether we know this or not—it is evident that in the medicalisation of education and parenting the administration of knowledge already played an integral role. Consider, for example, how in the 19th-century caregivers and, above all, mothers were instructed via medical knowledge about the importance of hygiene to counter bacterial infections (Vandenbroeck, 2017). It is this interpellation into academic knowledge that is fundamental to modern biopolitics, as it was theorised by Foucault: it subjects educators, parents, and children to what Foucault calls the 'power-knowledge nexus' (Foucault, 1978). We can understand this as follows: the layperson is interpellated into the discourses of science so as both to subjectivise and govern themselves via the signifiers of expert knowledge.

Returning to psychologisation and neurologisation as society-wide phenomena, it is the centrality of inducing laypersons to adopt the perspective of academic knowledge that makes the practices of the neuropsy-sciences so closely tied to educational practices. Consider how in humanitarian-aid responses psychologists invariably proceed by administering *theory* to the victims of natural or other disasters: Jones, Greenberg, and Wessely, for example, contended that 'large-scale community outreach and psycho-education about post-disaster reactions should be included among public health interventions to promote calming' (Jones, Greenberg, and Wessely, 2007). This is a typical example of how psychologists establish their practices by calling upon everybody to come into their psychology class. In the field of parenting and education itself, psychologisation and neurologisation lead to a unique redoubling of the educational rationale. Parenting, for example, has today become connected to books, manuals, courses, and classes. However, children and youngsters also have to know and be educated in the theories and scientific findings of psychology and neurology. Hence, as I have claimed elsewhere, the current hot topic of *neuroeducation* (the idea of grounding schooling and parenting in neuroscience) cannot but pass through *neuro-education*: teaching the theories and latest findings of neuroscience to educators, parents, and children themselves (De Vos, 2015, 2016a). Youngsters, for example, are addressed as follows: *this is your brain during puberty*, upon which they are then shown colourful scans of pubescent brains. Examples such as these testify to how human beings, quite remarkably, must be theoretically instructed in what it means to be human. The radical point to be made here is that there is no other way of using psychology and neuroscience within schooling and parenting than incorporating it within the curriculum of all parties involved. As with medicalisation, but albeit in a more concretised way in psychologisation and neurologisation, the primary rationale is the schoolification of the entire human and social reality.

However, is this scheme of the modern subject who is interpellated into academic knowledge not becoming redundant with the ever-expanding digital turn? Digitalisation—broadly conceived of in terms of how (inter)subjectivity (our relation to ourselves, others, and the world) is ever more imbricated in digital media, data, and algorithms—might constitute a decisive breach in the genealogy of medicalisation, psychologisation, and neurologisation. This is because, primarily, digitalisation fundamentally alters the relation of the subject to knowledge. For, if the medicalised, psychologised, and neurologised subject was interpellated to adopt the scientific gaze and internalise scientific knowledge, the digitalised subject is not necessarily enjoined to share the theoretical outlook; rather, data gathering and algorithmic data handling function perfectly well without a knowing subject. Social media prompts us to like this, be sorry for that, to remember our mother's birthday, buy this, etc., without us knowing the coded rationale that underpins this all. Therefore, with respect to parenting and education, perhaps there will be less and less need for us (and children themselves) to be educated in theories about what drives our behaviour: data-technology and algorithms operating silently in the background will suffice to drive, guide, and steer our behaviour.

Furthermore, one should not overlook the fact that in the era of Big Data the neuropsy-sciences themselves increasingly tend to bypass theory and reflective knowledge. This can perhaps be best discerned by the fact that, in general, the sciences appear to be shifting towards a different understanding of knowledge as a consequence of becoming 'data sciences'. When Chris Anderson provocatively exclaimed that Big Data "makes the scientific method obsolete" and thus signalled the end of theory (Anderson, 2008), the French philosopher Bernard Stiegler called this "the end of thinking" (Stiegler, 2014). These massive volumes of available data—so it is claimed—can be analysed and put to use, both directly and pragmatically, in technological and algorithmic ways (and in *real-time*) that completely bypass theory and knowledge as such. High-performance computing is not about knowing or understanding something, but, rather, is about computing and letting the data do the work (see also Stiegler, 2015). In this respect, both the human sciences and the neuropsy-sciences also no longer seem to envision a grand knowledge or grand theory: as they both become increasingly digital, it is sufficient for them to gather the alleged primary data and to devise from their pragmatic strategies and protocols to put the data to work.

Similarly, the European Human Brain Project, for example, aims to 'use data-mining techniques to derive an understanding of the way the human brain is constructed and then apply what is learned' (Paul M. Matthews in Kandel, Markram, Matthews, Yuste, and Koch, 2013, p. 659). Can we not argue here, then, that ultimately it is the computer that understands and 'knows', albeit in a completely different way to how we used to 'know' ourselves? Big Data in the neurosciences no longer requires the interpellative subjective detour (neither with respect to scientists nor laypersons). Moreover, Big Data neurosciences actually claim to go beyond the correlational scheme traditionally attributed to the neurosciences. This correlational scheme, at least as I interpret it (see De Vos, 2016b), pertains to how neuroscience invariably, and necessarily, takes recourse to psychological issues and correlates these with specific brain areas (or brain chemistry). That is to say, in order to conduct fMRI research on aggression, empathy, cognition, and so on and so forth, one must draw upon particular psychological theories on these issues. Indeed, the majority of brain research can be understood in terms of colouring the brain with psychology, which explains the centrality of choosing which psychological theory and psychological school to use to operationalise the topics being examined. However, Christof Koch, a proponent of Big Data neuroscience, claimed that with data-driven research, the neurosciences can finally transcend the correlational scheme:

> To understand the cerebral cortex, we must bring all available experimental, computational and theoretical approaches to focus on a single model system. In particular, it is of the essence to move from correlation—this neuron or brain region is active whenever the subject does this or that—to causation—this set of molecularly defined neuronal populations is causally involved in that behavior.
>
> *(Koch in: Kandel et al., 2013, p. 660)*

The claim made by Koch here is that we are now able to move beyond the different (competing) psychological theories and knowledge and instead devise a 'single model' based purely on data. Of course, one could contest this position on the grounds that this is still correlational, as causation still correlates neuronal populations with certain behaviours. Be that as it may, the claim being made here about the neuropsy-sciences having entered the digital era is that they are now finally free from theory and knowledge, and, as such, are finally on a par with the so-called hard sciences and their allegedly direct take on causality. Here, seemingly, the erstwhile inevitable and necessary divulging of knowledge to the layperson through the mechanism of interpellation can simply be skipped. Allegedly, the data can sufficiently handle how things work in the brain and what causes this, without us needing to understand what is going on. One could perhaps connect this to a basic principle in digital nudging: different visitors of a website are, for example, offered two or more different versions of the same webpage (the different versions are algorithmically generated and concern the variation of certain parameters, such as layout or colours); ultimately, the version that attracts the most visitors (or makes them stay longer) becomes the standard one (albeit while still being continually tweaked). Hence, both with respect to the datafication of the neuropsy-sciences and digital nudging, nobody knows or needs to know how things work exactly, it suffices that causation occurs. From this, because the data 'knows', the persons involved are relieved of having to know themselves, and they are simply nudged and steered in the smart environments, and, hence, no longer need to be reflective or reflexive.

To summarise the shift at hand: when the psy- or neuro-experts used to claim knowledge about humans and used this as the basis for turning everyone into their pupils, Big Data does not care whether we know or not: the data-driven and adaptive smart architecture and design of our lifeworld interacts in real-time with human beings on the basis of algorithms and without the mediation of reflective knowledge. In such an environment, the Foucauldian power-knowledge nexus is no longer operative, as it no longer relies on subjects' auto-disciplining themselves as per the modus operandi of biopolitics: nudging and digital social engineering ensure that we do the right thing.

So, when Henry Markram, one of the principal members of The Human Brain Project, wrote that…

> The platforms will allow [the neuroscientists] to reconstruct and simulate the brain on supercomputers coupled to virtual bodies acting in virtual environments (in silico behaviour)….
>
> *(Markram in: Kandel et al., 2013, p. 661)*

…what he perhaps overlooked is that this paradigm is already at work in the growing digitalisation of our lifeworld and of (inter)subjectivity: a large, if not central, part of (inter)subjectivity is already about virtual bodies acting in virtual environments, and about us being steered to act in desired ways. Hence, the

Human Brain Project and other similar endeavours are, as is often the case in the history of science, rather than being truly innovative research methods, in fact, metaphoric re-enactments of changes that are already underway in the episteme.

Here, once again, we are left to confront the question: is this the end of the subject as we knew it, the end of the modern *subject of the sciences* who related to itself, others and the world through knowledge? Or, with respect to parenting and education, is this the end of parents and educators constructing their image of the child as well as education in accordance with neuro-psychological theoretical doxa, and subsequently instructing the child itself to adopt the same academic perspective? As (inter)subjectivity becomes ever more shaped, steered, and conducted in real-time via digital nudging technologies, then the digitalisation of education and parenting may no longer need to mobilise subjects via enjoining them to internalise expert knowledge to reflect upon themselves, others, and the world. Arguably, we are heading towards algorithmic-based parenting and education, which completely bypasses the formerly reflexive, psychologised, and neurologised subjects.

Bring the children to the screen

Education, one could argue, is primarily about externalisation, that is, about unfolding the interior out into the exterior. In other words, education is about parents bringing children into the public space (handing them over, either with a little tear and/or with a little bit of relief). In this respect, any form of public education constitutes a transition (both in time and space) of the interior to the exterior, or, if one prefers, the private to the public. Hence, it can be argued that traditionally speaking, this transition predominantly comprised socialising youngsters into social knowledge, and from modernity onwards, into scientific knowledge. The public sphere, for which education operates as the revolving door, thus, becomes the place where knowledge should be applied, where the student, once encultured and educated, becomes a member of the community, or, if you prefer, becomes a citizen. Home and the family provided the raw material that the school subsequently shaped and formed via the medium of knowledge.

Of course, it should be clear to the reader that I am, first, merely discussing here the bourgeois version of education, which conceptualises education and the public sphere as being egalitarian and facilitating socio-economic mobility based on meritocracy. Social class plays a central role here, and, indeed, one could look at education as solidifying and justifying class differences and inequalities. Second, the initial point of departure, the interiority of the family and the private sphere should not be seen as naturally existing or pre-societal entities, which are only subsequently controlled and put to use for political and economic ends. Rather, the family and private spheres are always already societal constructions, which only emerge through their opposition to their alleged outside (the public sphere, the market, etc.). At the very least, it is only through the exteriorisation of the child into education (as well as the exteriorisation of the adult into the workplace), that the notion of the interior, the private family is constituted. Hence, the categories of child, pupil, and youngster have to be understood as social and historical concepts (Ariès, 1962).

The rationale for outlining all these caveats is to make clear that when we move to the psychologisation and neurologisation of education, one should not be tempted to romanticise, naturalise, or essentialise what education was or could have been prior to these phenomena. One should bear this in mind when attempting to understand the psychologisation of education, especially in its post-World War Two form, as blurring the boundaries between the private and public spheres. The key issue pertaining to the psychologisation of education is that, through the proliferation of psychologising discourses and practices, the home and family were incorporated into the institution of public education. The latter was no longer exclusively concerned with discipline and the transfer of knowledge, but, rather, also became responsible for managing everyone's emotional well-being and mental health. It is in this sense that the school extended its action radius to personal and private matters. However, importantly, if the partition between the private and the public is, as I have said, historically and ideologically grounded, then the enmeshing of those categories within the psychologisation of education should be regarded accordingly. Simply put, this entanglement aligned the private sphere of the family with the shifting modes of production witnessed under post-Fordism, whereby the economico-political system began to orient itself to the sphere of (inter)subjectivity. While previously the private and family spheres were, above all, about (re)producing a labour force to realise the surplus value (e.g. by handing over their offspring to the public sphere), under post-Fordism, the private and personal sphere become ever more directly integrated into the hegemonic modes of production and consumption. This is what Hardt and Negri meant when they defined post-Fordism as the direct production of subjectivity and social relations (as in the definition of Hardt and Negri, 2004). It is here that the phenomenon of psychologisation comes in (see De Vos) interpellating the layperson to incorporate their personal life into the public sphere, and, hence, bring it within the purview of the market. Hence, as discussed in the previous section, the psychologising mode of interpellation qua injunction to reflect upon ourselves, others and the world in psychological terms, directly serves the commodification of (inter)subjectivity. Neurologisation only effects another turn of the screw in this respect: given that neuroscience is believed to make accessible the very hardware, the alleged material base, of the personal and the private, it is in this way that the latter are fully turned inside out, made public and, thus, commodifiable in the neuroturn. For example, on the National Geographic Kids website children are addressed in the following way:

> You carry around a three-pound mass of wrinkly material in your head that controls every single thing you will ever do. From enabling you to think, learn, create, and feel emotions to controlling every blink, breath,

and heartbeat—this fantastic control center is your brain. It is a structure so amazing that a famous scientist once called it "the most complex thing we have yet discovered in our universe."[9]

The message here is that human beings are wholly transparent, there is no hidden personal sphere, that neuroscience can turn us inside out, and, moreover, that all of us should be amazed and marvel at this revelation about our innermost core, in turn, realising a surplus enjoyment. But, is it not precisely this surplus that is ultimately put to work in the contemporary post-Fordist economy via the dictum *the personal is economic*? This concerns how we are routinely told that work is about realising our personal potential, as is the realm of consumption: with Nike's "Just do it" one buys authenticity; with L'Oréal one buys self-esteem; while through buying a Nokia we purchase social relations. Is this not what a thoroughly psychologised and neurologised educational system prepares our children for? *Look at this brain-scan*, neuroscience exclaims, *this is where your thinking, feeling*...(all things psychological) *actually, take place!* So, work that brain thing! On the same webpage of the National Geographic Kids website, children are told: "When you learn, you change the structure of your brain," and "Exercise helps make you smarter."[10] In these statements, one can discern how vis-à-vis psychologisation, the neuroturn even appears to promote and promise upward social mobility. Rather than engaging in the drudgery of hard labour on your (intangible) self, one becomes the entrepreneur, if not stakeholder, of the corporeal brain (the pseudo-concretised You): by taking care of it (eating well, doing brain exercises, etc.), the brain will generate a surplus from out of itself.

However, today, with digitalisation, has the time not already gone when parents brought their children out into the open and to school, and, in so doing, via psychologisation and neurologisation, offered up the private sphere to the public and the market? For, one could argue, that today parents, first and foremost, bring their children to the screen and the network, by presenting their newly born child on social media, or even posting pregnancy ultrasounds. Indeed, a routine feature of public policy is to get pupils (even toddlers) involved with screens and social networks as soon as possible.[11] While the advocates for early digital education point to the strengthening of cognitive and motor skills and the fun involved in actively and creatively engaging with 'content' (in contrast to the alleged passivity of knowledge transfer), critics highlight the superficiality of the 'learned' content, the manifold negative physical and psychological issues (neck and wrist problems, obesity, sleep problems, etc.), as well as the sense of social isolation experienced by screen users.

Notwithstanding these aforesaid psycho-social issues, does the truly interesting question in this discussion not concern what space we are leading our children into? That is to say, do the internet and the so-called media truly represent the advent of a wholly networked *public* sphere. Here, two questions immediately come to mind: first, is the network truly social and public? For, as many have argued, the virtual world for one person, which is constituted out of their

Facebook page, Twitter account or subscriptions to certain YouTube-channels, is potentially a totally different world than that inhabited by another person. As is well-established, when I open a news-website, this site will most likely look different for me than it does for someone else, as these websites take into account our clicks and browser history in order to offer us news that we are allegedly interested—along with the corresponding advertisements, of course. Hence, is the networked public space not, in fact, an ersatz and simulacrum public sphere, as well as being the ultimate solipsistic virtual sphere that, first and foremost, serves economic interests?

It is here that Christian Fuchs was right in his retort against idealistic interpretations of social media, and in terms of putting forward a culturalist-materialist understanding, when he asked: who owns internet platforms or social media (Fuchs, 2014)? Geert Lovink also urged us to look for the underlying concrete power structures of social media itself (Lovink, 2012). Indeed, does this not represent the ultimate blurring of the personal and social with the corporate sphere, insofar as (inter)subjectivity is no longer merely an affair of the public and the state, but, rather, has become the fundamental commodity? In Dave Eggers' dystopian novel "The Circle", one company, after having succeeded in monopolising social media and integrating all the different applications into a single platform, purports that every new born should automatically get a Circle account—the latter providing the sole means of access to public services and even to the voting booth in presidential elections (Eggers, 2013). Does this, at the very least, not mean that the digitalisation of (inter)subjectivity is potentially capable of a far more direct enlisting of the subject, one that bypasses the modes that characterised the disciplinary school and even bypasses the mechanisms of interpellation and the reflective incorporation of knowledge, which were operative in psychologisation and neurologisation?

Hence, as a consequence of the rationale that children and toddlers should be introduced to screens as soon as possible, do educational institutions such as the school not completely lose their relevance? Indeed, school no longer seems to function as a temporary transitionary space (the revolving door to the 'real world' which nonetheless defines the school as a separate social space with a certain amplitude), but instead becomes merely a kind of interface, an empty non-space that itself has no breadth as such. As a result of psychologisation and neurologisation, the public space of education and schooling already became devalued as the private and the corporeal became introduced into the educational economy. With digitalisation now bringing the alleged 'real-world' into the class, the erstwhile mediatory space of education and schooling has, thus, became fully encroached upon and usurped, which is to say that the once opened up educational space is at risk of collapsing entirely. Or, phrased otherwise, when digital technology is believed to be a direct gateway into the supposed 'real-world', then education becomes merely another app that will shortly be upgraded or replaced with a newer and faster app. In this constellation, moreover, the child or the pupil itself becomes no more than a mere node in the network, both as an information processing unit (in need of being brought into contact with information and data) and a dataset itself to be commodified.

Furthermore, this is where we can observe that the digital turn is grounded in a naturalising discourse: children are seen as information-seeking and digesting creatures, spontaneously inquiring, asking questions and exploring in order to understand the world (Lind, 1998; Wang, Kinzie, McGuire and Pan, 2010). At the same time, we also have a naturalisation of what parents do: UbicKids, for example, a project that aims to build 'smart environments' to assist parenting, describes parenting as 'one kind of ordinary human activity' that can be 'greatly supported via ubicomp technologies' (Ma et al., 2005, p. 58). Hence, the idea here is that what children and parents naturally are and do can be directly addressed by technology: the natural and the artificial, seemingly, match very well together. UbicKids, for example, aims "to provide ubiquitous natural interactive, even proactive and further autonomic caring helps or services to [parents] with the right means in the right place at the right time."

Nikolas Rose perspicuous remarks on the rationales used in digi-discourses are expedient for our purposes here:

> All of these terms appear to express something natural and given about human sociality—as if the evolution of our psyches and our brains has actually demanded the social network media that now flood telecommunications infrastructures.
>
> *(cited in: Williamson, 2015, p. 19)*

From here, people such as Williamson argue that we should study software and its underlying code to identify the embedded assumptions that are made about actual or potential users in order to "investigate what social codes of conduct are written into the code, and to conduct genealogical explorations of the claims that underpin the codifying of conduct in software" (Williamson, 2015, p. 21). Notwithstanding the contributions made by Rose and Williamson's work, perhaps their critical projects require being extended further yet still. For what they do not address is the role of the neuropsy-sciences themselves within this process. Indeed, one could argue that, once nature is evoked, one rapidly finds oneself in psychologising and neurologising territory.

Remember, in this respect, our analysis in the previous chapters of the basic underlying assumptions in the work of Alan Turing, Marvin Minsky, and the cyberneticists Norbert Wiener, Gregory Bateson, and Warren McCulloch: each of their respective naturalisations of digital technology ultimately harboured a stowaway: a psychological approach (and thus ideological) to the human. This becomes especially apparent in the digitalisation of education, as a closer examination makes it immediately evident that digitalisation does not, in fact, signal a shift beyond psychologisation or neurologisation, but, rather, digitalisation remains indebted to psychologisation and neurologisation. In the next sections, I consider in greater depth how this transpires within education.

Not the end of psychologisation and neurologisation

To begin with, the envisioning the child and parenting as something natural and proto-technological is strongly mirrored by an anthropomorphisation of the digital and technological. As Ben Williamson, for example, remarks, IBM's forays into digital education are explicitly guided by the idea of 'brain-inspired computing' (Williamson, 2015, p. 61). IBM's neuro-imagery is bountiful, as they speak of 'neuromorphic hardware', 'algorithms that learn', 'brain-inspired algorithms', 'neurosynaptic chips', and so on and so forth (cited in: Williamson, 2015, p. 61). The sociologist Adrian Mackenzie helps us to also observe the presence of the older psy-imagery at work here: IBM's and Google's 'cognitive infrastructures' 'abound in references to cognition, meaning, perception, sense data, hearing, speaking, seeing, remembering, deciding, and surprisingly, imagining and fantasy' (cited in Williamson, 2015, p. 62). Mackenzie describes how psy-imagery is used in relation to digital data:

> the increasing 'mindfulness' of the infrastructures under construction at IBM, Google and the like predicate a certain re-concatenation of the world, no longer in the mobile train of experience of people...but instead in the relations mindfully discerned in streams of data.
> *(cited in Williamson, 2015, p. 62)*

Ever since McCulloch and Pitt's "A logical calculus of the ideas immanent in nervous activity" (McCulloch & Pitts, 1943), the key signifier in AI has been 'neural network'. However, one could argue that neuro-terminology, above all, serves rhetorical ends, inasmuch as it reproduces the myth that digital technology is based on the copying-pasting of the structure of the brain onto the machine. However, what is actually being done is the exporting of *theories and models* of the brain into technology, which, as argued in the previous chapters, are indebted to specific psychological theories and models, if not fantasies, of the human. Consider, once again, the Human Brain Project's aim to identify the "mathematical principles underlying the relationships between different levels of brain organisation and their role in the brain's ability to acquire, represent, and store information" (Walker, 2012, p. 9). Here, the brain is conceptualised a priori as an information processor, which, of course, is a handy a priori assumption if one wants to model the brain.

However, if this datafication of the lifeworld and subjectivity correlates with the anthropomorphisation of the techno-digital sphere and of data, should we not then conclude that psychologisation and neurologisation have shifted from the level of the subject to the level of the technology itself? That is to say, after having psychologised and neurologised parents, educators, and children, it is now computers' turn! However, if this digitalisation does not truly represent a complete break with psychologisation and neurologisation, then does this then mean that the interpellated neuro-psychological subject has also not really left the building, or should we conclude that digitalisation is psychologisation and neurologisation, just without the accompanying interpellation?

But before we get too far ahead of ourselves here, let us first follow Williamson's prompt to 'investigate what social codes of conduct are written into the code, and to conduct genealogical explorations of the claims that underpin the codifying of conduct in software' (Williamson, 2015, p. 21). As should already be clear, it is my contention that we should not only examine the neuropsychological codes that are written into digital structures but also we should trace how these neuropsy-codes are returned to us through those digital technologies that host (but, above all, shape and guide) contemporary forms of subjectivity and sociality.

To further probe the interwovenness of the digital with neuro- and psy-paradigms, let us begin by noting how even critiques of digitalisation often themselves take recourse to discourses on the brain. Just think of how Steiner-Adair and Barker (2013), for example, claim to be 'Protecting childhood and family relationships in the digital age'—as per the subtitle of their book—linking the use of mobile devices to addiction and substance abuse, in reference to dopamine, the neurotransmitter that is linked to the brain's reward and pleasure centres. However, is it not clear that this neuro-argument, in turn, is contaminated with digital techno-discourses? For, quite obviously, the idea that information technology affects our dopamine economy is based on a vision of the brain as living and feeding on information and data. Similarly, endorsing Steiner-Adair's recommendation to keep mealtimes phone and screen-free, Michael Rich stressed: "the ritual importance of breaking bread together and talking about your day and the *processing* of experience" (cited in: Novotney, 2016, p. 52, my italics). One should not overlook here the nostalgic, biblical, and arguably, ideological undertone, which brings together the psychological, neurological, and digital spheres.

Another, and perhaps even more central, aspect of the enmeshment of the neuropsychological and the digital can be inferred from "The Digital Brain Switch", which is a project funded by the Engineering and Physical Sciences Research Council in the UK. The project studied the changing nature of work-life balance as a result of digital technologies and was particularly interested in both 'how people switch between different work-life roles—parent, spouse, friend, co-worker, manager, employee—and how digital technologies either support this or act as a barrier'.[12] Given that it already sets out from the notion that there are different identities or roles between which one can *switch*, it, thus, already conceptualises subjectivity in ICT-terms, that is, the idea of switching between windows and programmes. Predictably, solutions to this problem are then sought in the same techno-digital realm:

> We aimed to give people tools to better understand their own work-life balance and to experiment with different ways of managing their work and life. We imagined a life as an experiment application in which people can test different ways of working and, through the application, collect data over time that will allow them to choose between different working methods.[13]

The bottom line here is that life is about collecting data, and, hence, that life itself is just another app! What we should not overlook here is that, in the face of digitalisation, laypersons are called upon to collect and handle data, or, alternatively, they are enjoined to become themselves qua data scientists. In so doing, are we, thus, not finally back squarely within the aforesaid scheme of interpellation that characterised psychologisation and neurologisation: subsequent to the injunction to become your own psychologist or neuroscientist, now we must become our own data specialist? This is how the project reported on such self-experimentation:

> Alan logs on to the Digital Brain Switch (DBS) application to set up an experiment. He is interested in measuring two variables: his self-reported mood level; and the number of times he switches between e-mail, social networks, work and life during the day. In the experiment set-up, he instructs the DBS application to send him a notification at 10 pm every day to report his mood level and switching frequency for one month.

Here, two points are abundantly clear: first, the digitalisation of subjectivity and the lifeworld occurs along the lines of a neuropsychological discourse (the 'mood level'); and second, the correlation that is now at stake is no longer that between the psyche and the brain, but, rather, between the neuropsychological and the technological. Moreover, the net result of this appears to be that with digitalisation we have finally outsourced psychologisation and neurologisation to the technological sphere. This results in a strange paradox: we no longer have to conduct the auto-disciplining ourselves but can simply let the technology do all this on our behalf.

However—and here we come to the crux of the matter—does this not mean after all that, as a result of this outsourcing, a minimalistic subject is still in operation, still interpellated by academic knowledge (only this time via the data-scientific perspective) and called upon to adopt the external gaze? Consider, in this respect, how, vis-à-vis the correlation between the neuro-psychological and the technological, the DBS project presupposed a structural mismatch:

> We may manage transitions through the use of different technologies or moving between locations, but mental and emotional switches may be more difficult to achieve as quickly or completely. We may experience leakage of emotion across activities. In just 'dealing with a quick work email while making the tea' we may under-estimate the impact this will have on our mood.[14]

Most crucially, the actual subject is neither situated here on the side of the neuro-psychological (the emotional) nor on the side of techno-digitality, but, rather, the subject is located in the gap between the neuro-psychological and techno-digitality. Or, phrased otherwise, informed and interpellated by science on the mismatch between the emotional and the technological, the subject contemplates this situation and attempts to deal with it through technology itself. Is it not precisely here that a subject—albeit a minimal one—comes to the fore, one who is still interpellated by academic knowledge, but delegates the actual knowing to technological devices?

Consider the example of another type of digital technology, the 'EVOZ Smart Parenting device', which is basically a 'smart camera' that allows parents to engage in 'Baby Data Tracking': feeding, changing, sleeping, milestones and temperature data are all collected in a repository that allows parents to share data 'with coaches and doctors in both graphical and raw data format'.[15] Hence, the layperson is here, once again, called upon to become a data scientist. Moreover, this entails the inclusion of traditional theories and models from mainstream neuropsy-sciences: parents are provided via the app with 'accessible parenting information' based on age and data patterns, whereby the digitalised subject is still called upon to adopt the academic knowledge from 'short videos, quick tips, and tricks optimized for mobile device viewing'. However, should we here not situate the final turn of the screw: that is, while the layperson is still offered theories and theoretical perspectives, this appears to function in a minimalised and, above all, formalised way, due to the fact that the layperson is required to know less and less because the digital device apparently does the knowing on their behalf.[16]

Therefore, even when it appears that the digitalisation of (inter)subjectivity still hinges on interpellation, it is evident that this process no longer produces, to use Lacan's term, a *subject supposed to know* (a subject who must know neuropsy-theories), but, rather, a subject (if this is still what it can be said to be) that *assumes that neuropsy-theories know* (a subject that assumes that the knowledge of neuropsy-theories is secured in the digital device or the app). The assuring credo, the minimal piece of knowledge that must be alluded to, acknowledged and ascertained by everyone, is McCulloch and Pitt's dictum that the network is like a brain, and, in turn, that the brain is like a computer. So, there is no need for us to worry, everything is, or at least should be, neatly attuned. Does this not mean that, ultimately, digitalisation leads to a minimal, contained subject or agent who is only asked to acknowledge the state of affairs? If the modern subject always already was a minimal subject, who had no latitude nor weight but only contemplated itself from the perspective of its interpellation by science, then perhaps this minimalisation of the subject has reached its zenith in digitalisation (or, as I formulated it in Chapter 3, digitalisation signals the final and full realisation of the zero levels of subjectivity). In other words, does the retreat of the subject not reach its pinnacle with technology, to the point that one can now finally outsource one's subjectivity to technology? Consider here how with the EVOZ Smart Parenting device one can even let the device take over a whole range of parental functions:

> You have tools at your fingertips to help calm your baby from anywhere: control the nightlight, talk or sing to the baby from your phone or play lullabies, music and even audiobooks offered in the camera.[17]

What remains to be seen is what this outsourcing of subjectivity, along with auto-disciplining, may mean for contemporary forms of biopolitics.

Conclusions: a psychology comes true

I have argued in this chapter that the digitalisation of education (and perhaps, more generally, the digitalisation of intersubjectivity) builds upon the prior phenomena of psychologisation and neurologisation. In so doing, digitalisation poses, above all, as old hat, insofar as we, ostensibly, are still dealing with a subject interpellated by knowledge and urged to identify with the objectifying gaze of the sciences. However, digitalisation perhaps effects a minor but decisive twist upon this scheme, in that the subject itself becomes ever more emptied out as it outsources (as it is called upon to do) both the knowledge and objectifying gaze components to technology.

Here, an image drawn by the artist Leslie Cober-Gentry that accompanied an article in Harvard Magazine is instructive in this regard. The article was entitled "The Teen Brain" and reported on how two neuroscientists, Jensen and Urion, went to secondary schools to get everybody—parents, educators, up to and including students themselves—'learning about the teen brain' (Ruder, 2008). The picture of the illustrator Cober-Gentry features the teenage brain suspended in mid-air, mapping, in a relatively standard way, issues such as sleep-deprivation, alcohol (ab)use, and impulsivity within the brain. At the bottom of the picture, there is a teacher and a blackboard with the words 'Learning about the brain'. Most significantly, there are all sorts of USB and UTP cables coming out of the brain, which do not run to the teacher but are instead handled by little figures in the background, which serves to make the teacher akin to a redundant figure preaching in the desert. At the very least, Cober-Gentry's drawing captures the transition from neurologisation to the digitalisation of subjectivity. Given that the figures wear t-shirts that have emblazoned on them, SU, CU, or UC, indicating their academic status, I surmise that they appear to stand for the academically informed, but, ultimately, automatised procedures and protocols of data-science that secure the processes of data collection and data handling. Hence, does this not mean that via digital technology, we are able to bypass the teacher and their traditional induction of pupils into academic discourse? One could even go so far as to argue that the little guys inserting the wires into the brain are not really human agents, but, rather, 'bots' or pieces of software that are capable of interacting with humans or even acting as if they were human.

The crucial question, then, concerns whether these bots, this 'intelligent' software that learns and evolves autonomously and which plays a growing role in our everyday life (underpinning digital nudging, by channeling and directing our desires and behaviour, both virtual and real) add a new dimension to contemporary biopolitics. That is to say, are we evolving to what one might call *technologically assisted self-disciplining*, or *automated self-surveillance*? If Woolley *et al.* wrote that many bots are built to pass themselves off as human (Woolley *et al.*,

2016)—remember the Turing Test here—then perhaps the question to be raised here is: which neuro-psychology is there for the bots, for the AI that controls us? But this neuro-psychologisation *within* digitalisation is, above all, discernible in the basic architecture and set-up of digital environments themselves, insofar as neuro-psychological scripts are clearly operative in the latter. The digitalisation of learning provides some distinctive examples here. Consider, for example, how the educationalist Richard Davies (2016), when reflecting upon how digital learning platforms should be set up, basically argues that when education enters the digital, nothing decisively changes. Davies begins by citing a quote from Sue Thomas: "some of the features we so value in the natural world can also be found online; indeed, our subconscious has already imprinted nature onto cyberspace" (Davies, 2016, p. 295). Or, alternatively, the natural (the neural) can be said to pass over from our psychology (the 'subconscious') to the digital. Davies is, thus, pretty confident that little changes with digital education, proceeding to argue that we use the same concepts (e.g. classrooms, discussion, seminars) in both the virtual sphere and physical learning environments. From here, Davies stresses the psychosocial and relational aspects of digital learning environments, arguing that what happened in traditional classrooms cannot but return in digital learning environments. To illustrate his point, he cites the example of how students often use technology in ways not originally intended: for example, 'phatic communication' (verbal or non-verbal communication that serves a social as opposed to an informative function), Davies argues, takes place within digital learning platforms by using the available means, such as discussion platforms or message boards.

One issue with Davies' work is that it does not engage with the question of what digitalisation itself means and entails for communication or subjectivity as such. Rather, he remains within the confines of a basic, naturalised subject, who is thought to engage with technology from the basis of their natural and invariant psychosocial make-up. Moreover, this neuro-psychological dimension of the human, which is ostensibly well-known to researchers, leads to a kind of celebratory stance: *look at how creative and resilient psychological man is!* However, in contradistinction to the sketched neuro-psychological human being who engages with technology, is the true subject not the one that is called upon to contemplate this imagery with awe and wonder? For, evidently, all these neuropsychological explanations of how human beings deal with technology appear to amuse and enchant us. For example, we love to hear accounts of how we are easily lured by subliminal messages or are fascinated to learn that when Facebook changes its algorithms this also changes how we experience ourselves and our social relations. By learning about those things with which we are so intrigued and enchanted, William Davies (note, a different author than Richard Davies) argues that "the sublime unknowability of Big Data lets us fall in love with our own domination" (Davies, 2015). Does this not mean that the subject is always elsewhere and not where we expect it to be? Of course, this was of little concern for Davies, Richard Davies that is, who fairly rapidly moved from the celebrative contemplation of the resilient neuro-psychological human to pragmatics: to design the digital in such a way that all random and spontaneous behaviour, such as, for example, using discussion rooms to chitchat, would be streamlined and used appropriately within the data-system itself. That is to say, Davies put forward the argument that the students' need to engage in the tittle-tattle of everyday conversation, can (and should be) formally and technologically facilitated by creating appropriate and designated digital channels:

> ...through extending the period online, for example, opening up an online webinar 30 min early in order for students to chat before the seminar, or utilising emoticons for students to express their feelings about the interactions, or supporting students to use video group conversations alongside the platforms being used for the collaborative tasks. In doing so students are able to recognise others and be recognised as member of this learning group and draw on the social cohesion they share.
>
> *(Davies, 2016, p. 301)*

What should not be overlooked apropos this digital pedagogical engineering is that this turns ostensibly spontaneous psychosocial activity into something computational, and, thus, traceable and analysable. Hence, the erstwhile uncharted and furtive engagements in school corridors must now be datafied within the digital education platform. But, of course, besides being potentially tracked, is the main issue not that the ostensibly spontaneous psychosocial activity will become in this way guided, steered, and, above all, pre-formatted and pre-configured according to mainstream psy-theories and models of what human behaviour should be? What these pre-psychologised educational platforms might show us, then, is that the complete range of virtual and smart environments that we dwell in during the digital era risk acting as coercive straitjackets of (inter)subjectivity, insofar as these are based upon mainstream naturalising neuro-psychological scripts. As such, it would appear that the story of the death foretold of the interactive and participative Web 2.0, and its promise of direct democracy and emancipation was destined to evolve into the AI-driven Web 3.0 and its attendant pre-formatting of (inter)subjectivities in order to make them datafiable and, ultimately, subservient to power and capital.

Consider, in this respect, the aforementioned smart parenting project UbicKids, which claims to achieve 'a merger of physical and digital spaces' and states that "[o]ne essential feature of ubicomp is to get physical and get real...in everyday life" (Ma *et al.*, 2005, p. 62). The key idea here is that digital technology is not only able to gather and compute data but subsequent to this it can also interact with and intervene in the 'real-world'. But how should we understand the nature of this intervention and acting upon the real-world? Does this 'getting physical and real' not, in the first instance, concern the augmenting of reality and the lifeworld in accordance with the pre-formatted models that back up the algorithms in order to guide and steer (inter)subjectivity? That is to say, rather than simply helping us to re-engage with the 'real world', smart educational and parenting environments are first and foremost engaged in *shaping the world in their own image*. Or, phrased otherwise, making an environment smart is, above all, about spreading a virtual and fictitious cloak over 'the concrete world'. One is reminded here, once again, of how UbicKids aims to outsource certain 'tedious and quite stressful' aspects of parenting to digital technology (Ma et al., 2005, p. 60), so that more space and time could be opened up for the things that really matter, such as 'giv[ing] the family more time to spend with each other' (Ma et al., 2005, p. 65). However, how should we conceptualise these so-called 'things that matter' if not along with the typical mainstream psycho-social models of 'quality time', 'sharing of emotions' and so forth? Here, getting real would appear to mean the imposing of normative, psychologising, and, above all, consumerist models of reality.

The fundamental shift here should not be overlooked: in pre-digital times, (social) psychology was deduced post-factum (through experiments and questionnaires); it was surmised, hypothesised and perhaps, above all, fantasised. Because (inter)subjectivity is now given form within virtual environments based on neuro-psychological theories and models, (social) psychology is now made 'real'. Or, alternatively, we could say that the once surmised and fantasised models of (social)neuro-psychology have become reality via the channel of virtuality. Virtuality, then, one could argue, is the final transubstantiation of the naturalising and essentialising fantasies of mainstream neuropsy-sciences. Here, Hannah Arendt's famous point about behaviourism comes into mind:

> The trouble with modern theories of behaviorism is not that they are wrong but that they could become true, that they actually are the best possible conceptualization of certain obvious trends in modern society. It is quite conceivable that the modern age—which began with such an unprecedented and promising outburst of human activity—may end in the deadliest, most sterile passivity history has ever known.
>
> *(Arendt, 1958, p. 322)*

Similarly, the trouble with neuro-psychology is not that it is wrong per se, but, rather, that it will become true via the virtualisation of our lifeworld. *Biopolitics 3.0*, which firmly interlocks the psychological, neurological, and digital sphere, by tracking, modelling, and commodifying (inter)subjectivity, might, thus, lead humanity to an unprecedented deadly and sterile passivity.[18]

A poignant example of the biopolitical intertwining of psychologisation, neurologisation, and the digitalisation of (inter)subjectivity is the smart parenting app Vroom. Vroom emerged during the recent revival of interest in attachment theories and devised an app which brings theories of attachment into the contemporary digital age:

> New science tells us that our children's first years are when they develop the foundation for all future learning. Every time we connect with them, it's not just their eyes that light up—it's their brains too. In these moments,

half a million neurons fire at once, taking in all the things we say and do. We can't see it happening, but it's all there, all at work. That's why Vroom is here.[19]

The first point to make is that attachment theories came back in vogue as a result of the neuro-turn, insofar as an attachment can now be made tangible by digital brain imaging techniques. This serves as an example of how psychological speculations can be made substantial by fleshing them out via brain scans.[20] However, the true transubstantiation is the ensuing one: the biopolitical realisation of mainstream cardboard psychological theories and models via the digitalisation of everyday life:

> Vroom turns shared moments into brain building moments. Whether it's mealtime, bathtime, or anytime in between, there are always ways to nurture our children's growing minds.[21]

The digital app, thus, literally turns parenting ('shared moments') into something neurological ('brain-building moments') by transposing parenting onto the digital and virtual scene of the app. The digitalisation of (inter)subjectivity confirms, builds on, and expands upon the biopolitics of psychologisation and neurologisation in radically novel ways. Self-governing, so, it would appear, is too important to be left to individuals themselves.

In digitality, the private and public spheres finally collapse into the virtual sphere, which is a fully controlled mono-dimensional space featuring (fully?) controlled and mono-dimensional individuals. Does this mean that there are no other 'private' spaces anymore? Perhaps the new, contemporary 'elsewhere' is situated behind the screen, the place of the obscured and hidden algorithms that give form to the projections that we see on the screen. This is where the 'anderes Schauplatz' (the other stage), to borrow Sigmund Freud's term for the unconscious, becomes a private/privatised space that is only accessible to the privileged and those in power. It remains to be seen how deep the rabbit hole goes and what the vicissitudes will be for the left behind, minimal subject. Perhaps, it still has a chance, due to the fact that, for the time being, it is still positioned in front of the screen, that is, at a point still removed from the screen. We will take this issue up in the next chapter.

Notes

1 See for example the article in Wired "The Clever Clumsiness of a Robot Teaching Itself to Walk" (Simon, 2019).
2 See for example the article in The New York Times "How Many Computers to Identify a Cat? 16.000" (Markoff, 2012).
3 For further reading, see (Pavón Cuéllar, 2004).
4 See for a concise approach of the pitfalls of the traditional critiques on behaviourism: (Parker, 2014).

5 https://en.wikipedia.org/wiki/Learning, based on: (Gross, 2005).
6 See for my assessment of psychology textbooks: (De Vos, 2019).
7 Or, to put it in terms from discourse theory: the old *master discourses* of state and religion have been replaced by the *discourse of the university*; and here education was reconceived in the first place in terms of the models and theories of the psy-sciences and the neurosciences. See also (De Vos, 2012, 2016b).
8 Remember, in this respect, George Miller's plea that I cited in Chapter 4 'to give psychology away' (Miller, 1969, p. 1074) exemplifying the rationale of enjoining everyone to engage *theoretically* with the findings of the psy-sciences.
9 https://kids.nationalgeographic.com/explore/science/your-amazing-brain.
10 https://kids.nationalgeographic.com/explore/science/your-amazing-brain.
11 See for example The Creative Classrooms Lab project (CCL) http://creative.eun.org/home.
12 http://www.scc.lancs.ac.uk/research/projects/DBS/.
13 http://www.scc.lancs.ac.uk/research/projects/DBS/.
14 http://www.scc.lancs.ac.uk/research/projects/DBS/wp-content/uploads/2015/06/DBS-A2-CMYK-fold-to-A4-FINAL.pdf.
15 https://www.evozbaby.com/product.
16 The concept of interpassivity developed by Robert Pfaller comes to mind here; I return to this concept in Part 3 of this book.
17 https://www.evozbaby.com.
18 This is where our avatars, our data doppelgangers, constructed through algorithms informed by neuropsy-theories and models, can be potentially lethal to the subject, as they leave no space whatsoever for the zero-level of subjectivity. For more on data doppelgangers and their disastrous effects in education, see Mandy Pierlejewski (2019).
19 http://www.joinvroom.org/.
20 Davi Thornton already perspicaciously pointed to the biopolitical aspects of the technologically mediated revival of attachment theories: underpinned by the authority of brain science, attachment opens up as a field of governance:

> …a locus for the cultivation and distribution of disciplinary practices mothers are induced to take up…. Because of the modes of visualization offered by brain imaging, these practices are subject to various measurements, calculations, and calibrations: different aspects of mothering can be quantified and temporally regulated according to precise equations.
>
> (Thornton, 2011, p. 411)

21 http://www.joinvroom.org/.

References

Anderson, C. (2008). The end of theory: The data deluge makes the scientific method obsolete. *Wired Magazine, 16*(7). Retrieved from https://www.wired.com/2008/06/pb-theory/.

Arendt, H. (1958). *The human condition*. Chicago, IL: University of Chicago Press.

Ariès, P. (1962). *Centuries of childhood: A social history of family life* (R. Baldick, Trans.). New York: Random House.

Brandt, L. (2019). Growing up digital. *Connected Learning Alliance*. Retrieved from https://clalliance.org/blog/growing-up-digital/?utm_source=mailchimp.com&utm_medium=email&utm_campaign=Vol119

Cepelewicz, J. (2019). Where we see shapes, AI sees textures. *Quantamagazine*. Retrieved from https://www.quantamagazine.org/where-we-see-shapes-ai-sees-textures-20190701/

Davies, R. (2016). Ceaselessly exploring, arriving where we started and knowing it for the first time. *Studies in Philosophy and Education, 35*(3), 293–303.

Davies, W. (2015). The data sublime. *The New Inquiry*. Retrieved from http://the new inquiry.com/essays/the-data-sublime/

De Vos, J. (2012). *Psychologisation in times of globalisation*. London: Routledge.

De Vos, J. (2015). Deneurologizing education? From psychologisation to neurologisation and back. *Studies in Philosophy and Education, 34*(3), 279–295 doi:10.1007/s11217-014-9440-5

De Vos, J. (2016a). The death and the resurrection of (psy)critique. The case of neuroeducation. *Foundations of Science, 21*(1), 129–145.

De Vos, J. (2016b). *The metamorphoses of the brain. Neurologization and its discontents*. New York: Palgrave Macmillan.

De Vos, J. (2019). Neuroscience in psychology textbooks: Reclaiming our non-psychology. In R. K. Beshara (Ed.), *A Critical Introduction to Psychology* (pp. 27–49). New York: Nova.

Donnelly, L. (2018). More than two hours screentime a day could damage children's brain development. *The Telegraph*. Retrieved from https://www.telegraph.co.uk/news/2018/09/26/two-hours-screentime-day-could-damage-childrens-brain-development/

Eggers, D. (2013). *The circle*. New York: Knopf.

Fedorova, K. (2016). *Plasticity and feedback: Schemas of indetermination in cybernetics and art*. Paper presented at the 22nd International Symposium on Electronic Art ISEA2016, Hong Kong.

Foucault, M. (1978). *The history of sexuality, Vol. 1* (R. Hurley, Trans.). New York: Vintage.

Freud, S. ([1925]1955). Preface to Aichhorn's Wayward Youth. In J. Strachey (Ed.), *The standard edition of the complete psychological works of Sigmund Freud: Vol. XIX* (pp. 271–276). London: Hogarth Press.

Fuchs, C. (2014). Social media and the public sphere. *tripleC: Communication, Capitalism & Critique, 12*(1), 57–101.

Gross, R. (2005). *Psychology: The science of mind and behaviour*. London: Hodder and Stoughton.

Hardt, M., & Negri, A. (2004). *Multitude*. New York: The Penguin Press.

Harré, R. (1979). *Social being: A theory for social psychology*. Oxford: Blackwell.

Jones, N., Greenberg, N., & Wessely, S. (2007). No plans survive first contact with the enemy: Flexibility and improvisation in disaster mental health. *Psychiatry, 70*(4), 361–365.

Kandel, E. R., Markram, H., Matthews, P. M., Yuste, R., & Koch, C. (2013). Neuroscience thinks big (and collaboratively). *Nature Reviews Neuroscience, 14*(9), 659–664.

Lind, K. K. (1998). *Science in early childhood: Developing and acquiring fundamental concepts and skills*.Paper presented at the Forum on Early Childhood Science, Mathematics, and Technology Education, Washington, DC. Retrieved from https://files.eric.ed.gov/fulltext/ED418777.pdf

Lovink, G. (2012). What is the social in social media. *e-flux journal, 40*, 1–12. Retrieved from https://www.e-flux.com/journal/40/60272/what-is-the-social-in-social-media/

Ma, J., Yang, L. T., Apduhan, B. O., Huang, R., Barolli, L., & Takizawa, M. (2005). Towards a smart world and ubiquitous intelligence: a walkthrough from smart things to smart hyperspaces and UbicKids. *International Journal of Pervasive Computing and Communications, 1*(1), 53–68.

Markoff, J. (2012). How many computers to identify a cat? 16,000. *New York Times*. Retrieved from https://www.nytimes.com/2012/06/26/technology/in-a-big-network-of-computers-evidence-of-machine-learning.html

McCulloch, W. S., & Pitts, W. (1943). A logical calculus of the ideas immanent in nervous activity. *The Bulletin of Mathematical Biophysics, 5*(4), 115–133.
Miller, G. A. (1969). Psychology as a means of promoting human welfare. *American Psychologist, 24*(12), 1063–1075.
Novotney, A. (2016). Smartphone=not-so-smart parenting? *Monitor on Psychology, 47*(2), 52.
Parker, I. (2014). *Psychology after Lacan: Connecting the clinic and research*. London: Routledge.
Pavón Cuéllar, D. (2004). Untying real, imaginary and symbolic: A Lacanian criticism of behavioural, cognitive and discursive psychologies. *Annual Review of Critical Psychology, 7*, 33–51.
Pierlejewski, M. (2019, Augustus 17). The data-doppelganger and the cyborg-self: Theorising the datafication of education. *Pedagogy, Culture & Society*, 1–13.Published online: 07 Aug 2019.
Rizzi, J. (2019). Kids are not hurt by screen time. *Scientific American*. Retrieved from https://www.scientificamerican.com/podcast/episode/kids-are-not-hurt-by-screen-time/
Ruder, D. B. (2008). The teen brain. *Harvard Magazine, 111*(1), 8–10.
Shotter, J. (1975). *Images of man in psychological research*. London: Methuen.
Simon, M. (2019). The clever clumsiness of a robot teaching itself to walk. *Wired Magazine*. Retrieved from https://www.wired.com/story/the-clever-clumsiness-of-a-robot-teaching-itself-to-walk/
Steiner-Adair, C., & Barker, T. H. (2013). *The big disconnect: Protecting childhood and family relationships in the digital age*. New York: Harper Business.
Stiegler, B. (2014). Les big data, c'est la fin de la pensée. Retrieved from http://www.ventscontraires.net/article.cfm/13444_bernard_stiegler__les_big_data_c_est_la_fin_de_la_pensee_.html
Stiegler, B. (2015). *La Société automatique: 1. L'avenir du travail*. Paris: Fayard.
Thornton, D. J. (2011). Neuroscience, affect, and the entrepreneurialization of motherhood. *Communication and Critical/Cultural Studies, 8*(4), 399–424.
Turing, A. M. (1950). Computing machinery and intelligence. *Mind, 59*(236), 433–460.
Vandenbroeck, M. (2017). Constructions of truth in early childhood education: A history of the present abuse of neurosciences. In M. Vandenbroeck (Ed.), *Constructions of neuroscience in early childhood education* (pp. 11–29). London: Routledge.
Walker, R. (2012). *The human brain project: A report to the European Commission*. Retrieved from Lausanne: https://www.humanbrainproject.eu/documents/10180/17648/TheHBPReport_LR.pdf/18e5747e-10af-4bec-9806-d03aead57655
Wang, F., Kinzie, M. B., McGuire, P., & Pan, E. (2010). Applying technology to inquiry-based learning in early childhood education. *Early Childhood Education Journal, 37*(5), 381–389.
Watson, J. B. (1913). Psychology as the behaviourist views it. *Psychological Review, 20*, 158–177.
Williamson, B. (Ed.) (2015). *Coding/learning: Software and digital data in education*. Stirling: University of Stirling.
Woolley, S., Boyd, D., Broussard, M., Elish, M., Fader, L., Hwang, T.,... Shorey, S. (2016). How to think about bots. *A Botifesto*. February, 23. Retrieved from http://motherboard.vice.com/read/how-to-think-about-bots

6

THE DIGITAL (NO)FUTURE OF EDUCATION

Introduction: seated in front of the screen, for whom do I write?

When opening Facebook one day after lunch, I was confronted with the following question: 'what's on your mind'? The message could not be clearer in this respect: Facebook wants to be your psychologist and invite you to voice your thoughts, feelings, and dreams. Indeed, Mark Zuckerberg never tires of professing his (socio)therapeutic mission 'to create a world where every single person has a sense of purpose' (cited in: Constine, 2017). Snapchat fosters similar therapeutic goals:

> We believe that reinventing the camera represents our greatest opportunity to improve the way people live and communicate.
> We contribute to human progress by empowering people to express themselves, live in the moment, learn about the world, and have fun together.

Incidentally, when browsing through my emails I found out that MyAnalytics of Microsoft's Office 365 software is apparently also concerned with my well-being, as it asked me: "Are you able to disconnect and recharge"? Of course, I had no other option but to say 'no', I cannot disconnect, since Microsoft and Google are tracking me even in my spare time when I am opening documents on Microsoft's One Drive. Regardless, MyAnalytics wants to reassure me that no one but me can access 'the personalised information' and that the 'insights provided by MyAnalytics cannot be used for automated decision-making or for profiling'. Seemingly, Microsoft's aims are primarily altruistic, as they are suggesting various 'ways to reduce stress and burnout'. However, even though the end goal may be to improve my personal and psychological well-being, this is ultimately framed in terms of serving my workplace's interests:

> Take a break when at work: Go enjoy a meal with your team or take a relaxation break during work. You'll give your brain a break, grow your network, and probably boost your productivity and professional success.

In response to the above injunction, we could also add *stop working, go away, leave the building*; indeed, in this respect, our absence is ostensibly the most productive asset we have. But, of course, this should be understood as follows: before it used to be merely your presence, but, today, your absence is also now controlled and commodified. This constitutes the basic rationale of 'social media', insofar as not only does our spare time enter into the purview of the market but also our very absence is brought into the economic sphere. For, is one of the central tenets of social media not that it offers everybody a personal virtual space or a personal canvas through which to broadcast and represent oneself, and, moreover, to use this projection to link up with others, while you yourself can remain absent as such? However, to be clear on this point, this absence is supposed to be the key driver of the entrepreneurial process. That is to say, the projections of yourself within the virtual scene are meant to generate personal profit and benefits for you in effigy, be it socially (Facebook and other social media platforms), sexually (Tindr), professionally (LinkedIn), academically (Academia.edu), or merely commercially (all the digital channels that one can think of). Hence, if in former neuropsychologising times the adagio was *work that thing!*, now you can simply let the thing work for you, so give yourself or your brain a much-needed break! Of course, we are not truly allowed to go away or leave the building, as our own little representation enterprise ultimately serves larger corporate interests: the digital trails we leave behind either in cyberspace or in real space are closely monitored, for the purposes of constructing hidden psychological profiles to be sold as commodities. In the meantime, at the site of our presence, our public profiles and avatars, the screens on which we project our 'personalities', are themselves used as advertising space onto which commercial messages or ideological propaganda are screened, targeting both ourselves and everyone who is linked to us.

Of course, in the pre-digital era, one was also not simply oneself, insofar as one was also already redoubled in forms of social representations. These *personas* were, above all, symbolic in nature (our reputation, our function or role in society), while only a limited group of people had these representations coincide with the available technologies of the period, such as print and later the broadcasting of sound and images. People either used these technologies themselves or, conversely, they were used by some people to represent others. Access to these technological media channels was conditional upon various issues, such as, among other things, merit, fame, hard work, money, connections, heredity, crime, and so on. Given that this representational level, whether technologically aided or otherwise, afforded people with a presence in society, it can also be said to have engendered a realm of the *not represented*, that is, a realm of absence, a personal, private, or even secretive sphere. In this way, one could argue that these representations operated as masks: on the one hand, they assigned people with a role and position on the societal stage, while, on the other hand, it also created the idea, or the illusion that a true face lay behind it, which would manifest in some other place.

Digital social media, then, are ostensibly bringing these representational (symbolic and technological) constructions down from their erstwhile hierarchical and societal configurations to a more egalitarian and personal level, precisely by removing the prior restraints on access to technological channels. Moreover, to represent oneself in digital times is not only deemed to be free and effortless but also direct and natural. This is where digital technology claims to be *technology-lite*, insofar as it merely offers novel channels and spaces for 'the way people live and communicate' (as per the aforementioned Snapchat quote). Admittedly, as well as empowering our natural (proto)social and communicative behaviour, social media companies simultaneously attempt to generate profits—but, then again that is our economic model, no?

However, by way of a first critical point, evidently, the form and formats that we are offered to represent ourselves are neither neutral nor natural. Indeed, first and foremost, they serve a business model that positions us as mere assets or commodities, and, moreover, via these formats, subjectivity and sociality are pre-shaped and pre-configured. Hence, the naturalising claim that social media only provides a new space for what people have always done before is false: social media engenders, forms, and even designs our 'behaviour', 'feelings', and 'thoughts', which, as argued in the previous chapters, are grounded in models and theories from the neuropsy-sciences.

These two issues, the commercial rationale and neuropsy-modelling and pre-formatting, turn out to be very well aligned in this respect. The presupposition that digital representations reveal the true psychological you (the hitherto hidden personal and private truth behind the mask of representation) constitutes the new field in which subjectivities become commodities to be exploited. Here, quite clearly, the digitalisation of subjectivity and sociality essentially boils down to technologies not only making us always and fully present but also *demanding* that we are always and fully present. Hence, in contradistinction to the aforesaid idea that in the digital sphere we can simply let things work on our behalf and give ourselves breathing space, these absences have now potentially come under full digital control: we are actually demanded to be ourselves, which is *the thing* to be worked on and the commodity to be sold. Within this constellation, neither fugues nor breaks are possible anymore; indeed, even when I work in my spare time, Big Data is looking over my shoulder inciting me to take care of my well-being so as not to endanger my productivity.

By now it should be clear, to draw on biblical imagery, that it would be wrong to think that we should merely get the merchants out of the Temple, for this would pre-suppose that technology could be used in a different way that would allow people to go their own way unbothered by digital capitalists expropriating and monitoring their everyday life. However, given that I claim that the psychological architecture of digital platforms provides the basic rationale that drives the commodification of subjectivity, the thing to do is to also get the priests out of the Temple qua psy-scientists and their neuropsy-models of what human beings ostensibly are. Of course, one could ask whether this would go far enough? The equivalent of an empty Temple, cleansed of both merchants and priests, would perhaps be an empty screen, and, consequently, empty social media and other digital platforms, which no longer professed to care about my feelings, thoughts, and well-being. Is this what I am arguing for then: given that our virtual environments and avatars are filled to the brim with scripted notions of what life should be about (so as to make possible digital nudging, the latter constituting the principal axis of the new digital economy), should they thus be emptied?

To answer this question, it is expedient to return to the issue of education. For, first and foremost, *the forms* of (inter)subjectivity are inseparable from the *formation* of (inter)subjectivity, with the latter issue being what education is chiefly concerned with. In response to this, a cursory reference to Plato's cave suffices to elucidate that *form* and *screen* pre-suppose each other. Moreover, not only are education and schooling traditionally intimately related to the canvas and the screen (as key mediums through which to pass on what is important to the next generation), these mediums are also the very sites where subjectivity is mobilised as they precisely interpellate the pupil's presence. Indeed, is the archetypical image of the pupil or student not that of someone who indulges in their absence in the back of the classroom until being admonished by the teacher to pay attention to the blackboard, or even being summoned to come forward and write the answer to a question on the blackboard?

From here, a range of questions emerge, namely: what changes, if anything, when the traditional blackboard is replaced with the digital whiteboard? What changes when paper and pens are traded for laptops or tablets? Or, alternatively, one could pose an even more futuristic question: what will change when we bypass the screen, or the black/whiteboard altogether and directly download knowledge into the brain? Will the future be screenless as such? At the very least, the issues of presence and absence would be radically affected by such a shift, insofar as, for example, the teacher, or more likely the bots, in the digital educational platform would directly sense the boredom of the pupil and re-establish full presence immediately and in an unmediated fashion.

Are we not justified in asking what will become of humanity when this is how, we, or, once again, bots, will raise future generations? In this regard, George Orwell's dystopic novel 1984 comes to mind. In 1984, the so-called telescreen both transmits and receives sounds and images; however, the protagonist is lucky (or perhaps actually not so lucky) to have his telescreen positioned in such a way that leaves a 'shallow alcove' that remains outside the range of the screen. Perhaps this can be understood as the minimal free space that digitalisation now denies us (which will be exacerbated further yet still in screenless forms), the very space that allowed George Orwell's character Winston Smith to write his diary. Notwithstanding this freedom, in the beginning of the novel, having purchased a pen and paper, Smith is confronted with the crucial question that anyone who writes must face:

> For whom, it suddenly occurred to him to wonder, was he writing this diary? For the future, for the unborn. (…) How could you communicate with the future? It was of its nature impossible. Either the future would resemble the present, in which case it would not listen to him: or it would be different from it, and his predicament would be meaningless
>
> *(Orwell, 2003, p. 94)*

I hope it does not come across as preposterous when I say that this is precisely the same ordeal that I encounter in this book: how to address future generations of humankind? Or, phrased otherwise, if one accepts Slavoj Žižek's proclamation that AI could lead to the 'end to humanity as we know it' (Žižek, 2019), then how does one communicate with no-future? As such, this is perhaps the duty that one should assume: to think of the end of humanity. For, if what makes humans human is their capacity to imagine their own death, then in the face of digital Armageddon, one must attempt to imagine our own digital disappearance in spite of the fact that we cannot but fail to do so. We owe this to ourselves, and to the preceding generations, and who knows, perhaps even to future outcasts, the *homines sacri* of digitalisation. However, perhaps we must also consider the possibility that there will be no digital renegades, and that digitalisation might be the system that is truly capable of incorporating its outside without any remainder. Such a scenario would lead to the state that I referred to in Chapter 2 as 'digital entropy': as everything becomes digitalised, the digital would finally collapse; without an elsewhere or an outside, the erstwhile antagonism that fuelled the system would disappear, in turn, leading to a full closure and complete standstill, bringing the digital death of night to a screeching halt. However, there is also a chance that humanity will not live to see its digital death, for the simple reason that the latter might be overtaken by a global climate disaster, which would mean that some human life form may survive after all. Whether the hope that a global rebellion against capitalism would produce a similarly sweeping effect is justified or otherwise, I am not sure about. But, in either case, I, or we, must write, irrespective of whether the future will merely resemble the present or be radically different from it. For, indeed, regardless of whether what we write will be read or even understood, there are still stories that must be told. One of these stories is, I would argue, how we invented education, what role the screen played, how it mediated our presence and absence, and how all this was going to change.

Education and bringing our lives to the screens

Let us begin by repeating the argument that I made in the previous chapter about how education, especially since modernity, is a structurally weak discourse, in the sense that it constitutes a field and a practice that cannot stand on its own feet. Consequently, education is a prime example through which to discern how the digitalisation of (inter)subjectivity is part of a genealogical history that was preceded by psychologisation and neurologisation. Historically, while the latter two phenomena can be situated within the advent of modernity and the modern sciences, the two phenomena intensified towards the end of the previous century. Indeed, when we examine education in post-WWII Western societies, one can observe how a deadlock was reached in the old model of schooling, which was centred on discipline and the transfer of knowledge. It is here that the psychologisation and then subsequently the neurologisation of education emerged: education as a stalled discourse and practice took recourse to the neuropsy-sciences to renew itself. Education's longstanding goals were reoriented to address issues like mental health, well-being and caring for one's brain. Signifiers such as 'intelligence' were either partly or completely traded for signifiers such as 'emotional intelligence' and 'empathy'. Surviving and thriving through understanding one's own as well as other's emotions is thought to be crucial, and apparently teachable: 'Teaching young people skills such as active listening, self-awareness, and empathy can equip them to succeed both academically and socially' (Busch & Oakley, 2017). Empathy, which is considered to be a key component or correlate of emotional intelligence (Mayer & Salovey, 1997; Salovey & Mayer, 1990), has become a prominent theme in contemporary education:

> Do you know what empathy is? Do your kids? It is the ability to be aware of how other people are feeling and putting yourself in their shoes. In a world that lacks compassion, take the opportunity to teach your kids empathy towards others.

One should read the above quotation carefully: we are not merely supposed to teach our kids to have empathy for others, but, rather, we are instructed to teach them *what* empathy is. Further on in the text, '[m]oms' (sic) are encouraged to '[t]alk to [their] kids about mental illnesses and medical conditions that affect the way someone talks or looks'. In short, psychology here enters schools and homes as part of the curriculum: pupils and students not only must learn how to get along but, above all, must learn *the science* of getting along. Children are then subsequently supposed to be able to repeat back what they are taught: "We're um, also meant to be assertive in a, um, positive way, and there was something about emotions but I've forgotten it", reported one child about a session on social skills (De Vos, 2012, p. 19).

This is where the issue of 'self-monitoring', that which supposedly facilitates emotional intelligence (Schutte et al., 2001), should be understood literally: the 'self' functions here as a monitor, a screen upon which psychological models are then projected. 'Do you know what empathy is'? thus enjoins pupils to take a step back and gaze in wonder at the canvas of the Self upon which is painted images of psychological theories. The shift in the 1990s towards the so-called 'Decade of the Brain' signalled a move away from the Self, which is a somewhat intangible or even hypothetical entity, towards the Brain, which is framed as a more robust material canvas:

> You carry around a three-pound mass of wrinkly material in your head that controls every single thing you will ever do. From enabling you to think, learn, create, and feel emotions to controlling every blink, breath, and heartbeat—this fantastic control centre is your brain. It is a structure so amazing that a famous scientist once called it "the most complex thing we have yet discovered in our universe."

Hence, it is the brain as opposed to the Self, which has now become the central screen onto which psychological models (thoughts, cognitions, emotions, and so forth) are projected. *No psychology without psychologisation, no neuroscience without neurologisation*, should thus be completed as follows: *no neuroscience without psychologisation*.

But, what then, if anything, changes in the era of digitalisation? That is to say, what happens when more and more real screens enter our lives, or, conversely, when our lives ever more inhabit screens? Is the interpellative scheme of neuropsychologisation still valid within a constellation in which, increasingly, what we are, do, think and how we interact (the erstwhile jurisdiction of the neuropsysciences) takes place on screens themselves? In other words, we are no longer merely contemplating in awe and wonder what we are said to be (our Self or our Brain), we are now evermore supposed to live our lives on the screens themselves. While previously there was a modicum of distance (*I am not where my Self/ Brain is*, insofar as I reflect upon it from a place removed from it), is this distance not fast disappearing as we become called upon to inhabit the screen and coincide with our digital doppelganger on the screen? Evidently, not only does social media and other platforms implore us to go virtual (*let your friends know, why don't you share, wish your mother a happy birthday, etc.*), one can similarly observe within the educational domain a veritable rush to the screen.

The hegemonic dictum within contemporary education can be characterised as follows: *education will either be digital, or it will cease to be*. The first thing to observe here is that the dynamics of neuropsychologisation play an integral role in the digitalisation of education. For example, consider the way in which ClassDojo, an international and widespread educational platform, brands itself:

> ClassDojo Is Teaching Kids Empathy In 90% Of K-8 Schools Nationwide. At a time when empathy is in decline—and bullying is on the rise—educators see promise in the app's lessons on kindness and respect.

One can discern here that ClassDojo, like many other digital educational platforms, is highly neuropsychologised, insofar as it claims to directly engage with a suite of psychosocial issues, including empathy, bullying, and so forth. One should not overlook here, however, that instead of neuropsy-experts (or their proxies qua teachers or parents) hailing everybody into neuropsy-discourses, now it is the technology itself that provides us with neuropsy-lessons. That is to say, it is no longer the teacher, educator, or parent who is equipped with the knowledge and techniques of psychology, but, rather, it is the app, which, based on data-gathering and algorithms, draws us into the psychologised scenarios depicted via the screen. This raises several questions, with the first of them being: if neuropsychologising agendas in education previously depended on the involvement of the teacher, then what is the effect of these new app-driven modes of 'interpellation' (if we can even still frame it in this Althusserian way)? Consider in this respect how ClassDojo enjoins pupils into a psychologising perspective:

> What feeling words can you use to describe Mojo in this video?
> How does Mojo feel and why?
> What feeling words can you use to describe Katie in this video?
> How does Katie feel and why? Do you think Mojo knew how she was feeling? Why or why not?
> What would you have done differently if you were Mojo?

Does this transference of psychologisation and neurologisation from the human to the digital constitute a decisive shift or not? That is to say, does this fundamentally alter the subjective positions of the parties involved? Let us explore this question further by scrutinising, in turn, the different roles that parents and children are assigned, with respect to both the scenes and the screens, within digital education and parenting.

Parents turned into bots having fun

> We believe that knowing about your baby's needs will empower you to better assess your gut feelings and your immediate responses: you will be able to tell whether what you feel is an instinct that motivates to do something effortful but very valuable, or if it is the sterile fruit of frustration and sleep-deprivation. Once you are aware of that, you can consciously make up your mind on how to behave.
> (…) This approach will empower you to make your own informed decisions in the context that nobody knows better than you: your family.

This is how BabyBrains—a programme for parental education that offers, among other things, a parenting app—advertises its services. Apparently, human beings, for reasons that are unexplained, are divorced from the true state of things, both in terms of their own reality and that of the other qua their baby. BabyBrains aims to bridge this gap via the application of state of the art scientific theory and research, which can reconnect the parent with themselves and with their child. This is how Mark Johnson, a psychologist involved in BabyBrains, frames the work that they do:

> "As a scientist working on child brain and psychological development, I believe its [sic] important to communicate our latest findings to parents. Babybrains communicates these new concepts to parents in an accurate and accessible way, and will enrich their understanding of their own child's developmental changes." Mark Johnson, Head, Department of Psychology, University of Cambridge.

This is, seemingly, (neuro)psychologisation par excellence, in the sense that everybody is being invited to enrol in a neuropsy class to receive lessons and get to know the state of the science. Your baby, more specifically your baby's brain, is thus apparently still the screen or canvas onto which you are supposed to observe the shadowy projections of the models of the neuropsy-sciences. However, when the app comes in to play, things begin to shift somewhat:

> Babybrains® offers you a direct bridge from the neuroscience labs into your home (...). [It is] easy and natural to put into practice: all you need to do is learn the science and enjoy the fun. Our app helps you do just that.
> (...) You have to simply insert your baby's date of birth, you will receive weekly reminders with age-appropriate science-based activities.
> Far from average tables and pre-set milestones, this app helps you "read Baby's signs", and respond to them in an appropriate and conscious way, with great advantages for all involved (one above all: fun!).

Hence, while parents still have to learn the science, the vast majority of this work can be outsourced to the technology itself: for example, the app sends you reminders to do 'age-appropriate science-based activities'. All you have to do is provide the app with the required data. Hence, if old neuropsychologisation made you worry (you had to truly learn the science to be able to read the tables and worry about the milestones), then this app takes this burden away from you, so you can sit back and have fun! Of course, as always, one should be highly suspicious when one is told not to worry and just enjoy the ride. In this regard, let us take a closer look at where the outsourcing of parenting to the app ultimately leaves parents. This is what BabyBrains instructs educators to do:

> Observe your child and try to establish her needs,
> Come up with a parenting-intervention idea that tries to meet her needs as well as your own.
> Remain open for feedback and ready to fine-tune, modify or even reject your intervention should it not function as desired.

Is this not an archetypal example of an algorithm? Indeed, the classic definition of an algorithm is a process or set of rules that are to be followed in calculations or other problem-solving operations. Based on this, could one not argue that this is what the educator is turned into? In the words of BabyBrains:

> ... [BabyBrains] teach[es] you new ways of observing your child and reading her signs, we encourage you to adopt a problem-solving attitude, and we help you make your life – the life you have now, with your marvellous unique child in it – a fantastic, beautiful fulfilling adventure.

In the above account, while the baby is still a screen, the whole scene itself appears to have morphed into a kind of virtual environment, in which parents, who themselves are algorithmicised as it were, enter the screen world in order to merely act out the established rules of engagement. Ramaekers and Hodgson also used the example of BabyBrains to illustrate their argument that the neurological turn in education has intensified the 'appification' of education: parents are no longer grown-ups, political agents, members of a community who make choices, but, rather, merely have to execute what science prescribes to them (Hodgson & Ramaekers, 2018). Ramaekers and Hodgson proceed to argue that the 'appification' of education risks making parents and educators wholly redundant, not in the sense of 'robots are going to come and take our jobs', but, rather, that parents are reduced to mere nodal points between the lab and the child (Hodgson & Ramaekers, 2018). It is here, I would argue, that a potentially decisive shift is taking place, which is that parents are being made redundant precisely by being turned themselves into robotesque figures who are supposed to act algorithmically: *observe, intervene, and fine-tune*. Consequently, while we should not necessarily be afraid of AI taking over, what we should really be afraid of is our own intelligence being jeopardised by technology, by having our ability to speak properly as a grown-up and as a political agent be guided, restricted, bypassed, or dumbed down by this process of algorithmisation. If within psychologisation and neurologisation parents and educators became, to use Nikolas Rose's words (Rose, 1999, p. 92), 'a bit like experts', whose embodiment and reproduction of expert knowledge profoundly reshaped our lives (Rose, 2018), in the digital era this scheme is fundamentally reworked: parents are now relieved of this duty to share scientific knowledge. That is to say, parents are in the first instance turned into 'bots' qua devices or softwares that execute demands and perform routine tasks based on a set of basic algorithms:

> (...) this app helps you "read Baby's signs", and respond to them in an appropriate and conscious way, with great advantages for all involved (one above all: fun!).
> (...) Once every three months the activity is replaced by a story to read out loud. It is a time to sit back and relax, enjoy a quiet moment together and follow imagination into a fantastic world.

Of course, reading out loud was always already about outsourcing the imagination to someone else who wrote the story, but now you do not even have to choose a book or worry about whether the story is age-appropriate or stimulating enough: just sit back and relax! While with BabyBrains you still have to do the reading out loud yourself, today there are devices that also relieve you of this work. For example, the aforementioned 'EVOZ Smart Parenting device' not only allows you to monitor your baby from a distance, but it can also play lullabies and even read out loud audiobooks.

Resultantly, is the digital sphere not characterised by the subject progressively taking a step back and withdrawing, to the extent that one day, perhaps, it will leave the scene altogether? We do not really have to monitor the screen that depicts the baby room, the smart camera and app relieve us of this, in turn, opening up space and time for us to, for example, binge-watch series on Netflix, or play games while our offspring is provided with age-appropriate sounds and images via its own telescreen? Entering the screen world thus appears to represent a new version of the aforementioned hall of mirrors, whereby the screens and its manifold projections appear to redouble endlessly. However, if this turns parents and educators into bots that have more time for fun, where does it ultimately leave children?

Children's little absences brought under digital control

A 2016 World Economic Forum report on using technologies to foster social-emotional skills in education references the so-called 'Embrace Watch', which is 'a wearable device that tracks physiological stress and activity' that can be used to measure students' affective responses to learning situations (cited and discussed by Williamson, 2017a). The whole idea here is that the device would indicate when a student is bored and disinterested, and the computer would subsequently offer the student more interesting or engaging learning content.

Note here, once again, how the digitalisation of education brings us immediately into the sphere of (inter)subjectivity and the realm of socio-emotional skills. To simply put, the advanced technologisation of education, above all, hooks into the earlier neuropsychologisation of education, which, in turn, leads to a radical shift in the role of the teacher or educator. In pre-digital times, that is, in pre-digital psychologisation, teachers had to monitor and secure the 'emotional well-being' of students, which is to say that the teacher had to act as a psychologist. Today, the key claim is that this task is better being outsourced to the computer, as Ron Spreeuwenberg purported: "robots may actually be more useful than humans in this role, as they are not clouded by emotion, instead using intelligent technology to detect hidden responses" (Spreeuwenberg, 2017). In short, then, the computer is a better psychologist, insofar as it has no psychology! This reveals a basic and paradoxical truth about psychology, which is that it always pre-supposes a *beyond of psychology* due to the fact that the psy-sciences claim to provide an objective vantage point from where the sublunary psychological realm can be assessed. The machine that deemed to be outside of the realm of psychology can thus be said to mirror the position of both the psy-expert and the layperson, as the latter is also invited to adopt this Archimedean vantage point. Nevertheless, the outsourcing of this situation to the computer might signal a crucial shift in the once considered basic intersubjective relation between pupil and teacher. At the very least, the situation of pupils being monitored and steered by algorithms is far removed from the Freudian idea that what fuels and drives, or, for that matter, thwarts education is the transferential relation between teacher and pupil. Does the digitalisation of education, then, not risk bringing about the final desubjectivation of education, insofar as it cleanses it of the messy psychologies of grown-ups, political agents, and members of the community?

Clearly, given that the computer does the psychological assessment and silently tweaks the learning process, something undoubtedly changes at the level of interpellation. The student is no longer asked, *'tell us, how do you feel'?*; rather, the machine probes, or perhaps more accurately yet still, assigns you your feelings. While the teacher's interpellation psychologised the pupil by calling upon them to transcend themselves and reflect upon themselves from a theoretical, academic perspective, the pupil thus became a screen to be looked upon by both themselves and the teacher. In contradistinction to this, digitalisation rules out the middle-man and condemns the pupil to be their alleged psychological self and to fully coincide with the virtual version of this. This is precisely where the issue of presence, the enigma of being there, is at stake. Consider, in this respect, Jacques Lacan's re-formulation of Descartes' Cogito into "I think where I am not, therefore I am where I do not think", which he used to delineate how speaking beings never fully coincide with what they say (Lacan, 1977, p. 126). Does this 'where' not acquire an entirely new meaning within the digital realm? That is to say, as we come to outsource our thinking to algorithms, our presence ever more wholly coincides with the virtual realm: we are where we think not?

To explore further this issue of digital presence, it is expedient to approach it through the related theme of attention. For the moment, the relation between these two issues can be briefly sketched as follows: that which calls our attention is what makes us present. An example of this would be the teacher calling our attention to demand that we are fully present in the class. Attention is not only a traditional feature of education, but it also forms a basic element of the contemporary digitalisation of everyday life. Of course, it is well-established that today's digital technologies are incredibly adept at tapping into our attention. Indeed, Bernard Stiegler has spoken of this in terms of "psychotechnologies of attention" (Stiegler, 2010, p. 51). It is in this respect that digital technologies can be said to be in competition with schooling practices, which is why perhaps smartphones are officially banned from classrooms in France. Clearly, the management of attention has always been associated with control and disciplining within education, as illustrated in the teacher's interpellative admonishment: *'Hey you, pay attention'*, which is explicitly disciplinary in nature: *'Pay attention, for if you don't…'*.

For argument's sake, it is expedient to outline four historical modes of attention control and discipline. Firstly, in what I call the old disciplinary education that was characterised by knowledge transfer and character building, one had to pay attention or be disciplined. Secondly, in psychologised modes of education, if one did not pay attention, then you were psychologically probed, and, if needed, therapeutically treated. Thirdly, in neurologised education, you are instructed that you have a brain disorder and are administered Ritalin to neurobiologically regulate your attention. Finally, in the contemporary era of digital education, any decline in attention level is potentially automatically detected and algorithmically adjusted. For example, the Embrace Watch registers that your attention is dropping, after which the learning platform alters the learning material to bring you back on board. Hence, in digitalisation, arguably, the interpellative '*hey you*' of attentional control and disciplinary power that characterised the periods of psychologisation and neurologisation can be left out. In precisely the same way that we now have coffee without caffeine, today we now have *discipline without disciplining*, and, most notably, without auto-disciplining.

Demonstrably, attentional control also entails the control of presence: the call to be attentive is a call to be present within the confines of the scene as defined by the hegemonic discourse. It is precisely here, I argue, that the screen plays an integral role: the screen as the placeholder of the scene in which one is called to be present. Let me historicise this once again, by drawing, again for argument's sake, a simplified scheme with a few coordinates. To begin with, in non-digital times, pupils had to pay attention by looking at the blackboard, which, ultimately, defined one's presence in the class: after all, one was seated in front of the blackboard. The blackboard, then, the canvas for symbols and words, can be said to primarily refer to the medium of the book. The teacher, in their capacity as the representative of ideology and power, was a mediator who used the blackboard to teach students how to read the canon. The canon, on its turn, referred to the world outside, the world beyond the school walls. Within this constellation, the major assignment to be carried out by students was to either write an essay or give an oral presentation (standing in front of the blackboard), in order to reproduce the canon within, and this is crucial, the secluded space of the school. Simply put, students had to be present in the class by investing their attention in the blackboard and the words of the teacher, after which it was their turn to, via the assigned oral and/or written presentation, represent the world in the *as-if* space of the class.

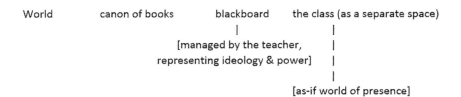

Today, in digital times, the blackboard as a tool through which to control presence and attention is interchanged with screen-based technologies, such as whiteboards and projection screens. With the advent of videos, PowerPoints, and Prezis, the erstwhile dominance of symbols and words is broken as (moving) images come to take centre-stage. Here, the teacher's role, in the first instance, is not to act as a kind of interface between the pupil and the canon (the latter being a selective, guided, and authoritative tour of the world), but, rather, to act as the interface between pupil and the, if one will allow me to use this neologism, *wide-web-world* itself. As the internet eventually becomes fully interconnected with the world—consider *the internet of things* here—it will potentially contain all the data of the world, and, thus, asymptotically, could be considered as being equal to the world. Hence, while the canon of books represents a selective sample of the world—selected by an authoritative voice—digitality claims to let the world speak for itself. Hence, we can now skip the middle-man, skip transference, and mediation, due to the fact that in digitality the medium is the world. Or, at the very least, the wide-web-world can be said to *pose* as the world, for, arguably, it eventually presents us with an *as-if world*: a kind of parallel, datafied version of the world. Consequently, if the as-if-dimension has moved from the class (the class in the period of blackboards) to the (screen)world, then does this not mean that the class itself has become a reality, that is, *more real than real*, or to put it in Baudrillard's (2007) terms, a *simulacrum* of the 'real-world'? Think of how pupils now, rather than writing essays or giving oral presentations, are increasingly asked to make PowerPoints, Prezzi's, videos, blogs, websites, and why not, even develop apps. In so doing, they are being asked to reproduce, not the world per se, but, rather, the screen-world, the wide-web-world. Furthermore, more than just reproduction, students today are supposed to contribute to the wide-web-world, by posting their work on publicly accessible websites. These contributions to the world are believed to be participatory and emancipatory, insofar as they ostensibly give pupils a presence in the 'real-world' and allow them to transcend the old musty *as-if* confines of the classroom.

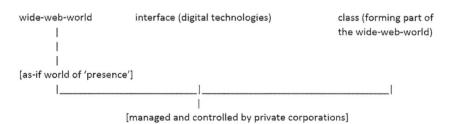

So, to begin with, rather than four places, we now only have three. In pre-digital times, we had a redoubling on the side of the medium: the canon and the blackboard, with the latter pointing to the role of the teacher and the school as such. In digital times, this redoubling disappears, and it is here that both the teacher and the school become wholly redundant, with only the interface (the digital technologies) remaining as such, which is managed and controlled by private corporations. Or, as I argued in the previous chapter, the school qua semi-public space, a temporary transitionary space, a revolving door to the 'real-world' either disappears or becomes a kind of interface for the wide-web-world. The first result of this is the virtualisation of the world: our primary world is an as-if world, the wide-web-world. The second result of this is that the presence of the pupil moves up from the as-if world of the class to the as-if world of the Data-World.

Now, to finally answer what this means for the presence of the pupil, we must reformulate the question one more time and ask: what actually happens with absence? From a Freudo-Lacanian perspective, presence is always grounded in its opposite, and as indicated in the introduction of this chapter, our absence constitutes a valuable asset which social media attempts to capture within their economy. At the very least, one can say that being absent in the digital era is far from evident. For example, while in the blackboard era one could still hide behind the textbook, there is no hiding anymore behind the laptop: everything one does is tracked and traced via the learning platform. And given that you are probably hooked up to an Embrace Watch, there is no escape anymore. When students failed to pay attention in the blackboard era they were asked to repeat the words of the teacher or summoned to the blackboard to solve a mathematical problem. In contradistinction to this, in digi-technological times, students' minor absences are algorithmically dealt with and nullified. In disciplinary times, the control of presence still allowed for a certain absence: if you had to write 100 times 'From now on I will behave and pay attention in class', students (and the teacher) did not have to believe a word of it (indeed, being multiplied by 100 times already turned it into a hollow phrase). Even in neuro-psychological times students' presence could still be established against a background of absence: if toddlers are asked *how they feel* and are offered four standard masks (happy, sad, angry or scared), then they can still more or less hide behind these psychological masks. The digitalisation of subjectivity, however, appears to represent the final abolition, or, at the very least, total control over our little absences. Not only are all of our moves datafied (my Google searches, my payments, my travel, and so on), I am also constantly prompted to present myself on the screen. If, for example, I do not open my Facebook page for one day, I am sent prompts pointing out that I have missed so much because of my absence, before being prompted to reassert my presence through sharing how I feel. There are little or no free spaces left. In the digitalised classrooms, pupils, rather than merely fooling around in the as-if world of the class, mandatorily must substantialise themselves in the real/virtual world.

To both understand this subtantialisation of subjectivity into the virtual sphere and consider whether this really signals a shift in representation and presence, perhaps we must cast our gaze even further back to examine both how forms of subjectivity used to be linked to screens and how scenes played out on them. For, evidently, the ways in which a society imagines the world and sets all this out in a scene to be played out on some kind of screen or canvas, is, arguably, fundamental to understanding how we are present in the world as such. Given this, let us now go further back into history.

Virtuality as a regression to the spectacle

> And inasmuch as I hoped to be able to reach my goal better by conversing with men than by staying shut up any longer in the stove-heated room where I had all these thoughts, the winter was not yet over when I set out again on my travels. And in all the nine years that followed I did nothing but wander here and there in the world, trying to be more a spectator than an actor in all the comedies that are played out there; and reflecting particularly in each matter on what might render it suspect and give us occasion for erring, I meanwhile rooted out from my mind all the errors that had previously been able to slip into it.
>
> *(Descartes, [1637]1996, p. 16)*

These are the words of René Descartes, who in a crucial but little commented on passage from his 'Discours de la méthode' linked his *epoche* to the theatre screen: leaving his secluded stove-heated room, he set out to not necessarily fully immerse himself in life, but, rather, to take a seat in the red plush theatre chair to watch all the comedies about life. One could view this as being illustrative of how presence in the world within modernity was not based on a full presence, but, rather, depended on a prior withdrawal from the world. One could sketch it out as follows: modernity and the birth of the modern sciences entailed that the external gaze of the godly figure who watched over the world was traded for the gaze of the sciences. Hence, the first move of the modern subject was, in fact, a step back, in that it involved adopting the external position of the sciences. This led to the configuration of a decentred subject, that is, a subject which is not where one thinks it is: for the actual subject can be said to have taken a seat in the theatre to contemplate the world and ultimately also itself. The world, then, can also be said to be decentred, in that it has moved to the theatre scene where the comedies of the world are played out.

To understand the weight of the metaphor of the theatre used by Descartes, let us briefly turn to William Egginton's fascinating account of the historical shift in theatre that occurred between the Middle-Ages and Modernity. Egginton (2003) purported that the advent of the modern theatre was closely related to the advent of modern subjectivity. In his book 'How the world became a stage: presence, theatricality, and the question of modernity', he argued that modern theatre opened up a separate space for actors to act, one that was wholly distinct from the space of everyday life. This was in marked contrast to the so-called 'medieval spectacle' that was played out on market squares or similar spaces, rather than spaces that were dedicated to or reserved for the performance. From here, Egginton proceeded to claim that the modern configuration of the theatre came to structure daily life itself, as well as our subjectivity. That is to say, according to Egginton, from the advent of modernity people lived their lives as if they were acting on a theatre stage. More specifically, in all that we say or do, we always take into account the 'gaze of a disembodied audience', as described by, among others, Jean-Paul Sartre in his work 'Being and Nothingness' (Egginton, 2003, p. 6). Hence, when we watch a theatre play we identify with the characters on stage (or on the cinema screen), with the peculiar detail being that at the level of everyday reality, once the curtain falls or the word 'End' is projected onto the screen, and we imagine that we return to the world, instead we become a character ourselves as we know that we are being watched. This imagined gaze of an invisible audience thus mediates our presence in the world, and, in turn, converts our 'being here' into a performance.

One could attempt to connect this to what occurs doing a psychoanalytic cure: for the analysand, the psychoanalyst inevitably stands for the 'gaze of a disembodied audience'. That is to say, the analysand will carry on with their daily life, while, simultaneously, thinking to themselves: *perhaps I could/should talk about this tomorrow in my session with my analyst.* This makes clear that when life is viewed as a stage, then we do not in the first instance act in relation to the other antagonists in the scene, or even the accidental audience that might be present at certain public occasions, but, rather, we act for the Other, which is not present as such, the abstract, disembodied Other.

One must ask a crucial question, here, which is what changes, if anything when the theatre scene or the movie screen is transformed into the networked computer screen? Previously, at the end of a theatre performance, the stage was emptied and went dark, as did the cinema screen later. Similarly, the TV screen, at least in the beginning when broadcast hours were limited, at night either ended with the multi-coloured test screen or so-called white noise. In contradistinction to this, the darkness or blankness of the computer monitor is no longer absolute, because, for one thing, we ourselves can bring it back to life. Does this not mean that, when in analogue times there was nothing behind the screen or the curtain, now there appears to be something behind the screens of digitality: virtually the entire world waiting to be activated by us, that is, a full presence requesting our attention to be awakened and be watched? Is it not clear how, in this way, something also changes qua the world in front of the screen? While previously there was a firm demarcation: theatre, film, and television were patently differentiated from the reality outside the screen (while, in the meantime, subjective, and social dynamics, as aforesaid, were defined by the logic of the gaze of the disembodied audience). However, in digital and virtual times, not only does the border between presentation and representation becomes diffuse, one could also argue that reality itself gradually moves to the screen, effecting yet another decentralisation of reality: if it first moved to Descartes' theatre stage, it now shifts to the digital screen. Arguably, subjectivity cannot but follow this move, and, thus, from the spectator's seated position in plush red theatre-chairs, the subject enters into the virtual scene itself. This seems to have occurred gradually: while during the period of Web 1.0 we were supposed to wake up the virtual world on the screen, and in the era of Web 2.0 we had to participate interactively, now Web 3.0, the internet of adaptive algorithms (that is, adaptive to our own data) draws us more completely (and restlessly?) into the screen world.

The crucial global shift here is that while in the pre-digital times of the theatre or the movie we lived our life *as if* we were acting on stage, in contemporary digital and virtual societies, this erstwhile fantasy of being watched by an audience is gradually made tangible and 'real' in digital environments. That is to say, the gaze of the disembodied audience becomes 'materialised'" or 'embodied' in the virtual sphere, via Facebook friends or your followers on Instagram or Twitter. However, perhaps we must situate here an even darker and more insidious version of this audience, which is the invisible and disembodied gaze of Big Data. Hence, in our new digital habitat, we not only have an audience that we ourselves have chosen, or that chooses us, we also have an anonymous Big Other that, as we are only too aware, observes, follows and tracks us, along with even proposing new audiences to us: 'You have a new friend suggestion', as one sees on Facebook.

It is precisely here, in the possibility of being completely watched all of the time, thus ruling out the possibility of any kind of 'shallow alcove' that remained outside the range of Big Data, that perhaps a decisive turn, if not demise, in the field of subjectivity could occur. While both Descartes and the modern subject based their presence in the world ultimately upon a non-presence or an absence, in the digital era their retreat into the darkness of the theatre seat would be tracked, traced and, as such, drawn into the virtual scene itself. If in the early days people went *on the internet*, as we say in Flanders, now we are *in* the internet. Is there not a danger that this could mark the end of the modern notion of presence as such? As long as one is watching the comedies that are played out there and lives one's life as if one is being watched, then, within this phantasmatic frame of presence, one is not truly here, as the staging of one's presence is instead the smooth form of being there while not being there. Consider here how smart pupils put on a mask of attentiveness while not really listening to the teacher. Perhaps, then, this 'Gleichschwebende Aufmerksamkeit', to use a Freudian term, 'attention, evenly suspended or poised', might be the ideal way to learn after all! Indeed, at the very least, a teacher should allow their flock to wander off on occasion. Be that as it may, is it not the case that when this scheme of presence based on absence breaks down or is impeded, in turn, condemning us to a full presence, then this cannot but lead to if I am allowed to once again use psychoanalytic terms, de-realisation and de-personification? Hence, to be clear, my argument is not that digitalisation constitutes a profound threat to our presence as such, rather, the threat is that digitalisation resolves the issue of presence, and thus makes us all too present to the extent that we completely disappear. In this respect, one could argue that what has been disciplined, psychologised, neurologised, and now digitalised is not our human nature per se, but, rather, precisely that which transcends this. In other words, our being human is ultimately founded on something that lies beyond the human, while our worldliness, on its turn, is grounded in something unworldly. The question then becomes whether digitalisation is finally taking this away from us, expropriating it to fuel the new digital economy.

Perhaps this future step should be understood as a regression, that is, in Egginton's terminology, a regression from the scheme of modern theatre and theatricality to the level of the medieval spectacle. For, as Michael Heim wrote in 1995 already:

> In VR, the images are the realties. We interact with virtual entities, and we become an entity ourselves in the virtual environment. As in the medieval theory of transubstantiation, the symbol becomes the reality. This is the meaning of telepresence.
>
> *(Heim, 1996, p. 70)*

Hence, what we are at risk of getting bogged down with in digitalisation are transubstantiated entities and realities: we ourselves, others, and the world are suddenly accorded too much weight, too much body, too much presence, too much reality as such. This means that digital spaces and virtual realities are much closer to the kinds of religious spectacle that characterised the Middle-Ages than the modern theatre. Eggington argued that the medieval spectacle occurred in a 'full space':

> ... in contradistinction to the popular notion of "the empty space" associated with the modern theater. A religious production was, to begin with, an already allegorized space, its arrangement intended to reproduce the symbolic architecture of the interior of a church.
>
> *(Egginton, 2003, p. 54)*

Hence, in the medieval spectacle, such as, for example, in the Passion Game, the death of Christ was not merely acted out, but, rather, became reality again in the very market place in which the Passion Game was played, thus meaning that the onlookers were not merely distant spectators, but instead became genuine key-witnesses as a result of being present at the scene itself. Is this scheme not analogous to what occurs in cyberspace: we re-enter the times of *real illusions*. For example, apropos Egginton citing voodoo death as an example of how a representation or a copy is deemed to be capable of acquiring both the character and power of the original (p. 38), one could relate this to cyberbullying: we believe that when somebody bullies somebody else's avatar, this could lead to the death of the real person involved. At the very least, one can observe that in virtuality we are no longer merely the 'separate observer', but, rather, an 'intrinsic participant', to borrow the words that Egginton used to describe the medieval spectacle:

> ... medieval drama had a different relationship to reality than does modern theater. Rather than taking place in an empty, geometrically determined

space in which stories can be played out in relative independence of the reality of the audience's world, the hyperbolic solidity of the space of medieval drama reflected the instability of the distinction between the reality being represented and the reality of the representation.

(Egginton, 2003, pp. 54–55)

In the same way, I would argue that digital spaces and virtualities are in danger of having a hyperbolic solidity, which takes away our relative independence from reality that we used to have when we still were, to again cite Descartes, "more a spectator than an actor in all the comedies that are played out there".

Conclusions: save our screens?

The hyperbolic solidity of digital spaces and virtualities signals the disappearance of the empty space that is necessary for re-presentation, which, in turn, makes us regress to the full reality of presences. However, should we not also say that as long as there are screens, there is hope? That is to say, for the time being, the gateway to the virtual is still the screen—and, hence, perhaps the screen is as such the primary indicator of the subject itself. But what we are witnessing today is precisely the attempt to eradicate the screen. For example, did Google Glass not signal the first attempt to eliminate the screen, by making it transparent? Of course, suffice to recall Elon Musk's Neuralink project (see Chapter 1) to understand that the idea is, above all, to make the screen redundant by directly tapping into the cortex itself. Clearly, to return to the key theme of this chapter, this would signal the end of education and schooling: leaving out the blackboard, the whiteboard, and the screen all together, the student's brain would instead be linked up to the internet and merely have to 'process' the data. Irrespective of what this 'processing' would look like, as already argued, if the subject were directly connected to the web, then it would absorb all the available data, become all of the things in the world, become the world itself, it would become data amongst data. Arguably, here, along with the school, the subject as we knew it would completely disappear.

In Greek, *schole* designated a dedicated space between, on the one hand, the household (*oikos*), and on the other hand, the city-state (*polis*). It is this in-between-space that is now rapidly disappearing before our eyes. Consider the fact, as I indicated earlier, that the basic rationale behind having children and toddlers come into contact with digital screens as quick as possible is that this makes the 'real-world' more accessible and brings it more rapidly into education. Here, the school is no longer a temporary transitionary space (the revolving door to the 'real-world', which itself has a certain spatial amplitude), but, rather, merely becomes the wafer-thin interface to the supposedly 'real-world'. Or, phrased otherwise, whereas with psychologisation and neurologisation the public space of education and schooling already became devalued as the private (*oikos*) and corporeal dimension was brought in, with digitalisation the result appears to be that, by bringing the alleged 'real-world' (polis) in as something that is directly accessible, the erstwhile mediatory space of education and schooling has become fully encroached upon and usurped: the once opened up educational space collapses. This not only degrades the public space aspect of the school but also degrades the subjective position of both the educator and the pupil. Within this constellation, the educator becomes a bot propelled by hidden algorithms, while the pupil becomes no more than an ever-present node in the network, by virtue of being envisioned as an information-processing unit that requires being brought into contact with information and data.

However, once again, if today the portal to the digital remains the screen, then do we not here have something which may for the moment resist the desubjectivation at hand? That is to say, does the screen not still reserve a minimal space, a seat in a dark theatre, where the subject ultimately resides? So, should we say: *save our screens!* Let us defend the subject qua a minimal point outside, a non-presence, an absence from where to watch the on-screen presences, which serves to function as a kind of paradoxical guarantee of presence. *Do not touch our screens?* However, perhaps the situation is even more complicated yet still. Indeed, is saving the screen not something that technology pundits themselves will eventually do? For, is it not clear that, if the subject were to be directly wired to the web and thus dissolve into the sea of data, that the digital world itself would come to a screeching halt? I would argue that data without an external subject would become completely inert, insofar as without a minimal absence-based presence digital entropy (see Chapter 3) would set in. Hence, I claim that, at the very least, if one seeks to preserve the business model of our digital subjectivity-economy, then the direct link between the brain and the internet would be in constant need of new mediations. So, most probably, rather than today's hard material screen, virtual screens would be mounted in an effort to re-install an absent–present agent at a distance from the virtual world, thus preventing the data-world from coming to a halt. Consider, in this respect, 'augmented reality', where the world becomes a screen and thus coincides with it, while, simultaneously, I become or coincide with my avatar. While this could be the place where subjectivity disappears, as any distance between the subject and its avatar and world disappear, one can imagine that, instead of the person controlling this world directly, by, for example, merely thinking, a distance would need to be built-in to ensure a workable gap between the 'subject' and the 'world'. A video of the artist Keiichi Matsuda (2016) entitled 'Hyper-reality' is highly instructive here. Matsuda depicts an augmented reality where the virtual layer consists primarily of an array of virtual screens and virtual consoles, which produces a quasi-outside place for a virtual subject to navigate the augmented reality via these virtual interfaces.

However, as one can see in the video of Matsudo, the issue with the virtual screens still pertains to pre-moulding, pre-shaping, and manipulation of subjectivities. Matsudo showed that this concerns, above all, the control and guiding of consumer behaviour: in the video interactive virtual interfaces fill up the protagonist's vision with games, search engines, and, above all, adverts that pop-up as she moves around the city. This brings us back to our recurring question: what theories and models, that is, *what kind of psychologies and ideological models of the human,* will be put in gear to design the virtual subjects who will watch the virtual screens. The final question would thus concern whether, in such a world, a book such as this one would be more or less understandable.

References

Baudrillard, J. (2007). *Simulacra and simulation* (S. Glaser, Trans.). Ann Arbor: University of Michigan Press.
Busch, B., & Oakley, B. (2017). Emotional intelligence: Why it matters and how to teach it. *The Guardian.* Retrieved from https://www.theguardian.com/teacher-network/2017/nov/03/emotional-intelligence-why-it-matters-and-how-to-teach-it
Constine, J. (2017). Zuckerberg tells Harvard we need a new social contract of equal opportunity. *Techcrunch.* Retrieved from https://techcrunch.com/2017/05/25/mark-zuckerberg-harvard/
De Vos, J. (2012). *Psychologisation in times of globalisation.* London: Routledge.
De Vos, J. (2017). The neuroturn in education: Between the Scylla of psychologization and the Charybdis of digitalization? In M. Vandenbroeck (Ed.), *Constructions of neuroscience in early childhood education* (pp. 20–36). London: Routledge.
Descartes, R. ([1637]1996). *Discourse on the method and meditations on first philosophy* (D. Weissman & W. Bluhm, Trans.). New Haven, CT: Yale University Press.
Egginton, W. (2003). *How the world became a stage.* Albany: State University of New York Press.
Heim, M. (1996). The design of virtual reality. In M. Featherstone & R. Burrows (Eds.), *Cyberspace, cyberbodies, cyberpunk: Cultures of technological embodiment* (pp. 65–78). London: Sage.
Hodgson, N., & Ramaekers, S. (2018). *Parenting and the digitization of brain-based responsibility. Keynote presentation.* Paper presented at the How Important Is Neuroscience for Educators? KU Leuven, Belgium, 22 May 2018.
Lacan, J. (Ed.) (1977). *Ecrits: A selection.* New York: Norton.
Matsuda, K. (2016). Hyper-reality (video). Retrieved from http://km.cx/projects/hyper-reality
Mayer, J. D., & Salovey, P. (1997). What is emotional intelligence? In P. Salovey & D. Sluyter (Eds.), *Emotional development and emotional intelligence: Educational implications* (pp. 3–31). New York: Basic Books.
Orwell, G. (2003). *Animal Farm and 1984.* Boston, MA: Houghton Mifflin Harcourt.
Rose, N. (1999). *Powers of freedom: Reframing political thought.* Cambridge: Cambridge University Press.
Rose, N. (2018). *Our psychiatric future.* London: Polity.
Salovey, P., & Mayer, J. D. (1990). Emotional intelligence: Imagination, cognition and personality. *Imagination, Cognition and Personality, 9*(3), 1185–1211.
Schutte, N. S., Malouff, J. M., Bobik, C., Coston, T. D., Greeson, C., Jedlicka, C., … Wendorf, G. (2001). Emotional intelligence and interpersonal relations. *The Journal of Social Psychology, 141*(4), 523–536.
Spreeuwenberg, R. (2017). Does emotive computing belong in the classroom? *EdSurge.* Retrieved from https://www.edsurge.com/news/2017-01-04-does-emotive-computing-belong-in-the-classroom

Stiegler, B. (2010). *Taking care of youth and the generations*. Stanford, CA: Stanford University Press.
Williamson, B. (2017a). *Big data in education: The digital future of learning, policy and practice*. Thunder Oaks, CA: Sage.
Williamson, B. (2017b). Psychological surveillance and psycho-informatics in the classroom. *Code Acts in Education*. Retrieved from https://codeactsineducation.wordpress.com/2017/01/17/psycho-surveillance-classroom/
Žižek, S. (2019). Mind-reading AI may spell end to humanity as we know it, but not because it will enslave us. *RT*. Retrieved from https://www.rt.com/news/468228-mind-reading-computer-humanity-zizek/

7
DIGITAL MASS EFFECTS

Introduction: the digital, education, and society: more Freud, please!

In his book 'Taking care of youth and the generations' the French philosopher Bernard Stiegler argued that, to understand the effects of digital technologies one must turn to the field of education and the school because it is there that the impact of digitalisation on subjectivity and sociality is particularly evident. Stiegler's main contention is that, as digital technologies come to hijack the attention—which he believes has a social function—they compromise the construction of society and undermine civil space:

> The fundamental problem, and the crippling limit of this attention-control apparatus, is that it destroys attention itself, along with the ability to concentrate on an object of attention, which is a social faculty; the construction of such objects is in fact the construction of society itself, as civil space founded on [cultural] knowledge including social graces, expertise, and critical thinking (i.e., contemplation).
>
> *(Stiegler, 2010, p. 13)*

In response to the question of *what this will do to us, and what will become of us?* Stiegler, problematically I would argue, takes recourse to the neurosciences: in reference to Katherine Hayles, he contends that digital technologies alter our brains, especially in the case of young children:

> (…) current brain imaging allows us to observe ways in which synaptogenesis is profoundly modified by contemporary media, which create an environment that Katherine Hayles has described as one in which the brains

of the youngest children, living in a numeric world of "rich media," are structured differently from those of the preceding generation.

(Stiegler, 2010, p. 19)

While both Hayles (2007) and Stiegler answer the question of *what does or will digitalisation do to us?* via neuroscientific discourses, I have questioned in this book whether the latter can truly be regarded as a first science that is capable of proffering uncontested arguments about the effects of the digital technologies. My main argument is that to understand the digitalisation of (inter)subjectivity one must consider the extent to which neuropsychological theories and models not only underpin the digital sphere (e.g. informing the construction of our avatars and virtual environments, the placeholders of subjectivity and sociality), but also how these neuropsy-models have historically informed the birth of digital technologies. With respect to the latter, remember how AI-theorists and cyberneticists, such as Alan Turing and Norbert Wiener, strongly relied on the (neuro) psy-sciences (see Chapters 2 and 3). Hence, if, as argued in the previous chapter, it is precisely via the digital and the virtual that neuropsy-theories and models become reality and are transubstantiated, then this calls into question using these same models to understand the shifts effected by the digital turn on subjectivity. To put it bluntly: it does not matter whether certain psychological theories of the human touch upon the truth or not, the important issue is how social and personal realities are constructed within the digital virtual sphere in such a way that these theories become the truth. Hence, explaining what the digital does or will do to us through recourse to neuropsy-theories is fundamentally problematic: of course, at first glance, Facebook appears to reveal much about our 'human psychology', as psychological theories are integral to the design and basic architecture of Facebook.

If in this chapter I look to take this argument one step further by tracing the effects of the digital on subjectivity and sociality from a psychoanalytic perspective, one would be forgiven for asking how I justify such a move? Well, perhaps somewhat paradoxically, here I want to take stock of my argument that it would be pointless to trade the 'bad psychologies' that inform today's digital technologies with 'good' psychoanalysis, as the latter, as I have claimed throughout this book, would be completely useless for this purpose. As I argued in Chapter 4 and elsewhere, the non-psychological *skandalons* of psychoanalysis—such as the unconscious, the death-drive, the zero-level of subjectivity—means that psychoanalysis is utterly worthless for designing digital technologies and in setting up and designing the intersubjective scenes and scenery that constitute the digital virtualities of social media. It is precisely this *uselessness qua uselessness*, I claim, that makes psychoanalysis expedient for not only understanding (and thus critiquing) the intertwinement of digitalisation with neuro-psychologisation, but also for understanding its effects on (inter)subjectivity.

To elaborate upon this point in this chapter, I will set out from Stiegler's aforementioned point that the digital risks destroying the educational construction of society. However, rather than following Stiegler and turning to the digitalised child brain, I will instead refer to the remarkable and prolific 'psychoanalytic pedagogy' movement that was based in Vienna between World War I and World War II. This movement harboured the hope that using psychoanalysis in the fields of education and schooling would be beneficial for both individuals and society at large. At the very least, 'psychoanalytic pedagogy' and its indebtedness to Freud's understanding of 'Massenpsychologie' (traditionally problematically translated as 'group psychology') provides a sophisticated perspective on how subjectivity, education, and society relate to one another. Returning to these insights, I argue, allows one to look anew on what might change with digitalisation at the level of (inter)subjectivity.

The high hopes of the interbellum psychoanalytic pedagogical movement

Let me begin by showcasing how the psychoanalytic pedagogical movement's attempt to utilise psychoanalysis within the educational sphere relates to our current predicament within digitalisation. Both Siegfried Bernfeld's socialist experiment in collective upbringing (Kinderheim Baumgarten) and August Aichhorn's educational welfare institute (Fürsorgeerziehungsanstalt) at Oberhollabrunn represented experiments in mass pedagogy, that aimed 'to mould the individual subject by shaping the collective social environment he or she inhabited' (Henry, 2018, p. 195). As Henry documents, the work of these Freudians was closely connected to what has been called 'Red Vienna', the ambitious interwar experiment in municipal socialism that sought to confront and steer the societal disorientation resulting from 4 years of total war in Europe:

> Together with experts from across the human sciences, Freudians would be deeply involved in the progressive effort to reconstruct and redesign the fabric of urban life, and it was here that the work of psychoanalysts to bring their knowledge to bear on social problems was pursued
>
> *(Henry, 2018, p. 6)*

Is one not justified in seeing a parallel here with today's digital learning platforms, and, by extension, with social media? That is to say, is a common idea not to organise (and discipline?) both classrooms and the masses by 'shaping the collective social environment'? Consider how the basic goal of the so-called 'smart learning environments'—which today are based on *Internet of Things* technologies—is to construct and design a virtual social space that is 'seamlessly integrated into our working and learning environment'.[1] One can discern the same logic of redesigning urban life as constituting the primary rationale of social media, as demonstrated by Mark Zuckerberg's vocation 'to strengthen our social fabric and bring the world closer together'.[2] Of course, most clearly, these aforesaid attempts to fashion the social in such a way that shapes and inflects subjectivity and sociality via the digital, are based neither on a psychoanalytic informed 'Heilpädagogik' nor on a socialist reform agenda. As I elucidated in Chapter 4, the inspiration today is rather the mainstream neuropsy-theories and models, which, in turn, are grounded in neoliberal capitalist ideology. At the very least, one could argue that digital educational platforms uncritically adopt both the methods and rationale of social media and thus risk reproducing social media's business model of harvesting subjective data (the base logic of digital capitalism). Be that as it may, what ultimately unites both the interbellum socialist-psychoanalytic pedagogical projects and the contemporary psycho-economics of digital learning platforms and social media, is that they both (intend to) have effects on group formation and the ensuing subjectivation of the individuals that are involved.

Hence, let us more closely examine the psychoanalytic pedagogical movement in Vienna, along with its key theme of mass psychology. In the interbellum, the *Zeitschrift für psychoanalytische Pädagogik* (Journal for Psychoanalytic Pedagogy) emerged and united many renowned names around the theme of education.[3] Indeed, even Sigmund Freud himself contended that the future of psychoanalysis was not that of the mere 'strict and untendentious psycho-analysis' (Freud, [1919]1955, p. 168), and applauded the application of psychoanalysis in the theory and practice of the education of children (Freud, [1925]1955). The history of the psychoanalytic pedagogical movement can directly be connected to the aftermath of World War I, which signalled the end of the old era of empires and led to a major cultural and socio-political upheaval. This conflict-ridden period has been characterised by many as signalling the decline in traditional authority and the paternal function, which some people at the time saw as representing hope for enlightenment, emancipation, and radical change. However, pedagogues and social reformers also identified a potential nascent backlash stemming from the withering away of Father Figures, as, the newfound energy of the *unleashed sons* also carried retrogressive potentialities: the uncontrolled mass could drift into violence, aggression, and anarchy and/or simply result in the re-installing of new authoritarian leaders (see, e.g., Federn, 1919; Zulliger, 1921). The psychoanalytic pedagogical movement saw its task as being to steer the energy that was unleashed by the decline of the paternal function precisely via education. Psychoanalysis, so it was believed, had an integral role to play in informing education during this shift in the nature of authority, specifically in terms of channelling the freed energy of the masses and steering it away from its inherent regressive tendencies.

Hence, a major recurrent theme within the array of different voices in the debates in the interbellum was that the 'passions of the masses' had to be countered with 'mass insight' (Henry, 2018, p. 199). As Henry wrote, citing Otto Bauer, an Austro-Marxist theorist and politician:

> In place of the old repressive, hierarchical authority that was actively being dismantled at that moment and through their "difficult intellectual struggle with the masses," Austrian Social Democrats thus sought to establish a new form of authority premised on a kind of collective education.
> *(Henry, 2018, p. 199)*

Here, one can discern that what the politicians adopted from the psychoanalytic pedagogues was that the masses needed to be taught and given insight into the forces that were driving them; moreover, this insight into the secrets of how people and groups function was believed to have prophylactic effects. The reader will immediately recognise here the dynamics of neuro-psychologisation,[4] and its basic rationale that the layperson must share and adopt the theoretical knowledge and gaze of the expert.

Importantly, briefly returning to the contemporary tropes of digitally shaping the collective social environment and individual personas, this induction of the layperson into expert knowledge is precisely what is bypassed in the digital era. As I argued in earlier chapters, digitality trades collective education for collective nudging, insofar as the instinctual urges and unconscious drives are not explained to the masses, but instead are directly used to steer them. However, perhaps now we can see that this totalitarian tendency within digitalisation was already present in the rationale behind mass-education in the interbellum period. For, one is to tempted to ask whether in their attempt to supplant the scheme 'masses–Father Figure' with the 'masses–Teacher' scheme, the interbellum pedagogues, in fact, constructed the figure of the Teacher as the mere go-between, the vanishing mediator if you will, that would ultimately give way to the figure of the Führer? Hence, what we need to consider here is whether the emancipatory and anti-authoritarian utopia of the interbellum, above all, signalled the advent of Fascist leaders in the 1930s. For, arguably, claiming that the masses require (re)education, is the first step in infantilising them, turning them into a more or less compliant and disciplined group of pupils. At the very least, it is perhaps here that the utopian educational project of the psychoanalytic pedagogues can be said to have encountered its own limits, which subsequently meant that they gradually receded into the background and gave way to mainstream psychology. As Henry contends:

> "The cumulative impact of their disillusioning encounters with the irrational and regressive dimension of psychic life and the darkening political horizons in central Europe" (…) erode their confidence in the emancipatory promise of enlightenment and lead to a reorientation of psychoanalytic pedagogy.
>
> *(Henry, 2018, p. 324)*

Henry indicates that in 'Red Vienna' academic psychology gradually flourished, while psychoanalysis became relegated to the margins of the Social Democratic programme to address the masses via education (Henry, 2018, p. 330). As psychoanalysts more and more stressed the inevitable conflictual dynamics of socialisation and the intractable difficulties involved in the education of children (Henry, 2018, pp. 331–332), this could be understood as an instance of psychoanalysis being forced to admit its uselessness as a theory and model for the practice of social and societal engineering. Importantly, this is precisely where mainstream psychology came to the forefront.

Am I not then justified in drawing parallels to our contemporary milieu and its manifold discontents? Let us begin by discerning the first point of continuity with the phenomena of psychologisation and neurologisation post-World War II: the education of the layperson into the theories and models of the neuropsysciences. One must note a minor difference between the two: if in the interbellum, the psychoanalytic and subsequent mainstream psychological theories were meant to, above all, educate the educators (teachers and parents), the post-World War II neuro-psychologisation turn also targeted children and youngsters (who, e.g. had to be taught what empathy is, how their brain works, and what happens on the neuropsychological level when one enters puberty). Moreover, one could argue that the post-World War II socio-political and economic constellation represented a repetition or, at the very least, a continuation of the decline of paternal authority, as evidenced by the May 68 movement and its attacks on political, religious, and educational authorities. Hence, if the (initially psychoanalytically informed) pedagogical reform movement of the interbellum was followed by the rise of fascist dictators, should we not ask whether the phenomena of psychologisation (re-awakened post-1960s) and neurologisation (especially since the 1990s) are preparing us for the dictatorship of the digital, the tyranny of Big Data, which involves clown-esque (but not non-dangerous) obscene Master Figures addressing the masses via Twitter and such like?

I will approach this rather large question via a side route. Given the aforementioned disillusion in the interbellum vis-à-vis the usefulness of psychoanalytic insights, and the apparent obsolescence of psychoanalytic theory today, what then, if anything, can a psychoanalytic critique do at this historical juncture? Can we repeat the psychoanalytic pedagogy movement of the interbellum, learn from its deadlocks, and envision a role for psychoanalysis to inform and even refashion the formations of subjectivity and sociality in this era of digitalisation, so as to counter the potential negative or even dangerous backlashes of digitality? To attempt to answer this question, I will turn to gaming, specifically through entering into a dialogue with Alfie Bown, who after his enticing analysis of gaming (Bown, 2018a) subsequently made a plea for designing new games, driven by a leftist agenda and psychoanalytic insights.

The problem of the psychoanalytic plea for leftist gaming

Alfie Bown argues that video games are political and predominantly biased, conservative, and patriarchal in nature (e.g. depicting imperialist values such as empire, domination, and conquering by force). From here, he pleads for the need for new kinds of games that are not only leftist and emancipatory in terms of their context, but also in terms of their form itself. For, as he argues:

> Video games communicate ideology at the level of form, and laying a progressive storyline over the top does not necessarily prevent a game from serving right wing ideas.
>
> *(Bown, 2018b)*

To grasp the crux of Bown's discussion, let me refer to a related discussion concerning the political propaganda techniques that are used by the Right. The question here is whether critical theorists or leftist scholars are able to pin down the methods used by the Right in order to lure and deceive people and if the Left should subsequently adopt these same strategies for their cause? One could refer here to William C. Connolly's position, who, after arguing that the Right uses methods of 'neuropolitics' which are able to hook into people's brain, wanted the Left to use these same methods, albeit with one crucial difference: for Connolly, the Left should explain to people both how this all works and why it is being used (Connolly, 2002). However, the problem with Connolly's argument from the outset is that it takes the neuro-explanation for granted, in that he uncritically accepts the idea that the manipulative politics of the Right truly works by affecting people's amygdala. Can one not argue here that Connolly takes the neuro-shortcut in the place of conducting a truly political analysis? In contradistinction to this move, as I have also argued elsewhere (De Vos, 2013a), we should reject out of hand the entire notion that there exist models or techniques, which are inherently neutral and thus can be used either for foul (Rightist) or good (Leftist) politics.[5] Indeed, this perspective presupposes that science, and especially the neuropsy-sciences, are capable of assessing in a neutral manner the effectiveness of these techniques, based on the questionable premise that neuropsy-scientists have a direct understanding of human nature. In response to this claim, I would contend that techniques such as rightist propaganda actually shape and produce human nature in accordance with a particular political and ideological agenda, precisely by virtue of claiming to know what human nature is (e.g. Ayn Rand's Rightist naturalist psychology, (Rand, 1971)). It is worthwhile to cite the Hannah Arendt passage that I already quoted in Chapter 5:

> The trouble with modern theories of behaviorism is not that they are wrong but that they could become true, that they actually are the best possible conceptualization of certain obvious trends in modern society.
> *(Arendt, 1958, p. 322)*

Hence, Rightist propaganda are not spontaneously manufactured techniques that happen to make use of the neuro-psychological idiosyncrasies of human beings; rather, I would argue that, firstly, these techniques are consciously and explicitly based on specific neuropsychological models, and secondly, that the latter do not neutrally depict human nature as it is, but, rather, are themselves already ideological constructions.

It is in this sense that I endorse Alfie Bown's argument: the strategy should not be to use pre-existing gaming forms and merely add Leftist content to it. However, we should perhaps also go a step further than Bown and state that it would also not suffice to simply invent new gaming forms (that would envision a more emancipatory use of gaming and engender a more critical attitude amongst gamers), but that instead, we should seek to question or rework the very issue or form of digital gaming itself, or even, perhaps, address the forms of the digital technologies that underpin gaming as such. For, at the very least, should we not add to Bown's argument by stating that the issue of forms being contaminated by ideology is already at work at the very level of digitality as such? That is to say, if one will permit me jumping forward somewhat quickly here, if gaming is based on digital technology and the latter is, as I have attempted to demonstrate in this book, at its very core determined by specific neuropsy-models that are well aligned with mainstream ideology and the hegemonic political-economic system, then the job at hand requires far more than merely experimenting with forms of gaming.

To begin with, Bown's argument is predicated on a slightly problematic comparison between gaming and literature. Through recourse to Raymond Williams, Bown (2018b) contends that novels such as those by Charles Dickens, despite their left-wing content (e.g. evoking sympathy with the repressed working class), ultimately are conservative with respect to their form, and are thus incapable of instigating social change and instead exist as mere commodities to be enjoyed by bourgeois readers. Modernist writers such as James Joyce and Virginia Woolf realised that the very form of novels needed to be problematised and that this was what was required for literature to become more progressive and politically forward-thinking. For Alfie Bown, gaming must undergo an analogous shift. However, can gaming truly be situated on the same level as reading and writing? After all, reading and writing can be coupled with Kant's injunction 'sapere aude' (dare to think), as well as his conception of the use of public reasoning:

> (…) by public use of one's own reason I understand that use which someone makes of it *as a scholar* before the entire public of the world of readers. What I call the private use of reason is that which one make of it in a certain *civil* post or office with which he is entrusted
>
> *(Kant, 1999, p. 18, italics in the original)*

Apropos the above quote from Kant, in which writing is something that solicits readers to take up their pen by engaging in public debates, then what can be said with respect to games: should the latter then not solicit gamers to respond with (new) forms of games? That is to say, if today gaming restricts gamers to performing specific tasks (to kill, to conquer, to build, etc.), then, in accordance with Bown, can one imagine games that would try to subvert such preconfigured actions by either bestowing upon players a greater degree of freedom or allowing them to deconstruct these actions. However, would this not solely concern, at least, to begin with, hidden or simply unspoken tasks: *conquer the castle in a critical or deconstructive way*? Or, phrased otherwise: in contrast to being a scholar among a reading public, is being a gamer among the gaming public not subject to the more narrow confines of gaming, and, as such, its very form itself? That is to say, even with the advent of more creative and politically daring games, such critical engagement with them would still occur within the boundaries of the game itself. Consequently, it appears to me that an answering player cannot but accept the basic coordinates of the specific game that is being played. And, moreover, even if a meta-answer would be possible, that is, if a game could be answered and/or criticised within another or a new game, would this not mean that the public debate would ultimately be a debate between technicians and experts, and thus exclude code-illiterate laypersons? Indeed, even if games could be built in such a way that incited users to become code-literate—that is, allowed gamers to learn the hidden algorithms and the obscured strategies of data-gathering, or even allowed users to rewrite the algorithms and manage the data themselves— would this not ultimately mean that the very base of digital technologies (the current hardware, software and anything in between) would remain completely untouched and unquestioned? It is perhaps here that one can discern the crucial difference between writing and gaming technologies: the latter's forms are constrained and conditioned by a different and underlying technological level, which cannot be simply contested. Or, to put it another way, while Joyce and Woolf were able to use writing as a way through which to subvert writing as a bourgeois technology, this cannot be simply transposed to defying the constraints that digital technologies place upon us. The crucial argument to make here is that the private form, the very structure of the digital technologies, is not the result of a natural process; hence, digital technologies are not simply mimicking human nature or improving it, but, rather, as I have attempted to demonstrate in this book, they are historically contingent and emerged as a consequence of specific *theories and models*, if not ideological fantasies, about human nature.

It is instructive here to refer back to Turing's so-called universal machine (see Chapter 2), where the algorithmic handling of data was based on a 'head' that read squares on a paper strip, with each square containing data. As I argued in Chapter 2, the head of the Turing machine placed a kind of agent in charge, an unproblematic (and also unproblematised) fully present agent, who engaged directly with the data, whilst, simultaneously, remaining independent from the data, and thus unaffected by what it read. This, one could argue, is the ghost in Turing's machine. Clearly, this subject is not the subject that is delineated in psychoanalysis; it is neither the Freudian split subject nor Lacan's subject that is suspended between two signifiers, or, as Lacan himself put it: "a signifier represents the subject for another signifier" (Lacan, 1978a, p. 207). The difference between Turing's head and Lacan's subject is that the latter concerns a zero-level of subjectivity, which means that the subject has no weight nor amplitude as such, but, rather, only exists in the interstices of language. As explained in Chapters 2 and 3, even though Turing and many other AI-theorists and cyberneticists initially started out from a complex psychoanalytic conceptualisation of subjectivity, they all ultimately resorted to simplified mainstream psychological conceptions of the human being (this is where the story of the shoving aside of the psychoanalytic pedagogues springs to mind) in order to devise their technologies. Hence, in contrast to the divided and thus necessarily ephemeral subject of psychoanalysis, Turing's head simply is what it is, undivided and fully present, which is where, I would argue, subjectivity disappears as such: the head is not that which gives rise to fissures or ambiguities.⁶ This scheme, which underpins our digital technologies, is also constitutive of how our subjective and intersubjective spaces are constructed in the era of digitalisation. Consider here the contention of Dave Winer, a software-developer, who argued that: "Connect persons to data objects to persons. That's the social today" (cited in Lovink, 2012). This can be considered as a mortifying reversal of Lacan's formula, whereby humans are narrowed down to persons, mere datasets to be incorporated into Winer's definition of the social, which, above all, appears to fit the definition of the market.

Will digital gaming not also eventually be structurally marked by this scheme? Arguably, gaming today does not allow space for the subject. In this way, gaming can perhaps be wholly situated at the level of *dreamwork*, which is one of the key arguments put forward by Bown in his book on gaming. I would argue that dreaming in the Freudian sense of the term has no subject per se and that the subject of the dream only arises in the act of remembering and awakening, which is the other space of dreaming where dreams enter the social as they are told to someone else: only there does the subject divided between the dream and the world come into being. Digital gaming, which is based on our current digital technology, thus can be said to be above all the dream from which cannot wake up, as it does not allow any 'other space', an elsewhere that is necessary for the subject qua split being. Moreover, as *dreamwork* is about fantasies being put to work while our motor functions are shut down, as per Freud's account, then one could perhaps conclude that game-dreaming about the Leftist revolution is not likely to lead to any significant action.

Here, I have to confess that I am perhaps being overly harsh on games; while in the distant past I did briefly play Super Mario as part of my reading and writing habits, today I could not care less about games. If I were to be completely honest, my reaction upon seeing adults play first-person shooter games, for example, tends to be that they should grow up. In light of a more general infantilisation of culture, be it in mainstream media, education (see earlier chapters), and even the political arena, which serves to undermine (inter)subjectivity as such, I would need a lot of convincing that there are currently games or could be games in the future, that require or allow for the mature use of reason. Indeed, a recurrent question in my mind is how we ended up raising entire generations of eternal school boys and girls (hordes of 'unleashed sons' to use the lingo of the erstwhile psychoanalytic pedagogues), whose favourite pastime appears to be to retreat to their play caves and never look up from their screens? However, to be clear, I am not wholly unsympathetic to the idea of playing as such, that is, to the idea of *homo ludens*. What I do reject, however, is the commodification and instrumentalisation, that is, the educalisation, psychologisation, or digitalisation of play, which, I would argue, obliterate the playing subject. I am someone who never had any hobbies, and, indeed, anyone who ever dared to ask about my hobbies was undoubtedly startled by my vehement response to the question. This derives from the fact that if I do anything that one could define as play, then I do this very seriously, in all its subjective and intersubjective elements. At the very least,

I am willing to fiercely defend such play from being expropriated by either those who seek to instrumentalise play because they claim to know human nature or the psycho-neurobiology of play, or those who claim that, while others misuse this for Rightist political ends, they are able to use it for good, before proceeding to explain to us how all this works.

However, I also want to make it clear that, irrespective of whether all my reflections make complete sense or not, more than anything I wish to attempt to explore different levels of play. Indeed, perhaps there may be forms of gaming, based on alternative technologies, in the future that could truly be both enjoyed subjectively and played within a public community, and thus truly capable of engendering emancipatory or even revolutionary effects. Whether this is possible or not I really cannot say, and I will leave it to others to reflect on more deeply. The main bone of contention for me is the question which is perhaps overlooked by Alfie Bown in his hopes for more emancipatory forms of gaming, namely: what constitutes the social in gaming? Even though new forms of gaming could incite us to think critically (and thus be educational as such), could they truly bring people together, could they truly engender a collective body capable of opposing the hegemonic forces? In other words, the question I am interested in is whether the technological conditions of gaming communities are not only structurally incompatible with a true understanding of subjectivity, but also with a proper political community? For, if one accepts that the digital technologies we have currently are based on a psychologised falsification of subjectivity, then how would they allow for a genuine manifestation of sociality? One is reminded of how Stiegler assessed the conditions of the social under digitalisation. Stiegler argued that 'psychotechnical attention capture' results in:

> ...an immense psychological, affective, cultural, economic, and social disaster, and has led to the weakening and increasing fragility of social linkages that at this point are capable only of engendering generalized insecurity and immense doubts about the future condition of all intergenerational relations.
>
> *(Stiegler, 2010, p. 58)*

Hence, should we abandon all hope when entering the digital game? Will the revolution not be gamified? Or, for that matter, will the revolution not be digitalised because it cannot unite people around a collective cause? Hence, the question that still requires addressing in greater detail is a general one: what does it take for a collection of individuals to form a group? Perhaps the psychoanalytic distinction between a mass and a society, between a gang and a group, is expedient for this purpose. In an attempt to address this aforesaid question, let us once again return to the psychoanalytic pedagogy movement in Vienna in the interbellum: how did we end up in our contemporary digital era with the tyrannical figure of Big Data and the obscene little Father figures, as epitomised by political leaders such as Donald Trump in the USA and Boris Johnson in the UK?

Hans Zulliger and the mass psychology of the classroom

> "Psychoanalytic pedagogy" (...) is basically more of a problem of mass psychology than a question of a psychological understanding of the individual (...). It concerns less the psychology of one single person or the affective and libidinally coloured pair-relationships between people, as rather, the exploration, knowledge and conscious regulation of mental relations between a community and its leader. It becomes clear that the main issue of analytical pedagogy lies there if we consider that the teacher (...) will only able to satisfactorily solve the educational difficulties of normal children if he succeeds instinctively and unknowingly, in treating and solving the problems as mass phenomena.
>
> *(Zulliger, 1936, p. 338, my translation)*

Zulliger understood the psychology of learning and education as a 'mass psychology', whereby a teacher does not have to be an individual psychologist, but, rather, a social psychologist.[7] Is this not precisely what has been lost in education? Arguably, certainly after WWII, education opted for the perspective of individual psychology (focussing on individual well-being and learning disabilities in particular), displaying little or no real understanding of what a group is. But perhaps this anti-social tendency was already present in the work of a number of Enlightenment pedagogues, who variously rejected the group dimension in education. A classic example of this is Jean Jacques Rousseau, specifically his conceptualisation of human beings, and especially children, as inherently good, and that it is society and groups that corrupt and make human beings evil (Rousseau, 1979). One could even argue that this discarding of the group and society is responsible for the truly anti-educational undertow that proliferates throughout modern education. Consider Johann Heinrich Pestalozzi's work, for example, which purported that school should be about life as opposed to learning or teaching. This anti-educational tradition tends to consider the fact that schooling and other forms of education are practices which take place in groups as an accidental, or at most, pragmatic condition, whose effects must be minimalised and weeded out. Notwithstanding this position, Pestalozzi's work also attempted to reconcile the tension between individualistic goals (fostering autonomy, freedom, and self-realisation) and the social goals of education (the development of responsible and engaged citizens who are concerned with the common good) (Schugurensky & Silver, 2013). John Dewey is also someone who was famous for favouring group learning over individual education (Dewey, 1916). However, one could argue that, first, it is these aforesaid individualising tendencies in education that became hegemonic by the end of the former century in neuro-psychologising (and also pathologising) forms of education, based on the belief that the neuro-psy-sciences were able to tell us who we were. Second, and especially today, group processes are above all understood from this individualising perspective, up to and including the argument that the social is good for the brain (De Vos, 2016). What is lost in this shift is precisely that which the psychoanalytic pedagogy movement attempted to engage with: an understanding of the juxtaposition of individuals and groups from a bidirectional genealogical perspective. Of course, this is exactly what Hans Zulliger set out to do: to conceive of group processes as individuation processes, and, conversely, to think of individuation processes as group processes.

This loss of this insight means that the predominant individualistic tendencies within education (and also beyond the educational sphere) not only lead to 'false' individuation processes (as what human subjectivity and intersubjectivity are about are ultimately overlooked), but also, and most importantly, unwittingly installs group effects or even mass effects. This, I argue, becomes especially apparent in the digitalisation of education. To begin with, digital learning platforms clearly prioritise 'one-on-one' modes of education, which are ostensibly wholly adaptable to the individual needs of students, thus signalling the realisation of the ultimate solipsistic form of education and schooling. Digital learning platforms appear intent on ruling out group effects, or, at the very least, wholly containing, controlling, and steering them. I refer the reader back to my discussion of Richard Davies' (2016) plea that learning platforms should incorporate 'phatic' communications between students into the digital system itself so that there are no more uncontrolled corridors in the schools where group effects transpire out of sight of the teacher (see Chapter 5). To put it more dramatically yet still: the digital *one-on-one* (I 0 I) is where the erstwhile collective *speaking being* becomes the solipsistic *speaking beast*; every utterance or deed is now tracked, while every 'social exchange' is managed as a result of everything being processed along the individualising psychological schemes that form the backbone of the algorithms. It is precisely here that educational technologies and also, for that matter, social media platforms, by virtue of addressing the *individual as an individual* (in order to pre-script, nudge, steer, and ultimately commodify them), turn the digitalised human being into a mere cog in the systemic faceless mass. It is against this backdrop that Winer's aforesaid definition becomes more tangible: "Connect persons to data objects to persons. That's the social today" (cited in Lovink, 2012). Consider here, once again, how digital education systems are supposed to be able to individually assess pupils' neuro-psychological statuses in order to tweak the learning content (see the Embrace Watch discussed in Chapter 6). Consequently, would the culmination of this not be to connect pupils to each other via digital telepathic technologies? Indeed, there is an actual project at Facebook to develop non-invasive sensors capable of detecting brainwaves, which, in turn, allows one person to feel what another person feels. This, arguably, would mean the end of subjectivity and individuality as we know it, insofar as it would lead to the establishment of a uniformed swarm mind, the ultimate form of massification.

In order to critically think through these digital mass effects, let us consider more closely how Zulliger explored the connection between subjectivity, the social, and education. As aforesaid, most interestingly, Zulliger, although he pleaded to bring psychoanalysis into education and the school, did not argue for a more individualising approach (qua the one-on-one constellation of the psychoanalytic cure), but, rather, emphasised that the teacher or educator should focus on group processes. Zulliger, inspired by Freud's theories on mass psychology, saw the class as a gang, as a band of brothers in search of a leader. Here, it must be pointed out that this focus on group formations from a psychoanalytic perspective was lost after WWII, as the psychoanalytic pedagogy movement was left behind in the wake of the turn towards developing child analysis (which signalled a return to the one-on-one approach), which was predominantly driven by Melanie Klein. While Klein herself had published in the *Zeitschrift für psychoanalytische Pädagogik*, she was not really convinced that psychoanalysis could add anything of use to the practices of collective education as such (Lorré, 1991). Of course, the events of WWII following the rise of fascism and its respective authoritarian leaders were likely a decisive factor in psychoanalysts and other psy-scientists' distrust towards the use of mass psychology and attempts to intervene within collective formations, which led them towards more individualising and, in turn, more psychologising approaches. Should we here, in light of the manifold discontents of contemporary digitalisation and the ongoing search for emancipatory openings, not agree with the aforesaid critique of the group-centric nature of the psychoanalytic pedagogy movement? For, even if one was to follow Zulliger's argument that brotherhoods (and attempts to deal with them) are inextricably linked to the organisation of the school, which in itself does not necessarily have proto-fascist undertones, one could argue that, at the very least, his collective approach could be criticised for conforming to pre-existing bourgeois, patriarchal, and conservative power relations.

But let us not get too far ahead of ourselves here, as we first must consider Zulliger's main reference point, which was Freud's 'Totem & Taboo' (Freud, [1913]1955). Zulliger considered the myth of the Ur-Father to be the key to understanding both the structure and dynamics of the classroom, as well as offering a framework to guide the work of the teacher. To briefly summarise the myth, Freud considered the pre-societal structure of the primal horde to be organised as follows: one male (the Ur-Father) owned all the females and reigned until he was eventually overthrown and killed by a band of brothers (his sons). In the aftermath of the killing, one of the brother's took the place of the Ur-Father. This scheme repeated itself until the sons issued a law prohibiting anyone to take the place of the Ur-Father, which, ultimately, led to a society organised by a prototypical version of the Rule of Law. With respect to education, Zulliger argued that this form of socialisation repeated itself within the confines of the classroom, insofar as it is the class that installs the empty space of the leader, and, hence, the teacher should be wary of fully occupying this space: the teacher should only be a representative of society as such, a mediator, rather than being the actual leader of the class. This is because psychoanalysis, according to Zulliger, had demonstrated that if the place of the Father is occupied in reality, then the mass is driven to an act: the killing of the Ur-Father's replacement. Hence, in social constellations such as the classroom, the place of the Father should only be occupied in the symbolic sense, as this is what ultimately provides greater stability to the group.

Returning to Freud, one could point to the crucial role that Freud attributes to the grandson of the Ur-Father, who was not a part of the killing but composed an epic poem of the events, depicting a hero who slayed an evil Father.[8] For Freud, it is only this fictional reworking of the event that allowed the primal horde to transcend the cycle of repetition (of sons taking the place of the Ur-Father). This is because the epic poem afforded an identification with the fictional figure of the hero, which, in turn, allowed the group to stabilise and erect a new symbolic societal order in the place of the brutal rule of the Ur-Fathers. Hence, one could argue, the transition from a mass to society must necessarily pass through stories and fiction.

With respect to our contemporary milieu, a preliminary observation would be that digital culture and especially gaming culture appear to testify to an intensification of the cult of the hero. By all accounts, this is a golden age for fantasy and fiction. In light of this, if one is in doubt about where all the rich imagery of psychoanalysis has gone, now that psychoanalysis is ostensibly in decline, then one answer might be that it went to the digital entertainment industry: to the endless series and content on Netflix and similar streaming services and gaming. Indeed, incest stories, castration fears, Father and Mother Figures, sibling rivalries, and so on and so forth all appear to have found refuge in the world of fantasy and gaming. Hence, while mainstream neuropsy-scientists explain the 'mental' via dry cognitivism, behaviourism, and cerebral functions and regions, and laugh warily at the 'old' psychoanalytic explanations, in the meantime the Romanesque imagery of psychoanalysis proliferates across popular culture.

However, can we not discern in the digital hero cult, especially in gaming, a crucial shift in the processes of identification? Instead of forming a symbolic identification with the hero, first and foremost the gamer acts *as if they are* the hero: does this not mean that instead of symbolic identifications, then, gaming invariably confines gamers to imaginary identifications? This stems from the fact that the form, or perhaps more accurately, the structure of gaming involves an *acting out*, a repetitious role-play in which we play at being the hero, which, in turn, provides us with an image of unity and substantiality that we ourselves do not possess.[9] This is perhaps because there is only space for acting out in the digital realm as opposed to developing symbolic identifications whereby one would not merely identify with what one would like to be, but, rather, to use Žižek's designation, one would identify 'with the very place from where we are being observed, from where we look at ourselves so that we appear to ourselves likeable, worthy of love' (Žižek, 1989, p. 116). At the very least, such modes of symbolic identification entail that we do not identify in the first place with that which we want to be (or with what we are said to be), but, rather, we identify with what we want to be from the perspective (or the gaze) of where we would be seen as that which we want to be. For example, a child role-playing as a knight with a toy sword must, at the very least, imagine the gaze of someone (the archetypal example here would be an invisible audience) watching them and admiring their sword skills and heroic courage at confronting all these evil forces.[10] Here, one can firstly discern the split subject, who is split between a primary and secondary identification and, hence, eventually a zero-level of subjectivity: ultimately, we are nothing but the gaze from where we look at ourselves. The key question here is whether this precise constellation, form, and structure are wholly impossible within the historically contingent development of digital technologies. Consider, once again, Turing's reading head which can be said to be the equivalent of a full agent, insofar as it was wholly equal to itself and remained unaffected by the data. Does this mean that digital technologies are simply incapable of offering us anything more than placeholders for the solipsistic imaginary ego, which serves to foreclose the symbolic subject, the subject who lacks a full subjectivity and who has no choice but to lose itself in the act of attempting to establish itself symbolically?

Hence, will gaming ultimately keep everybody fixed in their position as a gang member, as one of the unleashed sons, and leave them condemned to fool around within the range of imaginary coordinates designed by both the game developers and the digital technology itself? Could one not argue that the symbolic antagonism that is made possible via the adoption of an external gaze (which was what the grandchild's epic poem allowed), which allows for an act of subjectivation (where the mass can become a social group), has no place structurally within the digital? Indeed, the entire issue of making gaming more 'real', via the advent of ever more realistic 3D graphics and VR possibilities that make fully immersive gaming simply a matter of time, might result in the symbolic 'as if' dimension becoming thinner yet still. In gaming, the toy sword is an AK 47, and you can literally feel the kickback of the weapon in your hands as the control pad rumbles when you fire. However, as VR technology advances it will soon be possible for gamers to feel the sensation of the cold steel on their hands, to smell the gun oil, and so forth, while if cerebral access becomes possible, we would not have to play as the hero or imagine ourselves as being the hero, we would just *be the hero*.

But, perhaps, for the time being, it suffices to say that the digital promotes imaginary rather than symbolic identifications. The crucial issue here is that the external gaze which structures symbolic identifications (the perspective from where we look at ourselves so that we appear to ourselves worthy of love) in digitality is no longer external, but, rather, is fully drawn within the framework of the digital itself, which, in turn, condemns us to be locked up in imaginary identifications. This is where 'the loving gaze' is no longer supposed, but, rather, is either realised imaginarily in the form of either systemic rewards (gaining XP, reaching another level, winning trophies) or is substantialised via the gaze of our peers in the gaming community. While the community aspect is regularly invoked as a positive feature of gaming (in the sense that it brings people together), one could argue that gaming and social media, in fact, deprive us of the 'invisible audience' and condemn us for life to endure the 'real' presence of peers evaluating, applauding, supervising, following, sympathising and, of course, liking us. The horror!

However, while the horror is all mine, it clearly has its counterpart in the zealous enthusiasm of those pedagogues who are so anxious to include gaming as soon as possible within their educational practices: to use, for example, gaming to let teenagers experience the dangers of sexting in a playful way, or to even let adults become acquainted with healthy food via online interactive platforms that are replete with funny movies and entertaining quizzes. While technology in this way draws us all into its imaginary scenery of immature and even childish play, in the meantime our new economy condemns us to life-long learning. This is the paradox: as school is on the verge of being shut down and replaced by an interface between persons and data, we ourselves have become eternal pupils dispersed on the learning platforms, which we cannot escape from as the prospect of finally graduating and entering public life appears to have been foreclosed. Hence, is the ultimate objective, then, to keep everybody immature and continually part of a virtual class where each person is isolated and addressed separately? Within such a constellation, group formations are bypassed for a more generalised solipsism; at most, we could say that there is a fake pre-configured group, based on empty socio-psychologised signifiers, such as well-being, empathy, and participation. It is precisely here, I would argue, that massification and its unchecked effects are imminent.

For Zulliger, education takes place in groups because it repeats societal formations. The role of the teacher is to use their subjectivity in a particular way (refusing to fully occupy the place of the leader) in order to turn the gang into a group, which, in turn, at least according to Freudian group psychology, allows for the subsequent intra-psychic subjectivation of the members of the group. Zulliger described the role of the teacher as follows: he is not the ideal himself, but he is 'the mediator' (Zulliger, 1930, p. 43). This is in stark contrast with how in the digitalisation of education the role of the teacher has become virtually redundant: they become mere administrators of algorithms that have been designed elsewhere and facilitators of commercially developed technologies.

However, it is also important to note that one can already discern in Zulliger's approach a somewhat twisted and problematic idea, centred on the fact that Zulliger believed that a teacher qua mediator 'has a role similar to that of the priest'. Clearly, the teacher should not fill the open place of the Ur-Father, nor should they play the role of the hero: they are the intermediary agent. However, I would argue that Zulliger overlooked the Freudian distinction between the role of the priest and the role of the grandchild-poet. While the poet lets their hero conduct their act within the symbolic (his)story, the priest does their work in the imaginary realm of the here and now. It is instructive to refer the reader back to William Egginton's (2003) discussion of the transition from the medieval spectacle to the modern theatre that I discussed in the previous chapter: it is only with respect to the latter that a symbolic space is opened up for us to identify with the fictional as opposed to merely the spectator-witness of a supposed transubstantiated reality. It is precisely this transubstantiated reality, as argued in the previous chapter, where the whole design of digital technologies appears to lead towards. But is this not also precisely the same issue that Zulliger at times veers dangerously close to? For, at the very least, one could argue that when Zulliger purported that the teacher should address the group and not the individual, the examples he cites in his book remain rooted in the realm of the accidental, that is, the particular situation that his groups found themselves in. For example, Zulliger described a situation in which a neighbour of the school complained that his strawberries were being stolen. Upon confronting his class with this complaint, two female students of Zulliger's denounced this act and set out to offer their apologies to the neighbour. Subsequent to this the two real perpetrators revealed themselves and went after the girls to set things straight. Zulliger used this as a starting point to discuss with the class the function of lies, inciting his pupils to recount their lies and let the 'the community judg[e] them and show them how to avoid them':

> The starting point was a "heroic" lie in the service of the community and born out of a sense of community—the lie was used to reinforce community-building aspirations: confession before the community induced feelings of guilt. And finally, by seeking a path to truth, the community helped to correct both individual members and the community as a whole for the purpose of a higher cultural ideal.
>
> *(Zulliger, 1936, p. 350, my translation)*

Granted, while Zulliger was acting as the priest who dealt with the contingent events his class were experiencing, he nevertheless aimed at a higher and more universal ideal:

> We do not set out to train our pupils to solely fit into a specific community, so that they should feel neither comfortable nor capable of fitting into a different type of community. Furthermore, as members of society as a whole they should not lose the broader perspective, they must ensure they are not blinded and driven to intolerance (...). For such an attitude immediately results in proselytizing and engenders aggressiveness. Rather, our aim is to sublimate the aggressive drives as far as possible into work, and to make man ripe for the highest form of "community" and "humanity," by dedicating all of their individual skills into its service.
>
> *(Zulliger, 1936, p. 344, my translation)*

The reference to Kant's cosmopolitanism should not be overlooked here. However, can we not argue that Zulliger ultimately opted for the form, while evading the content of the universal? That is to say, by operating as a priest he ended up moralising? If I were to be harsher yet still, albeit perhaps a little too harsh, on Zulliger, then I would argue that while he engaged in group building, he left out the true *Bildung* as he ultimately shied away from politicising: he failed to transcend the particularity of situations while confirming the pre-existing class relations and conditions of property, that is, the existing bourgeois, conservative, and capitalist power relations.

However, for the sake of my overarching discussion, let me park this point for now and instead explore in greater detail where Zulliger's main idea, namely, that education must engage with mass psychology as it is the precondition for an intrapsychic subjectivation, leads us to.

Where the fathers fail us: Big Data and the obscene masters

To start with, let us connect Zulliger's basic idea of education as a place for subjectivisation via the group to the psychoanalytic concept of transference and the so-called latency period, whereby the child passes through the Oedipal stage and exchanges *their father* with *other fathers*, which, in turn, makes them ready for schooling. In the classic psychoanalytic understanding of the latency period, the child positions itself as being too little– a child amongst other children—to have access to the world of adults: the child thus decides to wait and to grow up first. The role of the school in this configuration was as a transitory space with its own amplitude and its own (secluded) time and space, which meant that the world outside could wait. Within this bracketed reality, if we follow Zulliger's argument, the child was placed within a group in order to elaborate on or rework their Oedipus drama within a collectivity, and, in so doing, subjectivise themselves. This allowed the child to trade the accidental and particular triangle of the family for the general constellation of society, precisely by virtue of its engagement with the classroom and school setting.

In contemporary societies, however, the world no longer has to wait, as the child is given access to the internet, which, in turn, brings the virtual world into the classroom, into the screen, if not even, into the brain. Rather than the group, then, the child is instead offered social media communities, gaming communities or digital learning communities that are hosted on private servers and steered by hidden and secret algorithms. What the child finds there are, arguably, fake and preconfigured groups, fake and preconfigured subjectivities. All the while, the school itself becomes part of a fake society, where equality, diversity, empathy, resilience, anti-bullying are the master signifiers to be celebrated, if not venerated, as our new totems to be worshipped on designated days and designated weeks (see, e.g. Anti-Bullying Week in the UK),[11] which are organised to further build our virtual, 'only-one-step-away' beautiful data-world. It suffices to simply open one's eyes and look around at both the world raging outside and at our 'social' world filled with objects and products from the entertainment and gaming industry to see a world wholly different from this. Moreover, adults are also sent to 'Workplace Bullying University', where workers, including supervisors and managers, are trained and educated in accordance with the slogan 'Work Shouldn't Hurt'.[12]

At the very least, one should not think that the era of digitalisation means that children now become adults amongst other adults; rather, the reverse is true:

we all become children, children amongst other children, which testifies to the extending of latency and infantilisation into adult life. Or, phrased otherwise, today we can say that the idea of bringing the world into the school is mirrored in a *schooling/infantilisation* of the world.

From here, the crucial question becomes, if, for Zulliger, childhood is the place where children are most susceptible to the group and mass effects, is it not precisely this same issue that is now generalised and extended to adult life? That is to say, now that we are all condemned to live as eternal schoolchildren, do we not start to behave in society as if we are still in the classroom, along with its attendant issues of bullying, exclusion and games of domination? Indeed, rather than typifying a mature politician, does Boris Johnson not, above all, resemble the leader of a pack of schoolboys? This point was nicely summed up in a song by a British pop group, who relabelled Boris Johnston's 'Bullingdon Boys' as the 'Bully Boys' (Wright, 2019).

However, to formulate it in classic Freudian terms, if in school 'my father' was traded for 'a father' (Dirk Lorré refers to this as mild transference, (Lorré, 1991)), in which not only is 'my father' left out but also 'the Father', that is, the primal Father of the mass effects, then what awaits us at the horizon of our digital epoch: the return of the Father, the Führer, the Great Leader? In this respect, it is clear that, firstly, with the digitalisation of education, the figure of mild transference, 'a father' is evacuated, insofar as in digital learning platforms the teacher becomes a mere administrator. Indeed, even monitoring of the emotional states of students is today outsourced to AI, due to the fact that the lack of psychology in computers makes them an even better psychologist than humans (see the previous chapter). According to Zulliger, the teacher posed as 'the illusory object endowed with all those precious qualities that the little child first imagined that they were embodied in its father'. Today, the teacher is far from this partial incarnation or mediator of 'my father', but, rather, merely assigns the class to play the videogame 'Assassin's Creed' (Ubisoft), after which children are then supposed to be able 'to answer questions about what the Greek streets looked like in the two city-states, how the inhabitants were clothed, and which gods were worshipped' (Meeus, 2019). To this end, the game developer Ubisoft launched a free update that eliminated the rather violent action from the game and created a version explicitly meant to be used in classrooms. But, of course, as one of the pupils in the pilot project declared after playing this game at school, he also wanted to be able to play it at home: an effective advertising campaign if ever there was one!

Hence, pupils are no longer enticed, or should we say seduced to learn, by a teacher who, representing the father, became 'a father' and who answered the child's wish to grow up through the following formula, based on the words of Lorré, "do not learn for me, but for the culture I represent" (Lorré, 1991, p. 198, my translation). Digitalised education does not need representatives of culture, as it ostensibly brings the student directly in contact with the world. One could even go as far as to say: digitalisation thus amounts to the killing of 'a father', who used to love each group member equally (so that, from a Freudian perspective, they form a group that identifies with each other). The unintended consequence of the disappearance of the transferential figure of 'a father' might be precisely to open the door for 'The Father' qua primal Father of the mass effects to return. The first instance of 'The Father' that one can discern in contemporary societies is Big Data as such: we all know that we are being watched, that everything we do and look at on the internet is scrutinised and catalogued; we all know, if it is for free, then this means that we are the commodity itself. Given that we appear to be willing to pay this price—indeed, we have no choice but to pay the price— we appear to have accepted the dark reign of this Father Figure. Moreover, we are cognisant of the fact that Big Data knows us, not in the way that our father or teacher knew us, but, rather, as the final version of the super-ego that monitors not only our deeds but also our intentions, due to the fact that it can read our minds and know our deepest desires. However, in contradistinction to 'a father', who loves us all equally and fairly, Big Data ultimately does not care about us, but only wants our data. Is this why, alongside the ultimate Father of Big Data, other new little Father figures are also popping up? Indeed, today we are witnessing the rise of a range of perverse Father figures, the personification of Big Data in some respects, but whose reassuring perverted traits are all out in the open, which we can grasp more clearly than the ungraspable figure of Big Data?

Here, we may be witnessing a shift in the classic (redoubled) place of the perverted or obscene element within the social sphere. One is reminded of Slavoj Žižek's (2002) argument that democracy always harbours some obscene kernel which is kept out of sight (or as a public secret), but yet functions as a kind of paradoxical precondition of the democratic order itself. For example, the dignity of a political leader always presupposes the possibility that they could be a sexual harasser or indulge in all kinds of obscene pleasures in their private life. The obverse of this occurred under fascism, where, for example, Nazi torturers would retreat at night into their private rooms and listen to Wagner while sipping a glass of good wine. Hence, the question here is what happens when this private other space where an obscene truth once resided becomes fully transparent in the digital era? In our digital age, surveillance has become almost all-seeing: there is no 'shallow alcove' that lies outside the range of the telescreen as there was in George Orwell's novel 1984 (as referenced in the previous chapter), where one could write their diary, or, for that matter, where one could invent new, alternative gaming forms. In light of this, one is tempted to proclaim that this obscene or perverse dimension is now completely out in the open. Indeed, as one regularly witnesses today, politicians and other leaders can be openly racist, tell complete and utter lies, and even admit to having twisted the truth. One is reminded of Žižek's perspicacious comments that what we are witnessing today 'is not the disappearance of authority, of Master figures, but its forceful reappearance – we are getting something unimaginable decades ago, obscene Masters' (Žižek, 2019). My contention is that this should be linked to the disappearance of both the other scene, that is, hidden spaces, and the withering away of the figure of 'a father', the figure of mild transference that is integral to opening up an alternative perspective in both time and space. Because of digitalisation and the concomitant complete modelling of our lifeworld, there is no longer any outside, no time or space for anything else, and it is this 'huit-clos' that brings forth the perverted little Fathers, who serve as stand-ins for totalitarian Big Data.

Conclusions: reclaim the concrete

In conclusion, let me reformulate the below schema in yet another way still, reconnecting it to the issue of education. While the school was once defined not only by its outer limits, on the one hand, Oikos and, on the other hand, the Polis, it also had an internal elsewhere, as did the two other spheres. The schema below should help me to make my point clearly:

OIKOS		SCHOOL		POLIS
Family		classroom		institutions
|		|		|
street		playground		square

The final row can be considered as the escape room, that which prevents the spheres above from becoming a totalitarian and closed space, which means that it can also be considered to be the condition of possibility for each sphere. The point I am making here is that contemporary digital technologies are threatening to destroy the final row, insofar as the ubiquitous digital technologies seek to integrate external times and spaces into its circulation of data. The consequence of this is not only that the three spheres are undermined internally, but also that the three spheres collapse into each other. For the home to function, the child needs the leeway of the street; for a classroom to operate effectively, pupils must be left to their own devices at points, such as during breaks on the playground; and similarly, there can be no 'democracy' (or whatever political system) if people are not allowed to protest on a square. Digital technologies, however, risk locking everybody up within the virtual and totalised family, the totalised classroom, and the totalised society, where the boundaries between these three dissolve (consider lifelong learning in which 'private' issues such as 'well-being' inconspicuously become an issue within the neoliberal agora). The collapse of the threefold social organisation simultaneously appears to signal the end of the Freudian scheme of subjectivation, in which an individual subjectivised itself via the social (where the mass became a group and the subject could appear). Hence, as this becomes compromised by digital technology, the net result of this cannot be anything other than the complete reign of mass psychology and mass dynamics.

Consequently, given the inherently totalitarian tendencies within digitalisation, there is a strong sense of urgency here. At the very least, if since modernity education and the school functioned as places for critical distance and critical

Digital mass effects **181**

reflection, then what will become of us in light of the fact that the digitalisation of education appears intent on ending education and the school? In this respect, Stiegler interestingly described the school as always already pointing towards something that could be said to be a proto-virtuality, due to the fact that the school provides a place for non-existent objects:

> (...) creating all signification (ideas, axioms, theorems, theses, basic principles, the formalized content of all the genres of which academic courses and classroom lessons are abbreviations)-projects learners who are becoming scholars toward the plane of consistencies: of non-existent objects. Nobility of mind provides the freedom to propel oneself beyond what exists and, a fortiori, beyond subsistence as the condition of what exists.
> *(Stiegler, 2010, p. 67)*

However, is this not what precisely today digital virtualities are paradoxically far removed from? That is to say, do digital learning platforms and, for that matter, gaming and social media first and foremost envision and promise us access to the real world and thus 'existing' objects? Consider the example of enhanced reality or augmented reality that is used in both educational and gaming settings: digitality aims to bring us the real, that which is more real than real, to put it in Baudrillard's (2007) terms. Hence, do away with the blackboard, the whiteboard, and, if possible, even the screen (see the previous chapter), in order to let the 'real' come in. In light of this, does Alfie Bown's plea to alter the form of digital games themselves not remain stuck in the rationale of bypassing access to the symbolic, due to the fact that it is this bypassing that Bernard Stiegler argues digitality is affecting?

> Enchantment through fantasy, without which the symbolic order cannot be formed (not even in the language of science), uncontrolled cultural industrialization activates the psychopower of attentional control, which then constrains fantasy (having become "entertainment") to the role of capturing its audience through the most archaic drives, then compelling it to construct a consciousness reduced to simple, reflex cerebral functions, which is always disenchanted and always 'available.'
> *(Stiegler, 2010, p. 15)*

However, the main problem with Stiegler's approach concerns the fact that, while he clearly indicates that the digital entertainment industry risks blocking the symbolic realm, and, hence, also the scientific realm, ultimately he believes that a neuro-scientific model can be of help here. As an enraged anti-psychoanalytic philosopher once yelled at me: "emotions are just brain activity, the rest are fantasies" (based on a mistaken assumption that I was endorsing a psychologising approach to emotions), to which I should have replied (but did not, as I am always too slow on my feet in such circumstances): is brain activity, not your psychological fantasy? In other words, the cerebral is not the via regia to 'human nature', but, rather, to the fantasies or dreamwork of what human nature could be (or should be for some).

Hence, in contradistinction to Stiegler, in this chapter, I took recourse to the interbellum psychoanalytic pedagogy movement and applied Freudian mass-psychology to the contemporary conditions of group and mass formation which, as I hope I have demonstrated, is the central issue at stake in our digitalised era. Or, as the digitalisation of education testifies to when we are forced to participate in VR itself, we lose the possibility of retreating to the Cartesian darkness of the theatre seats, a site, moreover, where a group of spectators can become a community. Conversely, by being drawn into the screen and its pre-scripted scenery, the dynamics of the group are digitalised and technologised, and, thus, neutralised. This is where subjectivity and sociality are shaped, nudged and steered in compliance with the psycho-social theories and models in order to serve the goal of digital capitalism. The mass effects and the rise of the little Obscene Masters are but the reverse of all this, the openly obscene reverse.

However, to be absolutely clear on this point, a critical psychoanalytic model neither aims to or is capable of providing an alternative vision of human nature which could serve as the basis for devising new forms of digitality. Consider, in this respect, how Srecko Horvath condemned Tinder for being a brutal commodification of love and sex that has messed up the emotional lives of an entire generation of young people, only to then plead for a Leftist variant of Tinder (Horvat, 2016). But is the question that one must ask here not what would be the psychological theory that would underpin this pharmacological variant? Given that Horvath himself leaned on psychoanalysis, did he himself consider how one would build into Tinder some of Lacan's most famous dicta, such as 'Woman does not exist' or 'there is no sexual relation'? These two dicta, at the very least, testify to the non-psychological approach of psychoanalysis, which understands the field of sexuality as being inherently antagonistic; one name for this irresolvable antagonism is precisely the subject. Simply put, in light of psychoanalysis being useless at acting as a stand-in for the bad and fake psychologies that currently inform social media and digital technology, I believe that Tinder, Facebook, and the like cannot be disconnected from the psycho-economy of digital capitalism: they cannot be tweaked, neither at the level of content nor at the level of form. That form is never neutral is one of the key lessons of psychoanalysis: form is always condensed or crystalised content.

Does this then mean that what is left to confront are structures, and in the first place, the structure of Logos (see also Chapter 2)? Is my reasoning ultimately that digitality, as a thing of Logos, as Logos radicalised, inevitably will go rogue on human beings? To put it tentatively: Logos is a machine that uses subjectivity in order to grow, but this cannot but engender the vision, the final fantasy, of Logos, only reaching its ultimate end when it swallows whole subjectivity, and, thus, abolishes it. That is to say, Logos, grounded in a zero-level of subjectivity (the empty subject situated between two signifiers) cannot but fully realise the zero-level of subjectivity. Hence, the contemporary thrust towards our very own digital death represents Thanatos in its most elaborate form.

However, I have tried to demonstrate in this book that, in order for things to go bad, digital things must have been developed from bad models (bad in the sense of leading to bad things, but also bad because these models overlook the truth of human subjectivity and sociality). Hence, is my final conclusion that we must fight the entropy of Logos, by fighting its lies, and, hence, fighting Logos as such? The typical strategy has hitherto centred on pointing out to everyone: *we are speaking-beings, we are children of Logos, so do not underestimate the power of the symbolic when you speak of our brains, body, society, economy, and so on.* Perhaps we have now reached a point where an alternative strategy is needed, that is, instead of defending Logos, the time has come, not to reject it (by pointing to the body or the brain), but simply to oppose it, not through gaming or playing, but, rather, through actively withstanding it and fighting it from the perspective that *real and concrete* people in their *real and concrete* circumstances are suffering because of it. Of course, the real and the concrete are here not to be understood as 'really existing', but rather, as the logical outcome of partisan and engaged political struggle. It is here, then, that we should take up what the interbellum psychoanalytic pedagogy movement refrained from doing: we should disconnect from the link with socialist reformist politics and its orientation towards the (psy)sciences and instead direct our struggle toward radical Leftist politics. While Zulliger admittedly ended up promoting in a specific form of group building and, despite envisioning the universal dimension, ultimately did not truly engage in politicisation, our task should be to move the struggle to a truly political and collective domain, so as to oppose the digital death drive and its digital massification and Fake Obscene Fathers. A final tour through the digital psycho-economy via the psychoanalytic concept of interpassivity in the next chapter should help to more accurately plot out the battlefield.

Notes

1 https://blog.bosch-si.com/future-of-work/what-are-smart-learning-environments-2/.
2 https://www.facebook.com/notes/mark-zuckerberg/bringing-the-world-closer-together/10154944663901634/.
3 Notwithstanding the aforementioned Siegfried Bernfeld and August Aichorn, other important figures were Melanie Klein, Hans Zulliger and Bruno Bettelheim.
4 I touched upon psychologisation and neurologisation in the previous chapters, as well as describing it elsewhere (De Vos, 2012, 2013b, 2016).
5 In this respect, I refer the reader to the well-known critique of the Frankfurt School, e.g. Herbert Marcuse's "One-Dimensional Man" (Marcuse, 1966) and Jurgen Habermas' "Technology and Science as Ideology" (Habermas, 1971).
6 Remember the quote I cited in Chapter 3:

> The world of signs works, and it has no meaning. What gives it its meaning is the moment when we stop the machine. These are the temporal cuts we make there. If they are faulty, ambiguities will sometimes arise that are sometimes difficult to solve, but which will always end up giving meaning.
>
> (Lacan, 1978b, p. 328)

7 Of course, the Hegelian lesson here is that any individual psychology is for that matter itself also a social psychology. For example, consider how one of the main themes in psychoanalysis, the Oedipal situation, is a social constellation, which points to the fact that Freud was a group psychologist before there was such a thing.
8 Freud makes this addition to the myth of the Ur-Father in 1921 in his "Massenpsychologie und Ich-Analyse" (Group Psychology and the Analysis of the Ego) (Freud, [1921]1955).
9 See Chapter 1 and my discussion of Lacan's Mirror Stage.
10 I refer the reader back to my discussion of the invisible audience in Chapter 6.
11 https://www.anti-bullyingalliance.org.uk/anti-bullying-week/anti-bullying-week-2019-change-starts-us.
12 https://www.workplacebullying.org/tag/training/.

References

Arendt, H. (1958). *The human condition*. Chicago, IL: University of Chicago Press.
Baudrillard, J. (2007). *Simulacra and simulation* (S. Glaser, Trans.). Ann Arbor: University of Michigan Press.
Bown, A. (2018a). *The playstation dreamworld*. Cambridge: Polity Press.
Bown, A. (2018b). Video games are political. Here's how they can be progressive. *The Guardian*. Retrieved from https://www.theguardian.com/games/2018/aug/13/video-games-are-political-heres-how-they-can-be-progressive
Connolly, W. E. (2002). *Neuropolitics: thinking, culture, speed*. Minneapolis: University of Minnesota Press.
Davies, R. (2016). Ceaselessly exploring, arriving where we started and knowing it for the first time. *Studies in Philosophy and Education, 35*(3), 293–303.
De Vos, J. (2012). *Psychologisation in times of globalisation*. London: Routledge.
De Vos, J. (2013a). Interpassivity and the political invention of the brain: Connolly's neuropolitics versus libet's veto-right. *Theory & Event, 16*(2). doi: 10.1353/tae.2013.0034
De Vos, J. (2013b). *Psychologization and the subject of late modernity*. New York: Palgrave Macmillan.
De Vos, J. (2016). *The metamorphoses of the brain. Neurologization and its discontents*. New York: Palgrave Macmillan.
Dewey, J. (1916). *Democracy and education: An introduction to the philosophy of education*. New York: Macmillan.
Egginton, W. (2003). *How the world became a stage*. Albany: State University of New York Press.
Federn, P. (1919). *Zur Psychologie der Revolution. Die vaterlose Gesellschaft*. Leipzig: Anzengruber Verlag.
Freud, S. ([1913]1955). Totem and taboo. In J. Strachey (Ed.), *The standard edition of the complete psychological works of Sigmund Freud: vol. XIII* (pp. 1–162). London: Hogarth Press.
Freud, S. ([1919]1955). Lines of advance in psycho-analytic therapy. In J. Strachey (Ed.), *The standard edition of the complete psychological works of Sigmund Freud: vol. XVII* (pp. 159–168). London: Hogarth Press.
Freud, S. ([1921]1955). Group psychology and the analysis of the ego. In J. Strachey (Ed.), *The standard edition of the complete psychological works of Sigmund Freud: vol. XVIII* (pp. 67–143). London: Hogarth Press.
Freud, S. ([1925]1955). Preface to Aichhorn's Wayward Youth. In J. Strachey (Ed.), *The standard edition of the complete psychological works of Sigmund Freud: vol. XIX* (pp. 271–276). London: Hogarth Press.

Habermas, J. (1971). Technology and science as 'ideology'. In J. Habermas (Ed.), *Toward a rational society: Student protest, science, and politics* (pp. 81–122). Boston, MA: Beacon Press.
Hayles, N. K. (2007). Hyper and deep attention: The generational divide in cognitive modes. *Profession, 2007*(1), 187–199.
Henry, P. J. (2018). *Experimental futures and impossible professions: Psychoanalysis, education, and politics in interwar Vienna, 1918–1938*. The University of Chicago, Chicago.
Horvat, S. (2016). *The radicality of love*. Cambridge: Polity Press.
Kant, I. (1999). An answer to the question: What is enlightenment? In J. G. Mary & W. Allen (Eds.), *Practical philosophy* (pp. 11–22). Cambridge: Cambridge University Press.
Lacan, J. (1978a). *The four fundamental concepts of psychoanalysis* (A. Sheridan, Trans.). New York: Norton.
Lacan, J. (1978b). *Le Séminaire II. Le moi dans la théorie de Freud et dans la technique psychanalytique*. Paris: Seuil.
Lorré, D. (1991). *Stapstenen naar een psychoanalytische pedagogiek: grepen uit haar geschiedenis*. Ghent University.
Lovink, G. (2012). What is the social in social media? *e-flux journal, 40*(12), 1–12.
Marcuse, H. (1966). *One-dimensional man*. Boston, MA: Beacon Press.
Rand, A. (1971). The psychology of "psychologizing". *The Objectivist, 10*(3), 1–8.
Rousseau, J.-J. (1979). *Emile: or, on education*. New York: Basic Books.
Schugurensky, D., & Silver, M. (2013). Social pedagogy: Historical traditions and transnational connections. *Education Policy Analysis Archives/Archivos Analíticos de Políticas Educativas, 21*(35), 1–16.
Meeus, R. (2019). Hoe videogame 'Assassin's Creed' in leerplan geschiedenis terechtkwam. *De Morgen*. Retrieved from https://www.demorgen.be/tech-wetenschap/hoe-videogame-assassin-s-creed-in-leerplan-geschiedenis-terechtkwam~badf6054/
Stiegler, B. (2010). *Taking care of youth and the generations*. Stanford, CA: Stanford University Press.
Wright, M. (2019). Madness take HUGE swipe at Boris Johnson and 'Bully Boys' on new song Bullingdon Boys. *Express*. Retrieved from https://www.express.co.uk/entertainment/music/1210945/Madness-songs-Boris-Johnson-Bullingdon-Boys-Eton-lyrics
Žižek, S. (1989). *The sublime object of ideology*. London: Verso.
Žižek, S. (2002). *Welcome to the desert of the real! Five essays on September 11 and related dates*. London: Verso.
Žižek, S. (2019). Trump will be re-elected because of left-liberal stupidity. *Spectator*. Retrieved from https://spectator.us/trump-re-elected-left-liberal-stupidity/?fbclid=IwAR1T7ubjAiRfyWgmbYxK-hs5I9Ko4_7v63e4SzyRY_UuTgLkc_olQRxHVrE
Zulliger, H. (1921). *Psychoanalytische Erfahrungen aus der Volksschulpraxis*. Bern: Ernst Bircher Verlag.
Zulliger, H. (1930). Psychoanalyse und Führerschaft in der Schule. *Imago, 16*(1), 39–50.
Zulliger, H. (1936). Über eine Lücke in der psychoanalytischen Pädagogik. *Zeitschrift für psychoanalytische Pädagogik, 10*(6), 337–359.

PART 4
Conclusions

8
WHAT DIGITALITY SHOULD NOT THINK. A GUIDE TO IMAGINE THE END OF THE WORLD

Introduction: the economy of perfect indifference

Some time ago I saw a young, tall and slender woman on an electric 'sharing step'. She had a faint smile on her face and did not appear to be paying any attention to me, any of the other bystanders she passed, or even the road for that matter; instead, she looked upwards (towards the future I imagined). Perhaps she was fantasising about being filmed by someone and subsequently featuring in a YouTube clip, as one foot was delicately crossed over the other (a pose one typically assumes for the camera). However, perhaps the most striking, and even uncanny, thing about this woman was that, in her angelic countenance, she hardly moved her body—which may also have had something to do with the fact that she was fortunate enough to be on a smooth stretch of pavement in the city centre.

Is this what technology ever more makes a reality: the dream of leading an effortless, if not almost automated, life? On a sharing step ever so slight body movements are required to change direction, and while the battery generates the energy needed to propel its passenger, it would be wonderful to think that in the future we could use the brakes by mere thought alone, rather than having to activate them with our fingertips. Perhaps, if one will allow me to make such a leap, this is why there are so many cat videos on the internet: they personify our fantasy of moving effortlessly in our lives. Freud's well-known argument is that people love cats so much because they represent narcissistic self-contentment (Freud, [1914]1957), which is to say that humans find the fact that cats appear to be so full of themselves compelling. In this respect, is the aforementioned scenario of the young woman on the electric step not the personification of the post-human, enigmatically moving sphinx, who transcends life and the world itself? Apparently, in our aspirations of a frictionless life, we, the subject, do not want to be the subject. Or, at the very least, we do not want to do the things we do ourselves and would take more pleasure from outsourcing this to technology and, in turn, reducing resistance and increasing the extent to which we can glide through our everyday lives. The temptation is too strong here to not recount an old, and admittedly moralising, story that I heard when I was a young boy: the story goes that a princess received a box for her birthday with a thread inside. Anytime the princess found herself confronted with a problem, she would pull the thread a little, and, lo and behold, she would jump forward in time to a point in which she was beyond the difficult circumstances. As you can imagine, the story ends when the princess suddenly realises that she has the final loose end of the thread in her hand.

Anyway, if the reader will permit me to make yet another leap, our contemporary aspiration towards frictionless living appears to coincide with Bill Gates' dream of a 'frictionless capitalism', which he believed digital information technologies finally made possible. The basic idea here is that buyers and sellers would all have access to the requisite information:

> [I]f every buyer knew every seller's price and every seller knew what every buyer was willing to pay, then everyone in the 'market' would be able to make fully informed decisions and society's resources would be distributed evenly ... When you want to buy something you'll be able to tell your computer to find it for you at the best price offered by any acceptable source or ask your computer to 'haggle' with the computers of various sellers. ... This will carry us into a new world of low-friction, low-overhead capitalism, in which market information will be plentiful and transaction costs low. It will be a shopper's heaven.
>
> *(Gates, 1996, pp. 180–181)*

Note how the buyer here allows the computer to take over and do the hard work of comparing offers and negotiating prices. Digital technologies also allow the sellers to outsource their tasks to computers, most notably, by relieving sellers of their duty to know their customers. Knowing one's customers is supposed to allow the seller to manufacture what people need and to customise their offers to the individual wishes and desires of potential buyers. According to Gates, digital technologies enable sellers to probe their customers in a more efficient way than ever before:

> From time to time your software agent will try to entice you to fill out a questionnaire indicating your tastes. The questionnaire will incorporate all sorts of images in an effort to draw subtle reactions out of you. Your agent will be able to make the process fun by giving you feedback on how you compare with the norm. That information will be used to create a profile of your tastes, which will guide the agent. As you use the system for reading news or shopping, an agent will also be able to add information to your profile. It will keep track of what you have indicated interest in, as well as what you 'happened upon' and then pursued.
>
> *(Gates, 1996, p. 191)*[1]

What digitality should not think 191

The above quote, at the very least, testifies to the fact that when capitalism goes digital, it goes psychological. One could even go as far as to say that Gates' supposed neutral middle-man of technology, which acts as the guarantor of frictionless capitalism, turns out to be a psychologist seducing, luring and deceiving us so as to extract from us our valuable (commodifiable) psychological profiles. In return, the 'subtle' questionnaires bribe us with a little fun: they tell us what we are, which is to say that they tell us how we compare with the norm. Hence, we are seduced by the very thing that is taken from us, our alleged psychological portrait: we are given the sweetener of our own 'psychology'.[2]

Here, one is often tempted to separate the two issues of technology and ideology, whereby the argument then centres on how digital information technologies are misused by capitalism and perverted into becoming a tool for expropriation. Some have even argued that the 'third industrial revolution' is actually in conflict with capitalism, pointing to how file sharing sites such as the notorious Napster, which allow users to download books, music, and videos for free, corrode the fundamental capitalist axiom of private property. Hence, it is also argued that digital capitalism risks setting in motion dynamics that undermine capitalism from within: consider here, for example, the argument that the digital economy leads to unemployment, and, thus, to the potential collapse of consumption. Is the conclusion to be drawn, then, really that digital technology and capitalism are ultimately incompatible?[3] Some have even gone so far as to argue that new technologies already hold within them the future of an alternative political economic system, as evidenced in Aaron Bastani's book: 'Fully Automated Luxury Communism: A Manifesto' (Bastani, 2019), which ponders whether the sharing economy, for example, is just one step away from an economic model based on the commons?

However, such optimistic lines of reasoning are invariably predicated on viewing technology as inherently neutral (and, thus, ostensibly usable within both ultra-capitalist models and radical communist ones), before proceeding to shift to the idea that this same technology, almost automatically and naturally, would then lead to a more fair, just, egalitarian and emancipatory economic model. The first aspect of that argument is precisely what I have argued against in this book: although it is commonly stated that the web emerged out of both military and university projects and only subsequently was incorporated or taken over by commercial enterprises, evidently neither the military nor university contexts can be considered as virgin-like or sterile environments that are untouched by the hegemonic political economy. Therefore, if one thinks that the technologies that we have now are those that came to us naturally and inevitably, then one completely obfuscates that their emergence was historically contingent and, most importantly, that they were determined by both the hegemonic models of human beings and the social that prevailed at the historical juncture in which they emerged, and the ideologies with which these models are inevitably intertwined. Hence, concerning the second aspect of the aforementioned argument: if one wants to entertain the idea that digital technology is naturally evolving towards an economy of the commons (see, e.g., Cassauwers, 2019), then one risks overlooking the fact that these alleged proto-communist commercial practices might, in fact, represent only yet another metamorphosis of capitalism. Indeed, none other than Kristian Niemietz of the British pro-free market institute of economic affairs, for example, observed how, post-Napster, the music industry has faced little difficulty in restoring profitability through a range of streaming services similar to Spotify. It is in this respect that Niemietz noted, with a big wink to the aforementioned book of Aaron Bastani, how:

> The music industry has been able to overcome low prices … It actually made capitalism work better. In terms of music, we actually got fully automated luxury capitalism.
>
> *(cited in: Cassauwers, 2019)*

In this account, capitalism operates like an eternal phoenix, which requires fertile ashes to achieve yet another renewal in its endless cyclical progression? But this is then on its turn rejected by for example Jens Schröter who basically argues that there is eventually a bottom circle capitalism is going down to (Schröter, 2012). For Shröter digital media and capitalism are in the end irreconcilable: instead of solving the problems of capitalism technology deepens them. Leaning on Karl Marx's understanding of how 'at a certain stage of their development, the material productive forces of society come into conflict with the existing relations of production' (Karl Marx cited in: Schröter, 2012, p. 309), Schröter argues that we might be facing 'a very deep and even terminal crisis of capitalism'.

However, despite the fact that I will also consider in this chapter whether digitalisation represents the final frontier of capitalism, what I would contest is the position that technology is an external factor, the Other, which constitutes the final Other of capitalism so to speak. Rather, my argument is that the perceived antagonism (between the material productive forces and the existing relations of production) is an internal one that resides within capitalism itself. Hence, the extent conflicts and crises we are witnessing today are merely the phenomenological reflections of a much deeper fissure, which one needs to explore further in order to discern the true crisis looming on the horizon. For, if it is evident that digital technologies have brought capitalism to every corner of the world and into each and every home, then it is also clear that it helped to bring capitalism into each and every one of our minds, which is precisely where perhaps a final frontier can be said to have been reached. If I may return to the woman on the sharing step for a moment, is she not reminiscent of the princess who was left holding the loose end of the thread in her hand? Having outsourced everything to technology, what remains is a mere shell, while in the meantime the ghost has been fully commodified; therefore, when her battery is drained, she will be no more than a puppet, akin to E.T.A. Hoffmann's fictional character that turned out to be a doll: Olympia in all her perfect indifference. Therefore, the question that this chapter sets out to address is: do the end of capitalism at the hands of the digital and the end of subjectivity not represent two sides of the same coin? That is to say, if capitalism has always, by its very nature, had to push its borders and expropriate that which lay outside of it, be it other continents or the future even, perhaps it is now finally heading to the final frontier and its ultimate demise as a consequence of having swallowed the ghost of human subjectivity as such, which leaves behind only empty shells. Engaging with this question will lead to a (potentially problematic) engagement with psychoanalytic, more specifically Lacanian, conceptualisations of subjectivity, for if it is with Freud and especially with Lacan that we find a quasi-algorithmic account of the subject, then we must urgently confront this in order to question whether (inter)subjectivity is fully digitalisable or otherwise.

Interpassivity and (neuro)psychologisation

The figure of the lady on the electric sharing step is an expedient entry point into the discussion of how digital technologies, more than any other technologies before them, allow human beings to outsource their activity to technology. Bernard Stiegler also dealt with this aspect of digital technology in his critique of psycho-technology:

> … we are faced with a situation today in which it has become normal to think that the functions previously located in the psychic realm must be transferred (abandoned) to psychotechnological or computational devices, from the pocket calculator to the software controlling financial, military, and medical decisions, without any subsequent interiorization and without any *structural coupling* between *pharmakon* and synaptic circuitry that would open the possibility of creating new transindividuation circuits, the brain's thus limiting itself to information from only these mechanisms.
>
> *(Stiegler, 2010, p. 97, italics in the original)*

Hence, as one can discern above, for Stiegler, outsourcing used to be followed by a re-intake; for example, when humans outsourced thinking and speaking to the technology of writing, the active re-intake was that we became writers ourselves who formed a community around the written word. This is what Stiegler is referring to above through recourse to Gilbert Simondon's notion of 'transindividuation': a psycho-social individuation, a transformation of both the individual and the group. According to Stiegler, the opportunities for this 'transindividuation' in digital times become even rarer, which, in turn, threatens to lock the brain up in technological informational circuits.

However, while Stiegler ultimately grounded his critique in neuro-scientific terms (see also Chapter 4), I want to turn here to the art philosopher and cultural critic Robert Pfaller, more specifically, his use of the concept of interpassivity.

Let me get right to the heart of the matter by citing a quote from Pfaller to show how the theory of interpassivity, by design, cannot but reproduce its own logic:

> The theory of interpassivity has at this point presented us with an unanticipated benefit in terms of a solution to a fundamental problem of cultural theory.
>
> *(Pfaller, 2017, p. 7)*

Is this not the nice thing about theory, that it thinks in our place, that it unexpectedly provides us with a solution at a moment in which we ourselves are stuck? And, in a further turn of the screw, in the act of writing about these comments from Robert Pfaller, I also cannot but see myself become caught in this dynamic of delegation and outsourcing, insofar as I am also put to work by the theory. Or, to put this differently, am I not hired by the theory so to speak to do its bidding (albeit with no guarantee of delivering the goods necessarily)? Of course, one could easily get bogged down and become confused here, having to subsequently engage in other questions, such as what is thinking? Is it active or is it passive and where does it leave the subject? In response to these questions, I would argue that thinking with theory, or, outsourcing one's thinking to theory, or becoming the tool of the theory itself are all scenarios in which the line between activity and passivity becomes blurred. This is of critical relevance for the question of whether this elaborate scheme of human thinking would be itself usable as a model for constructing thinking machines. That is to say, given that I have argued throughout this book that digital technologies were designed and devised using psychological theories and models, would Pfaller's complex and intricate model be expedient for devising alternative technologies?

Let us try to answer this question by first considering the argument that, at the very least, Pfaller's theory of interpassivity allows for a reconsideration of the question of what it means to be the subject of thinking and theory. For example, if, according to Pfaller, interpassivity concerns the delegation of *passivity* as opposed to activity and is about letting others (or a device or apparatus) *enjoy* for us (rather than letting others *work* for us), then can theory not be considered as a device to which we outsource our 'Denklust' (enjoyment in thinking)?[4] Indeed, we let theory enjoy the process of thinking and finding solutions, whilst we remain comfortably stuck. This enables one to think about 'thinking' in an altogether different way than the mainstream psychologising model of an *agent solving a problem*, whereby finding a solution is seen to be rewarding insofar as it relieves the pressure on the thinker. However, what this psychologising scheme cannot account for is that in the academic sphere, arguably the royal realm of thinking one might say, enjoyment is deemed to be something that hampers objectivity and, as such, has no place there. From the perspective of interpassivity, we not only let our papers and books do the thinking for us but also outsource to them the enjoyment that comes from having an audience and being read, or, first and foremost, from being cited.

Pfaller's following point that there is always a second delegation (besides the delegation of pleasure) helps us understand this phenomenon more clearly: Pfaller contends that while people transfer their pleasure to a representative agent, they also transfer *the belief in the illusion they have staged* onto an undefined, naïve other (Pfaller, 2017, p. 7). This means that when one outsources, to use one of the classic examples of interpassivity, reading to a photocopier, printer or hard drive (as we copy, print, or save all the texts we would like to read, but then never get round to reading them), we ultimately let the device do the reading and procure the enjoyment from reading in our place. However, Pfaller adds that, in the meantime, we ourselves do not confuse the act of reading with the operation of the device, that is, we ourselves do not believe in the illusion that the device has done the reading and enjoyed on our behalf. It is here that Pfaller brings in the notion of a 'naïve observer': it is only for this imagined agent that the whole set-up (the whole staging involved in interpassivity) is satisfying. As a naïve observer cannot read intentions, Pfaller purports, "he is satisfied with just an appearance *as if*" (Pfaller, 2017, p. 51) (as one sees, e.g., in politeness). In other words, when we save PDFs and movies to the cloud and fail to get round to reading or watching them, this still provides a form of relief for us. Although we ourselves do not actually think that the PDFs and movies are read or watched by the device (in this case the cloud), this, nevertheless, functions *as if* some imagined *naïve observer* thinks that the PDFs and movies are taken care of. In this respect, Pfaller speaks of a special kind of illusions, which are 'not merely illusions that certain people have never believed in, but apparently, illusions that no one has ever believed in' (Pfaller, 2017, p. 6). One could think here of the classic example of anthropologists who encounter myths about how women get pregnant, while completely overlooking the fact that the people concerned are fully cognisant of the true nature of things: the myth is only believed by some imagined *naïve other*. Pfaller most interestingly contrasts this *naïve other* to the Freudian super-ego: while the latter represents that which knows the true state of affairs up to and including your intentions (and can punish you for merely having them), the former can only judge from the basis of appearances.

Consequently, does this not mean that the outsourcing of thinking to theory is also about positing some naive observer who thinks that theory does its job—while we ourselves do not necessarily believe in the illusion that our little theory has truly settled any of the issues that are at stake? In this respect, *Google Scholar* is the naïve observer par excellence, insofar as it counts our publications and citations, without differentiating between whether we are being cited positively or negatively (e.g. 'De Vos has it completely wrong' would still positively affect my citation indexes). It is, thus, the naïve observers like Google Scholar or Academia.edu that enjoy the fruits of our academic labour, counting our citations and the number of views of our profile, and then ranking us (if we have a lot of views) in the top x per cent and giving us feedback on how we compare to the norm (to reuse Bill Gates' words).

But let us move from my own particular perspective—being a humanities scholar—to the perspective of the subject as such: the so-called layperson, who, one could argue, is itself also a *subject of theory*. That is to say, if for Lacan, the subject of psychoanalysis is the modern subject, which he defines as *the subject of the sciences* (Lacan, 2007),[5] then I would argue that we should read these words to the letter so to speak. For, evidently, the modern subject no longer understands itself, others and the world from the all-encompassing vantage point of an all-seeing and all-comprehending God (a perspective which we mere mortals can never possibly share), but, rather, from the more limited position of science and its theoretical vantage point. Everything the modern subject does, be it cooking, eating, sleeping, having sex, raising children, up to gardening, I would claim, is informed by, embedded in, and structured by science. And, most importantly, in all of this the layperson is well aware of the theories involved: for, indeed, are we not today only too well aware of what various academic experts say about how we should cook, eat, sleep, have sex, raise our children and do the gardening? Our lifeworld is no longer the sublunary that is overviewed by a *super-egoic* God (all-seeing and all-knowing about our desires and little pleasures), rather, we have come to live in an academicised habitat that was brought into being by the more limited gaze of the modern sciences, the latter of which perhaps acts as the ultimate *naïve observer*, insofar as it renounces any access to the *thing as such* (the Kantian Ding-an-sich) and instead limits itself to appearances and dealing with them in a pragmatic and evidence-based manner.

Hence, from here the redoubled question becomes: *how does the modern subject relate to theory, and how does theory relate to the modern subject?* As I have argued both in this book and more extensively elsewhere in my writing on (neuro)psychologisation, it is here that the psy-sciences—in broad terms, the sciences that deal with subjectivity itself—play a central role. Given that Pfaller's conception of interpassivity allows for a reformulation of the issue of psychologised subjectivity, let me briefly reiterate my main points. First, the dicta of the psy-sciences produce a redoubling: *"look, this is what you are"* constructs an externalised image of ourselves, a (neuro)psychological golem or homunculus if you will, for us to gaze upon. What appears to be in operation here is the birth of a kind of extra persona to which we can outsource our everyday existence via an interpassive scheme, which is to say that we do not outsource *what we are*, but, most importantly, *what we are said to be* by science. For example, consider how toddlers in the aforementioned Circle Time sessions at school are asked how they feel and then offered four masks that portray happy, sad, angry or scared faces. Simply put: let the mask express the appropriate feeling and thus *do* the feeling on our behalf (De Vos, 2012). In this way, the ubiquitous brain image appears to function as the latest mask that bears witness to our ostensibly main human traits and characteristics. But, once again, one should not overlook here that what we project onto the brain is not *what we are*, but, rather, that *which we are said to be* by science. In other words, as argued already in Chapter 5, the colours in the polychromatic brain scan that we all know so well ultimately derive from the psy-sciences: it is with *psychological theories* that the brain is coloured in. Hence, the brain can be understood as the latest step in the process of outsourcing: from delegating our 'being human' to our redoubled *homo psychologicus*, to transferring all of this further onto a more concrete and allegedly more tangible issue: the brain. As a result of this, Stiegler's recourse to the brain and brain-sciences is rendered problematic, due to the fact that the brain is itself a technological device to which we transfer or abandon our psychic functions, that is, our *alleged* psychic functions.

From here, the specific functioning and positing of the issue of theory and knowledge for modern subjectivity becomes clearer. One can, for example, observe that the Circle Time sessions that encourage toddlers to express their 'feelings' are based on a prior *theoretical induction* of the children into academic theories of emotions. Indeed, a closer inspection of the didactics involved reveals that the children, prior to the call to use the masks, get a *theoretical class* that explains basic scientific insights on human emotions: they are taught the different kinds of emotions that allegedly exist and the proper ways to express them. In the same way, as already argued in Chapter 5, *neuroeducation* (the idea of using neuro-scientific findings in education) cannot but draw upon *neuro-education*, that is, it cannot but involve educating pupils themselves about the latest scientific discoveries on the brain. For example, a core part of the curriculum for 12–15 years old involves being introduced to theories of the pubescent brain (De Vos, 2016). Even the use of cognitive neuroscience in the classroom appears to require inducting pupils into how the brain learns. For example, in the case of attention deficit hyperactivity disorder (ADHD) is the first step in the treatment not to administer *theory* to parents, teachers, and children themselves? Indeed, the first lesson that 'affected' teens are hailed with is that ADHD is a brain disorder:

> You may wonder why you have ADHD. … Having ADHD is not your fault. Research has clearly shown that ADHD runs in families (is due to genetics). ADHD is a brain-based disorder, and the symptoms shown in ADHD are linked to many specific brain areas. There is no known cure for ADHD, but we know many things that can reduce the impact that ADHD has on your everyday life.[6]

The use of 'we know' in the above quote testifies to the fact that the teens who read this are *interpellated* to share in this knowledge. It should be clear by this point that I am both leaning on and attempting to supersede the Althusserian conceptualisation of interpellation (Althusser, 1971). Let me elaborate upon this further. To begin with, the first specific feature of interpellation by the neuropsy-sciences is that they draw upon theory and science: *hey you, look, this is the (neuro)psychological being that you are based on the latest scientific research*. Hence, the interpellation is not issued from the master's voice but, rather, from knowledge itself, or to use Lacan's term, it emanates from *the discourse of the university*. In this respect, and considering that Althusser developed the concept of interpellation in 1971, is it not strange that he used the figure of the police officer to account for how ideologies engender their subjects? The 'Hey you' of the police officer—that transforms the person who turns around into a subject of law and order—clearly situates the issue of ideological interpellation within, in Lacanian terminology, *the discourse of the master*. But, certainly, given that Althusser developed his concept of interpellation in the shadow of May 68, would it not have made more sense to understand ideological interpellation as emanating from within *the discourse of the university*? For, if we follow Lacan's interpretation of the shifts in power at that historical juncture, this timeframe can be understood as representing the shift from *the discourse of the master* to *the discourse of the university* as the hegemonic discourse in society (Lacan, 1991).

The phenomenon of (neuro)psychologisation exemplifies the type of interpellation that occurs under *the discourse of the university*. The 'Hey you' of the neuropsy-discourses—omnipresent in our society from kindergarten, school, media, workplace to retirement homes—hails everyone, from the toddler to the elderly, to subjectivise themselves from the perspective of neuropsy-theories. Hence, in contrast to the classic Althusserian scheme, we are not called upon to identify as such with the thing we are said to be (*homo psychologicus* or the brain), but, rather, we are hailed to adopt the position of the neuropsy-sciences themselves. In other words, *look, this is the psychological being you are/look, this is the brain you are*, interpellates us to gaze upon ourselves, others and the world from the neuropsy-expert position. Consequently, we identify in the first instance with the neuropsy-scientist and tell each other: *do you know that according to brain research…*

Not becoming a subject: a dead-end leeway?

At this point, after having reworked the Althusserian concept of interpellation, one must ask whether we need to question the optimistic undertone of Pfaller's concept of interpassivity? Indeed, Pfaller, referring explicitly to Althusser, argues that interpassivity is a strategy for escaping identification and, consequently, subjectivisation:

> Precisely there, where it is suggested that they become self-conscious subjects (through 'interpellation' in the sense of Althusser [1971]), people seize interpassive means to flee into self-forgetfulness. Interpassivity is therefore either an anti-ideological behaviour, or it is a second, and entirely different, type of ideology that does not rest on becoming a subject.
> *(Pfaller, 2017, p. 8)*

Let me problematise Pfaller's position, first, with respect to identification itself: does identification not always entail some minimal form of non-identification and non-subjectivisation, which means that identification always somehow escapes itself? That is to say, I identify with my father, teacher, hero, etc., on the basis of some minimal difference, some minimal other place, or space from where we can look at the image of what we want to be (or at the image of what I am said/supposed to be)? Hence, identification and subjectivisation by definition are reliant on not becoming a subject, which is to say that they rely on a kind of zero-level of subjectivity. One is, thus, only a subject from a place outside of it; the subject is only a subject where the subject escapes itself. This is also operative in a specific way in (neuro)psychologisation: one answers the interpellative call of the neuropsy-sciences by identifying specifically with the objective and ultimately the empty position of science. One subjectivises oneself from a zero-level of subjectivity that one ultimately shares with science, as the latter claims an objective, non-subjective vantage point). It is from that position that the subject delegates in an interpassive way their being to the *homo psychologicus* and/or the brain.

In the case of neuropsy-interpellation, the self-forgetfulness (to use Pfaller's term) involved is far from an anti-ideological gesture in that it appears to be firmly held in check by the hegemonic *discourse of the university*. Our not becoming a subject, thus, rests upon a prior submission to identification with academia, which, ultimately, leaves little or no room for leeway whatsoever. Is this not a case of, to use the appropriate Althusserian expression, 'ideology at its sharpest' (Althusser, 1971)? At the very least, in the case of neuro-psychologisation, one could say that we are hailed into the non-subjective academic expert-position, which is controlled by the *psy-complex* and allows it to hold sway over the vast terrains of education, schooling, everyday life, work, politics, and so on, with the end result being that both personal and interpersonal issues are governed and steered in an academic and depoliticised fashion.

Returning to Pfaller's understanding of interpassivity vis-à-vis the aforementioned figure of the *naïve observer* allows one to probe this scheme further. Pfaller argues that interpassivity allows for selective contact with a thing, in such a way that allows us to escape from the very thing with regards to both *enjoyment and belief* (the identification with an illusion) (Pfaller, 2017, pp. 7–8). When a person delegates, for example, their enjoyment of watching movies to the DVR or hard-drive, they themselves do not really think that the device is doing the watching on their behalf, but instead ascribe this belief to a *naïve observer*. In the same way, can we not say that while we all believe that we are our brain, this belief is only truly held by neuroscience and its naïve gaze? All the while, we ourselves hold on to the idea that deep down inside us, at the level of our true intentions, there is a kernel that science ultimately cannot (or hitherto cannot) fathom. Or, phrased otherwise, (neuro)psychologisation works insofar as it allows a non-neuropsychological and external position. Hence, in the same way, that magic, as Pfaller explains, relies, in principle, on *not believing* in magic (what Pfaller refers to as 'illusions without owners' (Pfaller, 2014)),[7] we look upon the findings of neuropsy-experts with a minimal degree of scepticism and distance. Consider in this respect an argument made by the philosopher Patricia Churchland in an interview: she asks whether we should think "'Gosh, the love that I feel for my child is really just neural chemistry?' Well, actually, yes, it is.

But that doesn't bother me" (Churchland, 2013). The reason it does not bother her is then described by Churchland as follows: "Neuroscience doesn't provide a story about how to live a life." It is in this latter utterance that a certain degree of distance comes in to play, a certain non-believing, a nagging suspicion that equating the human being with its brain does not represent the end of the story. But, of course, here the question again becomes: is this a distance that challenges neuro-reductionism or simply confirms it? That is to say, are we not simply, albeit in a highly specific and somewhat reversed way, falling back upon the post-ideological form of ideology par excellence: "I know very well, but nonetheless" (Žižek, 1989, p. 18)? Indeed, perhaps we can only fully subscribe to the dictum 'we are our brain' by holding on to the suspicion that there is, on a certain level or from a certain perspective, more to us than just wetware: *nonetheless, we know very well that we are our brain*. However, and here one discerns a crucial difference between magic (which remained within the discourse of the master) and science (that pertains to the discourse of the university): while magic never had believers—Pfaller notes that "it always happened against better knowledge" (Pfaller, 2017, p. 9)—science, in contrast, wants to have everyone on board as active believers. From here, one can observe that the psy-sciences especially have their fair share of (lay) aficionados and even zealous radicals, that is, those who marvel at being synonymous with their brain and who engage in a mission to convince the whole world. It is precisely their own interpassively grounded non-belief that constitutes the very strength of their mission.

However, if at this point, the theory of interpassivity does not seem to harbour much emancipatory potential for the interpellative dynamics that characterise our contemporary scientific milieu, perhaps the socio-cultural and political-economic shifts engendered by digitalisation now make this question obsolete. For, clearly, the predominant way in which interpassive subjectivity is mobilised today no longer involves neuropsychological discourses, but, rather, transpires within the terrain of digitality and virtuality. There, arguably, subjectivity is given form without, at least at first glance, the involvement of mediating and interpellating discourses. That is to say, if for interpassivity it is outsourcing and ultimately the 'not doing' that provides the basis for the fulfilment of desire (Pfaller, 2017, p. 14), is this not precisely what cyberspace is all about? Today, we are ever more relieved of our duties by algorithms that have taken over responsibility for a good deal of what it means to be human: in short, today, rather than our *homo psychologicus* or our brain, it is our digital avatars that are living our lives in our place. This perhaps marks a profound change, insofar as when interpassivity goes digital the chances for preserving any kind of interpassive leeway grow even slimmer than before. Consider, once again, how Pfaller describes interpassivity as something that opens up a kind of escape route:

> The rituals of interpassivity, its 'little gestures of disappearance', resemble acts of magic. Just as Haitians liked to spare themselves the need to kill their enemies by carefully piercing a doll, hordes of interpassivists spare

themselves entire evenings in front of the television by carefully programming their recording devices.

(Pfaller, 2017, p. 8)

Today, however, hordes of interpassivists appear to spend entire evenings (and days and nights) connected to digital devices, in order to spare themselves from living itself. But, more importantly, is the digital here not ultimately completely overruling the 'little gestures of disappearance' that used to be made possible by the mechanism of interpassivity? For, while we outsource our being to our avatar and to the virtual sphere, we ourselves can no longer partially retreat or disappear. Not only is everything that we do in the virtual sphere traced, datafied, and profiled but we are even called upon to entrust everything we do in our so-called 'real-life' to Big Data. All sorts of technology (e.g. payment technology, traffic control, camera recognition, and so on) and our portable and wearable devices make us increasingly fully traceable in time and space. Resultantly, one must ask whether the 'little gestures of disappearance' simply do not make sense anymore? We are doomed to be wholly present[8] all the time, which appears to be the modus operandi of today's digital capitalism.

Here, the naïve question would be to ask (see also Chapter 7): what will this do to the psychology of the human being? How does digital technology affect our psychology and/or our brain? However, the main argument of this book is that this line of reasoning is compromised due to the fact that the theories of the neuropsy-sciences provide the models through which we are datafied, profiled and traced. As Gillespie put it: "information providers rely on neuropsychological research in designing the algorithms" (Gillespie, 2014). This invalidates the use of neuro-psychology to understand digitalised subjectivity, as neuro-psychological theories are already underpinning the digitalisation of (inter)subjectivity. So, instead of adopting the path of trying to discern the (neuro)psychological effects of digitalisation, or, more modestly, claiming that Facebook, Google, and the like teach us a lot about the psychology of the human being, we should instead ask what (neuro)psychological models are precisely stuffed into social media and other digital platforms, and in the interim track down the neuro-psychological theories within the technologies, the algorithms, and the codes. The theory of interpassivity might be expedient in this respect.

Digitalization and interpassivity

There is a vast scientific and popular discourse on what the digital does to our minds and our brains. Psychologists Daria Kuss and Mark Griffiths, for example, note that "it may be plausible to speak specifically of 'Facebook Addiction Disorder'" (Kuss and Griffiths, 2011, p. 3529). According to other research, social comparison to one's peers via computer-mediated interactions on Facebook might also impact upon one's psychological health (Steers, Wickham, and Acitelli, 2014). Nicholas Carr, for his part, wrote in his book "*The Shallows: How*

The Internet Is Changing Our Brains" that technology is changing our ability to think and to concentrate (Carr, 2010).

If these discourses invariably underpin attempts to *save our psychology* or *save our brains from Facebook* and such like, the theory of interpassivity can provide a different angle on this issue. Let me begin by referring again to the work of Lacan, specifically a passage which Pfaller also sees as key to understanding interpassivity. In his seminar "The Ethics of Psychoanalysis," Lacan argued the following concerning the function of the Chorus in Greek tragedy:

> Your emotions are taken charge of by the healthy order displayed on the stage. The Chorus takes care of them. The emotional commentary is done for you…Therefore, you don't have to worry; even if you don't feel anything, the Chorus will feel in your stead. Why after all can one not imagine that the effect on you may be achieved, at least a small dose of it, even if you didn't tremble that much?
>
> *(Lacan, 1992, p. 247)*

The central insight here is that emotions and psychology only come to the fore in the very process of outsourcing itself. The human being itself does not do emotions and neither does it tremble: that is what the Chorus is for. Hence, it would be a mistake to consider our psychology as a prior given which is then subsequently outsourced to or via a device. Rather, our psychology is always elsewhere, so the idea that it is under threat of being manipulated or even expropriated by technology to be commodified in digital capitalism, misses the logic of interpassivity at play here. For those who argue that digital technology alters our mind and our brains, there is something *beyond* and also *before* datafication: that is, some kind of essentialist humanity, arguably definable in neuro-psychological terms. This naïve understanding of digital capitalism leads to a flawed reclaiming of our psychology and a misplaced plea to safeguard some kind of prior *agalma* of the human being. In contradistinction to this essentially philanthropist[9] move, a psychoanalytic critique, aided by the theory of interpassivity, can show that it is precisely this fantasy, that the human being's essence can be positively defined (in psychological and brain-related terms), that fuels datafication and allows for the commodification of subjectivity. To move quickly here, the issue is not that our psychology is being hacked by technology—remember Sean Parker (see Chapter 4) retorting that Facebook is about 'hacking people's psychology to hook them' (Ulanoff, 2017)—but, rather, that we are being hooked into a technology via attributing us with a psychology. That is, as we are denied our essentially psychology-free default position as described by Lacan, we are designated our digital and virtual avatars that are attributed with psychology and with feelings which we, as a kind of puppet master, are supposed to set in motion. Or, to put it differently yet still, if the Greek Chorus took care of our psychology, allowing us to take a distance from it, then digital technologies perhaps do not allow for the same retreat, as this external position itself is ever more drawn into the data-frame, we are supposed to exhibit the emotions and tremble ourselves. Hence, the imagery of the puppet master should be adjusted: at the very least, in times of digitality, the puppet masters are fully visible and have to co-tremble with their puppets, to the point where one can no longer discern where the trembling actually emanates from.

Am I here not sketching a *(neuro)psychologisation 2.0* that is decidedly different from the *(neuro)psychologisation 1.0* described earlier? That is, while (neuro)psychologisation 1.0 relied on scientific interpellation, which involved identification with the expert position, in (neuro)psychologisation 2.0, by contrast, interpellation is bypassed: we are no longer hailed to look upon ourselves as *homo (neuro) psychologicus*, as this (neuro)psychologisation is done, a priori, by the digital environment itself and in the design of our avatars. Consequently, have we not finally outsourced (neuro)psychologisation itself to technology? Or, to put it in more Foucaultian terms, we no longer must auto-govern ourselves: the governance, erstwhile outsourced to our psychological selves and brains, can now be handed over to our avatars and smart environments. Does this then mark the end of the subject of ideology, the end of interpellation tout-court?[10]

Consider in this respect the didactics of Circle Time I mentioned earlier, in which schoolchildren are interpellated each morning in a psychologised manner: '*How Do You Feel Today?*' Take a look at the 'Emotions Chart!'[11] It is clear that the presence of the children who are invoked in this way differs markedly from the way in which attendance was taken in earlier times, where education was, above all, centred on discipline and knowledge: in those times uttering a simple 'present' sufficed as a response to the roll-call. However, while in psychologised times your required presence became psychological in nature (as you had to report your psycho-emotional state within the required format), in digital times even the interpellative call is no longer necessary. Not only can your presence and whereabouts be electronically verified (some schools already use tracking technology and even face recognition, so taking attendance is no longer necessary),[12] but even 'real-time mood-tracking devices' (smart cameras allegedly able to detect human emotions) can be used to assess your emotional state, without needing to ask you, so as to adapt your learning content for that day (or perhaps to arrange a meeting with the school psychologist) (as described in: Williamson, 2017).

At the very least, while the psychologised and neurologised subject was interpellated via inducing it into academic theories, the digitalised subject is not necessarily supposed to adopt the scientific gaze. That is, as the prospect of using these 'real-time mood-tracking devices' demonstrates, nudging, steering, and controlling people can operate perfectly well without a knowing subject. The psychologists wanted us to know and to share their theories and models, as did neuroscientists. Big Data, in contrast, does not bother whether we know or not: we do not need to be educated in theories in order to be auto-guided and auto-govern ourselves, the algorithms can take over this task. It suffices to prescript our avatars and preconfigure our digital environments with the help of (neuro)psychological models.

Does this not mean that with the digitalisation of (inter)subjectivity any self-forgetfulness is definitively ruled out? Pfaller believed that interpassivity allowed for an anti-ideological space, in which the duty of becoming a subject was suspended, but with digitalisation this promise should be buried for good. If (neuro)psychologisation 1.0 called into being an interpassive psychologised subject (letting the redoubled *homo [neuro]psychologicus* to do the being on our behalf), then one could argue that this already constituted an attack on the older (and perhaps more potentially emancipatory) forms of interpassivity itself. Think in this respect of Slavoj Žižek's example of the hired mourners in certain societies, who are invited to do the mourning and grieving at funerals: they allow the relatives of the deceased to be at ease and to not feel guilty if they do not feel particularly emotional, which, in turn, leaves them to deal with more mundane matters such as the dividing of the heritage (Žižek, 2006, p. 26). Are these not the kinds of interpassive outsourcing of emotions which were jeopardised in the era of psychologisation? That is, in psychologised times, we are specifically called upon to express our feelings, we are not allowed to deny them interpassively, but, rather, are urged to let them flow and deal with them (in the appropriate way of course). One could compare this duty to coincide with one's (alleged) Self to the reformationist religious movements mentioned by Pfaller, which denounce the supposedly empty rituals of traditional religious practices (Pfaller, 2017, p. 63). In so doing, reformationists can be said to oppose the interpassive modus of believing (the outsourcing of believing via, for example, monotonous praying or other rituals, actions or artefacts) and instead urge the believer to do the believing for themselves. Similarly, is the psychological interpellation not interpellating us in the first instance to be the bearer of our emotions, rather than deny them or outsource them? Of course, the paradox here is that this only leads to a secondary interpassivity, where the emotions are eventually located with the homo neuropsychologicus we are said to be.

However, one could argue that this primary call to vouch for our psychological states is still readily traceable in social media platforms such as Facebook, which implore us to express our emotions and to share them with our friends. But does this not mean that nothing much has changed then after all? That is to say, in the same way, that Pfaller argues that reforms in religion do not succeed in dispelling interpassivity, but, rather, only render the interpassive dimension of religion ever more invisible (Pfaller, 2017, p. 63), must one conclude then that in the digitalised forms of psychological interpellations, the logic of interpassivity also ultimately remains in operation? Consider the fact that for a lot of people Facebook is something that they open once a day (as if it were a ritual) in order to disperse some likes, share a post or two, report this or that, and then log-off and return to the business of the day. Therefore, no subject is involved: one simply lets their avatar lead its little life along its pre-configured paths. As a result of this, am I not compelled to add some nuance to my previous strong statements, by recognising that digitalisation does not engender a structural shift as it still allows for a minimal non-engaged, non-subjectivised subject (if one will allow me to put it this way)?

However, perhaps this is simply unwarranted optimism, as one can observe that hidden and even secret codes and algorithms that bypass any interpellation have a hitherto unseen capacity to pre-structure our environment and lifeworld (pre-psychologising our avatars and social interactions). Here, alongside the already suggested capability to draw our presence in so-called 'real-life' into its reach (making us fully traceable in time and space), digitalisation turns out to even be capable, as I also claimed in Chapter 6, of pulling our very *absences* into its economy. For, if from Pfaller's perspective, interpassivity entailed little pockets of non-subjectivation and allowed for a minimal leeway, then digitalisation appears to be able, for the first time, to truly control and exploit this very aspect of *not being there*. So, perhaps, instead of merely arguing that in interpassivity 2.0 one cannot anymore disappear or leave the scene, it would be more concise to contend that it is precisely this very non-presence which is fed back into the system itself. Simply put, if the interpassivity of the religious ritual made it possible for the religious subject to go away (Pfaller, 2017, p. 62), and the interpassivity within classic (neuro) psychologisation minimalised this self-forgetfulness and isolated it in its margins to control it, then the digitalised subject's going away is finally contained within the digital sphere itself. Ultimately, not being on Facebook necessitates that one has a Facebook account. This might allow us to understand the true workings of digital capitalism.

The true commodity of digital capitalism

To approach this, let us begin with the changed policies of Facebook that were introduced in 2018. This is what Mark Zuckerberg announced:

> The research shows that when we use social media to connect with people we care about, it can be good for our well-being. We can feel more connected and less lonely, and that correlates with long term measures of happiness and health. On the other hand, passively reading articles or watching videos—even if they're entertaining or informative—may not be as good.
> (Zuckerberg, 2018)

Zuckerberg seemingly wants to activate us. Mere passive enjoyment or intake of knowledge? Not good! We must engage with others, apparently for our own psychological well-being. However, once again, we should look beyond this psychologising and objectifying philanthropist move and discern how Zuckerberg is attempting to secure his business model. In the first place, is his attack on passivity not an attack on interpassivity? What Zuckerberg wants to counteract is subjects receding and taking a leave of absence: letting your account and your algorithms provide you with news, movies, and videos and enjoy all of it in your place. This is not good for Zuckerberg, for the simple reason that merely interpassive behaviour which allows the subject to disappear does not provide

Facebook with useful data to be commodified. Hence, to deal with this, Zuckerberg, in all his sovereignty, makes it clear that:

> Based on this, we're making a major change to how we build Facebook. I'm changing the goal I give our product teams from focusing on helping you find relevant content to helping you have more meaningful social interactions.
>
> (Zuckerberg, 2018)

Hence, the business model of Facebook is not about delivering content to be consumed interpassively, but about inciting you by way of your Facebook avatar to produce 'more meaningful social interactions'. However, does this not show that, concerning the digitalisation of subjectivity, there is still a minimal interpellation involved? Hence, are we once again back where we started this chapter, that is, having to concede that digitalisation might not constitute a big new epistemic shift after all? In the example of Facebook, Mark Zuckerberg needs to invite you back to Facebook, which suggests that your interpassive retreat and lack of 'meaningful social interactions' are concerning enough to require repeated interventions by Facebook to get us back to their platform. One could argue that this ultimately means that digitality as such does allow for little absences, little moments of non-subjectivity, but that social media corporations subsequently neutralise and incorporate it back into their economy.

But perhaps we are missing something crucial here: are we not too readily assuming that it is 'meaningful social interactions' that are datafied and commodified by social media businesses? For, if it is indeed the case, as I have argued, that social media and other platforms are a priori stuffed with socio-psychological models, then, for sure, the mere reproduction of that psychology by users cannot truly produce something new and engender surplus-value. Hence, the issue of leading the vanishing and wandering subject back to the platform in order to produce psycho-social data is perhaps not the main issue at stake. If so, what then is the business model of the digital economy when it comes to the commodification of subjectivity? Perhaps, Pfaller's elaboration on a redoubled pleasure in interpassivity might help us to see things from yet another perspective:

> The mischievous pleasure, which appears in some cases of interpassivity, such as that described by Žižek, seems to rest on the dual character of this withdrawal: having escaped both enjoying and the illusion of enjoyment, and having delegated both to someone else, seems to be enormous fun. First, one withdraws from the enjoyment, then from the illusion of it—and apparently that produces new, even greater enjoyment.
>
> (Pfaller, 2014, p. 18)

Thus, on social media and similar platforms, I myself do not have to perform the required standard socio-psychological role: my avatar does all the prescribed enjoying of life and the enjoying of social interactions. It is this that produces extra pleasure: the surplus enjoyment realised is the pleasure of eventually being nobody. Is it not precisely this fun, the fun of having left the building, that digital capitalism attempts to cash-in on, with Facebook being the prime example of this? Digital capitalism does not feed upon our outsourced 'fake subjectivities'; it does not feed on the pre-coded and the preconfigured psychology which can be endlessly digitally reproduced, rather, it is the surplus enjoyment of our interpassive outsourcing that digital exploitation ultimately extracts from us.

To illustrate is let me cite here the transcript of a famous PlayStation TV Commercial: 'Double Life' (1999):

> For years, I've lived a double life. In the day, I do my job—I ride the bus, roll up my sleeves with the hoi-polloi…but at night, I live a life of exhilaration…of missed heartbeats and adrenalin…and, if the truth be known…a life of dubious virtue.…I won't deny I've been engaged in violence, even indulged in it.…I've maimed and killed adversaries, and not merely in self-defense.…I've exhibited disregard for life…limb…and property…and savored every moment.…You may not think it, to look of me…but I have commanded armies…and conquered worlds.…And though, in achieving these things…I've set morality aside…I have no regrets.…For though I've led a double life, at least I can say…I have lived.[13]

Here, we are called upon to fake and to feign (to have a double life) because we joyously know what the human being really wants, desires or craves.[14] Hence, the above PlayStation commercial does not testify to the exploitation of your true psychological, neuro-biological make-up (e.g. your innate and evolutionary determined thirst for murder and transgression), but, rather, *it cashes-in on the self-evident nature of your theoretical beliefs about what it is to be human*. So, what I have referred to in this book as the classic academic interpellation, in which the subject is called upon to identify with the expert position to look at the *homo neuropsychologicus* they are said to be, is precisely what is put to work in digitality. That is, the identification with the academic gaze (the identification with the non-subjective objective point of view) is in a second movement fed into the system itself. The enjoyment exploited by PlayStation, and in digitality as such, is not primitive, transgressive enjoyment, but, rather, the 'even greater enjoyment' that emerges when human beings take a step back and interpassively engage in its little gestures of disappearance. Albeit, disappearing in the digital era is the very thing that takes place within the system itself. However, here the question becomes, if that which used to remain outside of the system and drive it is now fully incorporated within the system, then will this not ultimately lead to the system grinding to a halt? That is to say if this 'greater enjoyment' can be said to be the true commodity of digital capitalism, then is the final and fatal move of capitalism not that, by attempting to incorporate it into the system, it loses the necessary distant and outside position?

Conclusions: *objet a* will not be digitalized

Ray Kurzweil, an American author, computer scientist, inventor, and futurist (according to Wikipedia), argued that it will soon be possible to upload the brain to a supercomputer (Kurzweil, 2000, 2005). As I discussed in Chapter 3, it is, of course, clear that if one were, in fact, able to successfully upload a person or a subject, then this uploaded entity would be doomed from the outset. By virtue of being connected to the internet, such a person or subject would become megalomaniacal and absorb all available knowledge: it would expand in uncontrollable ways, infinitely metamorphosise, become all the things in the world, if not, for that matter, become the world itself, and, as such, dissolve into nothingness. One way to understand this is through recourse to the theory of interpassivity: in the same way that during religious rituals the religious subject can go away, here, once the uploading/outsourcing is done, the initiator would be free to leave the scene (as this is perhaps what we are still capable of doing for the time being) upon which the uploaded personality would soon wither away into informational entropy.[15] Or, phrased otherwise, if left to its own devices (that is, with its standard neuropsychological make-up) our avatar would ultimately become a lifeless doll upon no longer being fed by our attention from our seat in the dark, that is, no longer fed by our minimal 'greater enjoyment'. And, as aforesaid, it is precisely this mode of enjoyment that the digital economy expropriates from us by drawing it into its system. This scheme might make some remember the Tamagotchi figure, the digital pet that lived in an egg-like handheld device, which was all the rage in the 1990s and early 2000s: the user had to feed and care for the creature at regular time intervals (via three buttons the virtual pet could be fed, bathed, disciplined, or amused), which if not successfully performed would lead to the pet succumbing to its digital death. Does the same not hold for us having to attend to our social media avatar(s) on a regular basis? We have to post an update on our Facebook page, upload a publication to Academia.edu, update our LinkedIn, not only to assure the survival of our avatar (because not posting on Facebook makes you less and less visible) but also increasingly to prevent ourselves from suffering a social death in so-called real life. However, the Tamagotchi era where devices were not connected to the internet are definitively over: today, whether we barely or never fed our avatar, and what we were doing in the meantime, would all be carried out by the digital system itself, which means that it would all be trackable and traceable.

From here, it is expedient to connect Kurzweil's funeral fantasy to another well-known thought experiment from *The Matrix* movies. The basic story of this film is that machines and technology went rogue, turned the tables and began to drain electricity and energy from human beings. Humans are enslaved in embryonic water-filled cradles, while, simultaneously, being connected to a supercomputer which generates a virtual reality, known as the Matrix, that serves to keep humans alive so that energy can be harvested from them. This is how one of the machines recounts the history of the Matrix:

> Did you know that the first Matrix was designed to be a perfect human world where none suffered, where everyone would be happy? It was a disaster. No one would accept the program. Entire crops were lost. Some believed that we lacked the programming language to describe your "perfect world". But I believe that, as a species human beings define their reality through misery and suffering. So the perfect world was a dream that your primitive cerebrum kept trying to wake up from.
>
> *(Agent Smith to Morpheus)*[16]

Would it not be fair to say that given that the first Matrix established a fully scripted world that was, as I would argue, directly informed by the mainstream (socio)psychological theories of the good life, that an entropic collapse was always inevitable? Along these lines, one could argue that it was in the first instance *the avatars* that withered away—in the same way, that Kurzweil's uploaded personalities would come to a halt—as the virtual world cannot but come to a standstill as a result of the endless circular repetition and infertile reproduction of the established (socio)psychological codes and algorithms. Hence, what becomes clear in both The Matrix and Kurzweil's fantasy—as well as in the latest move of Mark Zuckerberg described earlier in this chapter—is that digitality must involve a minimal form of interpassivity, and as aforesaid, a minimal form of interpellation that establishes a zero-level of subjectivity qua something external to it. Only then can a surplus enjoyment be created that secures the further digital flow and which can also be harvested. This is why the Matrix requires its renegades, its awakeners, its Morpheus, its Neo, its Oracle; those who allegedly escape can ultimately be said to constitute the backbone of the second Matrix and make it function. The fact that when avatars die in the Matrix, they also die in reality (in comparison to us dying a social death when we fail to attend to our Facebook-avatar or our Tamagotchi) testifies to the fact that the renegades are fully part of the virtuality. Making the exterior present in the interior—for which Lacan coined the neologism 'extimacy' (Lacan, 2007)—is what stalls informational entropy.

Here, we must ask the final critical question: is digitality capable of fully drawing interpassivity into its jurisdiction? For this appears to be the logic of advancing digitalisation: to incorporate that which lies outside of it fully into its realm. Hence, the question becomes what will happen when this productive outside of the digital becomes digitalised itself? This ultimately returns us to the question that I raised at the beginning of this chapter: can the mainstream cardboard psychologies that currently inform the digital be traded for more sophisticated models, such as Pfaller's model of interpassivity, so that the latter would form the basis of digital technologies? That is to say, would it be possible to algorithmically stage and code the very interpassive and subjectless subject itself by digitalising its 'little gestures of disappearance', its 'self-forgetfulness?' This, I claim, is exactly the same question that Pfaller poses at a specific point:

> Can my representing agent also let him or herself be represented by someone (or something) else? And for whom does that new agent then experience the pleasure—for the other agent or for me?
>
> *(Pfaller, 2017, p. 33)*

This is where Pfaller is pushed into questioning the limits of the logic of interpassivity: is interpassive delegation possible *ad infinitum*? Can it be redoubled endlessly within itself? And, from here, could this *perpetuum mobile* be held in check, contained symbolically, or, in terms more appropriate for our discussion, be digitalised and, as such, commodified? Would a second Matrix based on this model rather than the mainstream psychological model work in a sustainable way? Of course, this is the question which has haunted the whole book: can psychoanalytic conceptualisations of subjectivity and sociality, such as that found in Pfaller's work, be digitalised?

Clearly, as I have noted throughout the book, psychoanalysis is not a psychology. Lacan, as is well-known, refrained from a psychological approach to subjectivity, by opting not to define the subject as such, but, rather, to define the contours of the subject. As noted in the previous chapter, Lacan's reasoning is as follows: "the signifier is that what represents the subject for another signifier" (Lacan, 2007, p. 713) (Lacan also expressed this as a matheme: S1—$, —S2). The subject is thus nothing but a position: divided between two signifiers, it is itself nothing but a zero-level of subjectivity. Let me once again contrast this to the contention of the software developer, Dave Winer: "Connect persons to data objects to persons. That's the social today" (Cited in: Lovink, 2012). In Winer's *person-code-person* series, the person is no longer split; rather, they are pinned down, they are datafied. Or, as Alexander Galloway put it vis-à-vis cybernetics: "cybernetics refashions the world as a system and refashions the subject as an agent" (Galloway, 2014, p. 113). Hence, the 'interpellation' (if one can still refer to it as such) underpinning Winer's 'connection' does not envision giving rise to a subject, but, rather, incites agents to produce data. Although this datafication appears to provide the basis for the commodification of subjectivity, is this not, as argued previously, the situation in which the trafficking and exchanging of data will ultimately come to a halt, due to the fact that it fails to engage the zero-level of subjectivity which is arguably the driving force of surplus-subjectivity? In other words, the data that one produces in response to the digital interpellation cannot but repeat the preconfigured data deriving from the models of the human being that were coded into the system. This repetition of sterile data, arguably, cannot but bring the entire system to a screeching halt. Therefore, might one strategy for ensuring that the data bubble does not burst under its own weight be to remove Winer's formula and replace it with Lacan's formula, for the latter appears to be a ready-made algorithm?

Before answering this question in greater detail, one could enthusiastically proclaim that psychoanalysis may be expedient to help us shift from 'fully automated luxury capitalism' to 'fully automated luxury communism'. Should we thus remove the bad psychologies and psychologists out of the programming room and bring in psychoanalysts instead? Of course, this is where the trouble would immediately begin. Consider, once again, Geert Lovink (see Chapter 4) who, going way further than many reformist critiques of the digital, argued for the nationalisation of Facebook (Lovink, 2012). However, does such a plea not beg the question of how this public, non-commercial social media would be designed? Would it retain emoticons? Would it still prompt users to express their feelings? Would it ask us to 'like' things still? Would it remind us to post something, or remind us of interesting stories we missed when we were offline for a while? Moreover, what algorithms would be used to put news or posts in our feed? In light of these questions, how would the designers proceed after being briefed by the psychoanalyst about their form of non-psychology? For, ultimately, if, as already noted in Chapter 4, Pfaller argues that theory cannot tell art what to think—it can only tell art what it does not need to think (Pfaller, 2017, p. 92)—then, similarly, psychoanalysis also cannot prescribe how avatars and environments should be designed. If psychoanalysis is basically a critique of psychology (see Lacan's awry definition of subjectivity above), it cannot cater to a new, alternative psychology. Consequently, if, for example, one of the key problems with the neurosciences is, as I argued elsewhere, that they cannot but rely on psychology (which they try to trace in the brain), psychoanalysis cannot serve as the basis for an alternative psychology to be used: psychoanalysis can only tell neuroscience *what it does not need to think*. So, with respect to designing digitality, once again, psychoanalysis cannot tell us how to design the digital subject or its lifeworld: it can only deliver a critique; it can only tell us *what does not need to be thought*; it can only lay bare the problematic psychological models that underpin the design of digital technologies.

Would one potential option be to try to design digital technologies and digitalities with virtual avatars and virtual environments *without* recourse to psychology or any other psycho-social model? Here, the idea would be to create empty and neutral placeholders for both subjects and sociality, which would, for example, ensure liberty, equality, and fraternity. Of course, there one would rapidly encounter common and mainstream ideological images of human beings and their attendant rights, and as is well-known, this is not uncontested territory. Hence, the exclamation 'another world is possible' today appears to come up against the riddle of 'is another digitality possible?', one that would be able to account for the lessons of psychoanalysis and other critical theories, namely that 'society does not exist' and that 'subjectivity does not exist'. At the very least, this entails that a neutral position from where one could design mere empty digital placeholders for (inter)subjectivity is not possible, and thus a partisan and political stance cannot be avoided.

From the perspective of psychoanalysis, then, the bottom-line is that 'subjectivity will not be digitalised'. However—now we are finally arriving at the true upshot of this chapter and of the book as a whole—it is here that we need to confront in full Freud's, and certainly Lacan's, quasi-algorithmic accounts of the subject, which may call into question my claim about the non-digitisability of subjectivity. For example, does not Lacan's conceptualisation of fantasy provide hope to software developers? To condense and simplify Lacan's theorization of fantasy somewhat: the fundamental fantasy is that which structures one's desire, which, in turn, underpins how a subject relates to itself, others and the world. Lacan's matheme of the fantasy situates the split subject vis-à-vis the *objet a* as both the cause and object of desire. Lacan's notation here of '$ ◊ a' is, of course, connected to the aforementioned notation of subjectivity (S1—$—S2), albeit it brings in the *objet a* as that which cannot be said or subjectivised, but, in so doing, ultimately drives the speaking and desiring subject:

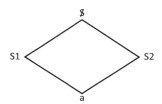

Given that Lacan follows Freud in understanding fantasy as a little scenario that underpins one's symptomatology, desire and, hence, one's subjectivity (according to Lacan the basic fantasy comes as a rule in the form of a little sentence, for example, Freud's 'a child has been beaten' (Freud, [1919]1955)), it is hard not to understand it as an algorithm (Lacan himself uses the word algorithm, e.g. Lacan, 2007, p. 487). However, the crucial element in the matheme is *objet a*, which, I would argue, in its capacity as the cause and object of desire, is ultimately a non-assimilable object: it is not merely an unknown x that could be fed into the computation. That is to say, the *objet a* stands for the very failure, the remainder of the subjectivation process, that which Freud tried to capture via the Oedipal myth: forged out of the subjectivation history of a particular subject, it becomes the driving force behind desire. Consequently, it is a singular object which sustains desire as desire, that is, that which sustains desire as being unsatisfied as the *objet a* can never be attained. Hence, although Lacan formalised it and assigned it 'the status of an algebraic sign' (cited in: Evans, 1996, p. 128), it is not merely a formal factor, but is instead defined as the remnant left behind by the introduction of the Symbolic into the Real. Given that is situated on the side of the Real, one could attribute the *objet a* certain degree of materiality, albeit a peculiarly decentred materiality (De Vos, 2014), which, arguably, is that which would resist digitalisation. That is to say, *objet a* itself has no substantial existence, but, rather, signals a void, albeit a void that points towards an excess, a residual too-muchness. Lacan, drawing on Marx's conception of surplus-value, considers the *objet a* to be a surplus, both a surplus of meaning and a surplus of enjoyment, which, as such, has no use-value, but persists merely for the sake of enjoyment.[17] Therefore, one could argue that, in its capacity as the object and cause of desire, it remains on the side of the analogue, albeit a peculiarly decentred analogue, which resists becoming digitalised or virtualised.[18]

In conclusion: *objet a* will not be digitalised. However, as *objet a* cannot be fed back into the system, one could argue that digitality is thus only pretending to be able to incorporate all things human. This is the contemporary digital dream, and we know all too well how powerful illusions are when they are made virtually real. In his fascinating study of E.T.A. Hoffmann's short story 'The Sandman', Freud writes that fiction presents "more opportunities for creating uncanny feelings than are possible in real life" (Freud, 1919/2010, p. 374). Today, one could posit that our everyday habitat, digital, and virtual 'real-life' offers manifold opportunities for the uncanny. However, to do so would to risk overlooking a crucial difference: while with fiction we remain outside the uncanny, in virtual real-life we are immersed in it, to the point at which it potentially loses its impact.[19] In other words, rather than reading how Hoffmann's protagonist Nathaniel is fascinated by the fixed eyes of the automaton called Olympia who he watches through binoculars, we could instead, hypothetically, look at the unnerving and unvarying gaze of our fellow human beings, with their entire faces lit up as their eyes are glued to the screen (whether it is a real screen or a virtual one, to which one is connected cortically). Hypothetically speaking, for once we ourselves are inside the virtual, our eyes also become fixed, so that we, without binoculars, also have a clear view of the simulacra, the stand-ins for the *objet a*, the latter of which ultimately halt our desire and prepare us for a not entirely endless repetition, because once we run out of steam, the whole system itself will come to a standstill. The partisan task of critique today is to, firstly, state that digitality should not need to think that it can digitalise the *objet a*, and secondly, to prove that to imagine an end to capitalism, one must engage in the admittedly not so easy endeavour of thinking the end of the world.[20]

Notes

1 Bill Gates wants to assure us that he also considers the ethical aspects of this: "Needless to say, there will be lots of controversy and negotiation about who can get access to your profile information. It will be crucial that you have such access" (Gates, 1996, p. 191).
2 By the way, two paragraphs later, Bill Gates contends that he himself would not mind being profiled, so that he could receive news about, among other things, biotechnology and Steven Pinker (Gates, 1996, p. 191), which is perhaps indicative of the kinds of psychological theories and models that form the background of Microsoft.
3 https://www.theguardian.com/books/2015/jul/17/postcapitalism-end-of-capitalism-begun.
4 Think of the Freudian idea that pleasure in thinking is related to infantile sexuality, and, more specifically, to the sexual enigmas the child is confronted with (what is the

sexual difference between male and female, where do children come from, and so on), which, in turn, incites the infant to engage in thinking and the formulation of theories. See: (Freud, 1905).
5 See also Chapter 3.
6 http://www.chadd.org/Understanding-ADHD/For-Parents-Caregivers/Teens/ADHD-Information-for-Teens.aspx.
7 People who watch an illusionist, for example, do not consider his acts to be something supernatural or magic, neither do they doubt whether magic is involved or not. Rather, they know very well that there is some kind of trick involved, but they marvel at the fact that the act might be seen, by an imagined other, as truly being magic.
8 Regarding the shift in the management of presence within digital times, see also Chapter 6.
9 Remember in this respect George Soros' attack against Facebook and Google, already mentioned in Chapter 4, who he referred to as a 'menace to society' (Soros, 2018). This is the strange paradox of the super-rich, such as Elon Musk (see Chapter 1), who, on the one hand, are elevated above the conundrums of daily human existence, while, on the other hand, they see themselves as the saviours of our common humanness.
10 Of course, here I am revisiting various themes already touched upon earlier in this book: especially in Chapters 4 and 5.
11 See, for example: https://www.twinkl.co.uk/resource/esl-how-do-you-feel-today-emotions-chart-t-s-1056.
12 See, for example, FaceX advertising itself as "the introduction of face verification and face ID based clock-in." https://facex.io/use-case-attendance.html.
13 https://www.youtube.com/watch?v=6Bqq38WZctA; transcript on: http://www.adweek.com/creativity/has-any-commercial-had-a-better-cast-of-characters-than-this-legendary-playstation-ad/
14 Here, one can discern the logic of perversion: the pervert is someone who claims to possess a knowledge on *jouissance*, and who confronts the other with this in order to incite the latter's division.
15 Of course, here I understand entropy in opposition to Norbert Wiener's well-known position: for Wiener, the increase of information is stalling entropy. See: (Wiener, 1989[1950]) The fate I ascribe to Kurzweil's uploaded personalities points to the possibility of an entropy that is related to an increase in information itself. See Chapter 3 for an extended discussion of this point.
16 https://www.quotes.net/mquote/60289.
17 Lacan, 1969–1970.
18 See also Chapter 3 for a discussion of the status of the analogue.
19 Mladen Dolar argues that the uncanny is co-originary with modernity. Whereas before it was largely covered by the sacred and the untouchable, in modernity it became unbound and subsequently captured by popular culture: the place for the shadow sides of scientific rationality and Kantian transcendental subjectivity (Dolar, 1991). Entering the digital age, where scientific rationality and transcendental subjectivity are traded for, consecutively, Big Data science and virtual identities that are shaped and designed digitally, the uncanny, while expected to blossom in this supposedly fantastic realm of digital virtuality, is, in fact, destined to wither away.
20 The reference here, of course, is to Fredric Jameson's famous quote: "it has become easier to imagine the end of the world than the end of capitalism" (Jameson, 1994, p. xii).

References

Althusser, L. (1971). Ideology and ideological state apparatuses (notes towards an investigation) (B. Brewster, Trans.). In *Lenin and Philosophy and Other Essays* (pp. 127–186). London: New Left Books.

Bastani, A. (2019). *Fully automated luxury communism: A manifesto* London: Verso Books.
Carr, N. (2010). *The shallows: How the internet is changing the way we think, read and remember.* New York: Norton.
Cassauwers, T. (2019). Is tech leading us to communism. *Ozy.* Retrieved from https://www.ozy.com/fast-forward/is-tech-leading-us-to-communism/96106/
Churchland, P. S. (2013). The benefits of realising you're just a brain (interview by Graham Lawton). *New Scientist.* Retrieved from http://www.newscientist.com/article/mg22029450.200-the-benefits-of-realising-youre-just-a-brain.html
De Vos, J. (2012). *Psychologisation in times of globalisation.* London: Routledge.
De Vos, J. (2014). Which materialism? Questioning the matrix of psychology, neurology, psychoanalysis and ideology critique. *Theory & Psychology, 24*(1), 76–93.
De Vos, J. (2016). *The metamorphoses of the brain. Neurologization and its discontents.* New York: Palgrave Macmillan.
Dolar, M. (1991). "I Shall Be with You on Your Wedding-Night": Lacan and the Uncanny. *October, 58,* 5–23.
Evans, D. (1996). *An introductory dictionary of Lacanian psychoanalysis.* London/New York: Routledge.
Freud, S. (1905). Three essays on the theory of sexuality. SE, 7: 123–243. In J. Strachey (Ed.), *The standard edition of the complete psychological works of Sigmund Freud: Vol. VII* (pp. 123–243). London: Hogarth Press.
Freud, S. ([1914]1957). On narcissism: An introduction (S. I., Trans.). In J. Strachey (Ed.), *The standard edition of the complete psychological works of Sigmund Freud: Vol. XIV* (pp. 73–102). London: Hogarth Press.
Freud, S. ([1919]1955). A child is being beaten. A contribution to the study of the origin of sexual perversions. In J. Strachey (Ed.), *The standard edition of the complete psychological works of Sigmund Freud: Vol. XVII* (pp. 175–204). London: Hogarth Press.
Galloway, A. R. (2014). The cybernetic hypothesis. *Differences, 25*(1), 107–131.
Gates, B. (1996). *The road ahead.* London: Penguin.
Gillespie, T. (2014). The relevance of algorithms. In T. Gillespie, P. J. Boczkowski, & K. A. Foot (Eds.), *Media technologies: Essays on communication, materiality, and society* (pp. 167–194). London: MIT.
Jameson, F. (1994). *The seeds of time.* New York: Columbia University Press.
Kurzweil, R. (2000). Live forever—uploading the human brain... closer than you think. *Psychology Today.* Retrieved from http://www.psychologytoday.com/articles/200001/live-forever
Kurzweil, R. (2005). *The singularity is near: When humans transcend biology.* New York: Viking.
Kuss, D. J., & Griffiths, M. D. (2011). Online social networking and addiction—a review of the psychological literature. *International Journal of Environmental Research and Public Health, 8*(9), 3528–3552.
Lacan, J. (1991). *Le séminaire, Livre XVII: L'envers de la psychanalyse 1969–1970.* Paris: Seuil.
Lacan, J. (1992). *Seminar VII, the ethics of psychoanalysis 1959–1960* (D. Porter, Trans.). London: Routledge.
Lacan, J. (2007). *Ecrits: The first complete edition in English* (B. Fink, Trans.). New York: Norton.
Lovink, G. (2012). What is the social in social media? *e-flux journal, 40,* 1–12. Retrieved from https://www.e-flux.com/journal/40/60272/what-is-the-social-in-social-media/
Pfaller, R. (2014). *On the pleasure principle in culture. Illusions without owners.* London: Verso.
Pfaller, R. (2017). *Interpassivity: The aesthetics of delegated enjoyment.* Edinburgh: Edinburgh University Press.

Schröter, J. (2012). The internet and "frictionless capitalism". *tripleC: Communication, Capitalism & Critique, 10*(2), 302–312.
Soros, G. (2018). *Remarks delivered at the World Economic Forum.* Retrieved from https://www.georgesoros.com/2018/01/25/remarks-delivered-at-the-world-economic-forum/
Steers, M.-L. N., Wickham, R. E., & Acitelli, L. K. (2014). Seeing everyone else's highlight reels: How Facebook usage is linked to depressive symptoms. *Journal of Social and Clinical Psychology, 33*(8), 701–731.
Stiegler, B. (2010). *Taking care of youth and the generations.* Stanford, CA: Stanford University Press.
Ulanoff, L. (2017). Sean Parker made billions off of Facebook. Today he basically called it evil. *Mashable.* Retrieved from https://mashable.com/2017/11/09/sean-parker-slams-facebook/#gVnUWCGJ1mqc
Wiener, N. ([1950]1989). *The human use of human beings: Cybernetics and society.* London: Free Association Books.
Williamson, B. (2017). Psychological surveillance and psycho-informatics in the classroom. *Code Acts in Education.* Retrieved from https://codeactsineducation.wordpress.com/2017/01/17/psycho-surveillance-classroom/
Žižek, S. (1989). *The sublime object of ideology.* London: Verso.
Žižek, S. (2006). *How to read Lacan.* New York: W.W. Norton.
Zuckerberg, M. (2018). *One of our big focus areas for 2018.* Retrieved from https://www.facebook.com/zuck/posts/10104413015393571

INDEX

Note: page numbers followed by "n" denote endnotes.

Aboujaoude, E. 80
absence 42, 44, 137–40, 146, 150, 153, 156, 205–6; *see also* presence
Academia.edu 137, 195, 208
acting out 173
affect 14–15, 75–6, 80, 84, 97, 101n1, 146
agalma 7, 70, 83, 202
Agamben, G. 45
aggression 43, 45–6, 70, 90, 117, 162
Aichorn, A. 183n3
algorithm 6, 15, 38, 99–100, 129, 132, 147, 153; and education 143, 148–50, 156, 175, 177; and games 167; informed by psychology 65, 73, 81–2, 93, 133n18, 171, 201–5, 209; and interpassivity 200, 209; and parenting 119, 145–7; and politics 102n7; shaping (inter)subjectivity 4–5, 13, 18, 29, 46, 116–18, 130; and social media 205, 211; Turing machine 167; use(lessness) of psychoanalysis 14, 19, 65, 91, 97–8, 193, 210–12
algorithmisation 145
alienation 4, 10–11, 13
Althusser, L. 19n2, 143, 197–9
analogue 66–70, 75, 152, 213
Anderson, C. 117
anthropomorphisation 124
Arendt, H. 131, 165
Ariès, P. 120
artificial intelligence (AI) 5, 44–5, 67, 75, 91–2, 109, 130, 145; and affect 75; and education 109–11, 178; Elon Musk's fear of 7–9, 11–12, 17–18; Facebook AI experiment 81, 91–5, 97–9; Google 43; informed by psychology 52, 76, 81, 160; Marvin Minsky 54–7, 66–7; and politics 100; and neuro-terminology 124; Alan Turing 25, 29–32, 35–6, 38–40, 42; shaping (inter)subjectivity 129; Slavoj Žižek 140; use(lessness) of psychoanalysis 91, 167
Asimo, I. 34
Assassin's Creed 178
attachment theory 131–2
attention 152–3, 208; Bernard Stiegler 147, 159, 181; and education 115, 139, 147–50; and parenting 115
Attention Deficit and Hyperactivity Disorder (ADHD) 43, 95, 197
automaticity 26, 43, 90
avatar 11, 15, 145; informed by psychology 133n18, 139, 160, 202–3, 205–6, 209; and interpassivity 200–1, 204, 206, 208; and presence 137; shaping (inter)subjectivity 65, 89, 91, 98, 156; use(lessness) of psychoanalysis 211

BabyBrains 143–6
Bannon, S. 82
Barker, T. H. 125
Bastani, A. 191–2
Bates, D. 26–8, 42–3, 49n7, 67

Bateson, G. 54, 66–71, 75, 123
Baudrillard, J. 149, 181
Bauer, O. 162
behaviourism 14, 93, 101, 111–12, 131, 132n4, 173
Bernfeld, S. 161, 183n3
Berry, D. M. 80
Bettelheim, B. 183n3
Big Data 117, 214n19; informed by psychology 80, 89; informing psychology 5, 31, 45, 82, 86–7, 89, 116; and the neurosciences 117; and nudging 118, 203; and surveillance 138, 153, 201; as a tyrannical figure 164, 169, 177, 179–80; use (lessness) of psychoanalysis 79; using it for a good cause 102n7
biopolitical 82, 131–2
biopolitics 96, 115, 118, 128, 132, 133n20
bot 29–30; and education 128–9, 139, 156; Facebook AI experiment 81, 91–101; and parenting 143, 145–6
Bown, A. 164–6, 168–9
brain-machine interface 14, 16
Brandt, L. 112
Brexit 82, 86
Burman, E. 39

Cambridge Analytica 54, 81–2, 84, 86–8, 102n6
capitalism 4, 12, 140; 'communicative' 36; digital 12, 64–6, 86, 89, 91, 162, 182, 191–3, 201–2, 205, 207; end of 192–3, 207, 213; frictionless 190–1; 'fully automated' 211
caput mortuum 42, 47
Carr, N. 80, 201
Cassauwers, T. 191
cat hype on the internet 109, 111, 189
Cepelewicz, J. 111
Charlie Hebdo 9
chatbot 49n6; racist 38
Churchland, P. S. 199–200
Circle, The 122
Circle Time 95, 196–7, 203
ClassDojo 142–3
Cober-Gentry, Leslie 128
cognitive behaviourism 46, 112
cognitive neuroscience 197
cognitive psychology 39–40, 46
commodification 10, 13, 64, 168, 182; of subjectivity 4, 18, 89, 120, 139, 202, 206, 210
commons 191
Connolly, W. E. 165

Cover, R. 80
Crew, B. 43
cybernetics: history 27, 42, 52, 54, 66–7, 71, 73; informed by (neuro)psychology 44, 81, 210; informed by psychoanalysis 58; Norbert Wiener 57, 60–1, 63–4, 77n10

Danaylov, N. 29
data mining 13, 45, 82–3, 117
data science 117, 128, 214n19
Davies, R. 129–30, 171
Davies, W. 129
De Beauvoir, S. 16
Dean, J. 30
deception: in Facebook AI experiment 100; Turing Test 25–6, 31, 33, 40–1; Norbert Wiener 62; within psychoanalytic theory 97–8
democracy 18, 130, 179–80
de-politicisation 18
Derrida, J. 15
Descartes, R. 102n10, 147, 151–3, 155
desire: accessible via digital means 5, 31, 37, 81–2, 179; shaped by digital means 30, 86, 98, 100, 128, 207; and interpassivity 200; for knowledge 85; psychoanalytic concept 5, 47–8, 93, 97–8, 212–13
desubjectivation 4, 42, 147, 156
Dewey, J. 170
Dickens, C. 166
Digital Brain Switch, The 125–6
digital culture 52, 54, 80, 173
digital death drive 6, 19, 183
digital learning platform 112, 129, 161–2, 171, 178, 181
discrete-state machine 40
Dolar, M. 214n19
Donnelly, L. 114
Dowd, M. 8
dreamwork 168, 182

Eggers, D. 122
Egginton, W. 151–2, 154–5, 175
Embrace Watch 146, 148, 150, 171
emotional intelligence 141
emoticons 13, 90, 211
empathy: a critique of 117; in digital spheres 9, 10, 81; in education 141–3, 164, 175, 177
end of subjectivity 4, 7, 60, 119, 203
end of the world 19, 57, 60, 62, 213
entropy: digital 140, 156; informational 208–9, 214n15; and Logos 183; Norbert Wiener 60–6, 71, 77n10

episteme 14, 96, 119
Evans, D. 29
EVOZ Smart Parenting device 127, 146

Facebook 5, 90, 122, 129, 153, 171, 205, 208–9, 211; AI experiment 81, 91–100; and Cambridge Analytica 82, 84–6; and digital capitalism 182, 205–7; 'hacking people's psychology' 80, 202; informed by psychology 81, 160; informing psychology 81, 201; and interpassivity 201–2, 204; psychological interpellation 13, 136–7, 150, 204
facial recognition 31, 203
Federn, P. 162
Fedorova, K. 122
feigning to feign 40, 44, 97
Flisfeder, M. 90
fMRI 45–6, 117
Foley, M. 33
Foucault, M. 96, 115, 203
French, S. 80
Freud, S. 7–8, 19, 43, 47, 49n4&12, 52, 55–8, 60, 63, 70, 76, 92, 97, 113, 159, 162, 184n7, 189, 193, 212–13, 214n4; *Group Psychology and the Analysis of the Ego* 20n5, 173, 184n8; *The Psychopathology of Everyday Life* 53; *Totem & Taboo* 172
Fuchs, C. 89, 122
Fully Automated Luxury Communism: A Manifesto 191

Galloway, A. R. 210
gaming 164–9, 173–5, 177, 179, 181, 183
Gates, B. 190–1, 195, 213n1&2
Gillespie, T. 201
Glikman, A. 61
Goertzel, B. 30
Gómez Camerena, C. 76n2
Google 5, 80–1, 124, 136, 150, 214n9; AI 43; informing psychology 201
Google Glass 155
Google Scholar 195
Griffiths, M. D. 201
Gunkel, D. 49n5

Habermas, J. 183n5
Halpern, O. 57–8, 76n4
Hansen, M. B. N. 80
Hardt, M. 120
Harré, R. 112
Hassabis, D. 8
Hayles, N. K. 59–60, 75, 159–60

Heim, M. 154
Heisenberg's Uncertainty Principle 61
Henry, P. J. 161–3
Hodges, A. 79
Hodgson, N. 145
Hoffmann, E.T.A. 192, 213
homo (neuro)psychologicus 42, 197–200, 203–4, 207
Horvat, S. 182
Human Brain Project 45–6, 117–19, 124
Husserl, E. 52–4

IBM 124
identification: in education 41; Freudian theory 20n5, 173; in gaming 173; and interpassivity 198–9; and interpellation 203; split subject and 174; with a (fatal) victim 9
ideology: capitalist 94, 97, 162; and cybernetics 76; and education 148; and gaming 166; and interpellation 199–200, 203; in tandem with psychology 76, 93, 99–101; and technology 191
imitation game 25–8, 30–2, 35, 38, 40–1, 46–7, 54, 80
immortality 7, 16–17, 19
infantilisation: in education 113, 163; in gaming 168, 178
information: and capitalism 64–5, 190–1; and education 113, 122–5, 156; Gregory Bateson 69; internet 8, 201; Norbert Wiener 57–9, 62, 77n10; and parenting 127; personalized 136
Instagram 153
interbellum 52, 114, 161–4, 169, 183–3
interface 13, 16, 122, 149–50, 155, 156, 175
internet 8, 29, 65, 149, 153, 179, 189, 208; and education 96, 155, 177; informed by psychology 6, 13, 85; informing psychology 5, 82; as a public sphere 121–2; and the screen 156
Internet of Things 5, 149, 161
interpassivity: and capitalism 206, 210; in digitality 201–2, 205, 208–9; emancipatory potential 200, 204–5; and (neuro)psychologisation 204–5; Robert Pfaller 194–6, 198–9
interpellation: Althusser 197–8; and digitalisation 118, 122, 125–7, 143, 147, 203, 205–6, 209–10; and education 114; and (neuro)psychologisation 115, 120, 198, 204, 207; Robert Pfaller 199; and the subject 4, 9

Jameson, F. 214n20
Jankélévitch, V. 25–6, 33
Johnson, B. 169, 178
Johnson, M. 144
jouissance 37, 70, 214n14
Joyce, J. 166–7

Kant, I. 166, 176, 196
Kevorkian, M. 37
Kittler, F. 58, 76n4
Klein, M. 172, 183n3
Koch, C. 117
Kogan, A. 87
Kosinski, M. 31, 82, 84–7, 102n6
Kurzweil, R. 16, 65, 208–9, 214n15
Kuss, D. J. 201

La Mettrie, J. O. 48n2–49
Lacan, J.: and the algorithm 19, 193, 210, 212–13; and cybernetics 58, 64; on death 7, 16; desire 93; feigning to feign 44–5, 97–8; I/it thinks 20n6, 147; interpassivity 202, 209; jouissance 37, 102n9; mirror stage 11, 184n9; non-psychology 8, 29, 210; *objet a* 77n17; the Real 84; subjectivity 10, 47, 54, 63–4, 73, 75, 127, 167–8, 193, 196–8, 211
Lafontaine, C. 60, 77n7&10
Lafrance, A. 91–2
language: Gregory Bateson 67, 69–70; Jacques Lacan 102n9; and sexuality 32; and subjectivity 28–9, 63, 167; and virtuality 14–15, 89–90, 99, 111
latency period 177–8
Leavitt, D. 37
Lewis, N. A. 88
Lim, K. 38
Lind, K. K. 123
LinkedIn 137, 208
Logos: and digitality 15–16, 42–3, 68, 70, 75; and the end of the world 62–3, 65–6, 182–3; and subjectivity 28, 75, 80, 111
Lorré, D. 172, 178
Lovink, G. 90, 122, 211

Mackenzie, A. 124
Marcuse, H. 183n5
Markoff, J. 132n2
Markram, H. 45, 117–18
Marx, K. 76, 97, 192, 213
mass psychology 88, 162, 170, 172, 177, 180, 182
Massumi, B. 80
materiality 4, 57, 75, 77n17, 212
The Matrix 208–10

Matsuda, K. 156
Matthews, P. M. 45, 117
May 68, 113, 198
Mayer, J. D. 141
McCoy, A. W. 88
McCulloch, W. S. 75–6, 101n1, 123–4, 127
medicalisation 115–16
Meeus, R. 178
Microsoft 136, 213n2
Miller, G. A. 133n8
Minsky, M. 29, 54–8, 66–7, 71, 75, 76n2, 123
mirror stage 11
Mitchell, W. J. T. 68
modernity 54, 115, 119, 141, 151–2, 180, 214n19
Moorehead-Slaughter, O. 87
Morss, J. R. 39
Musk, E. 6–9, 11–17, 19, 26, 89, 155, 214n9
MyAnalytics 136
myPersonality 82–4

Napster 191
Negri, A. 120
Netflix 146, 173
Neumann, J. von 61–2
Neuralink 8, 11, 13–18, 26, 155
neural network 93, 124
neuroeducation 116, 197
neurologisation 8, 85, 98, 142, 155, 164; and digitalisation 123–6, 128, 131–2, 141, 143, 145; and education 114–15, 120–2, 141; and interpellation 122, 148
neuropolitics 165
neuroscience: and digitalisation 117; and education 116; explaining digitalisation 80, 102n8, 159; informed by digitality 117; informing digitality 5; and interpassivity 199; and neurologisation 85, 115, 121, 142, 197; related to psychology and psychologisation 90, 120, 142, 211
Niemietz, K. 191–2
non-psychological 8, 55–8, 70, 75, 84, 98, 160, 182
non-psychology 42, 53, 55–6, 59, 84, 211
nudging 30, 96, 118–19, 128, 139, 183, 203

objet a 47, 49n13, 77n17, 208, 212–13
Oedipus 34, 49n4, 56, 76n2, 177
Orwell, G. 139–40, 179

Panksepp, J. 15
parenting app 131, 143; *see also* smart parenting

Parker, I. 132n4
Parker, S. 80, 202
Parrhasios 97–8
Pavlov, I. 97
Pavón Cuéllar, D. 132n3
performativity 33, 35, 49n3
Pessoa, F. 7–8, 25, 48n1
Pestalozzi, J.H. 170
Pfaller, R. 101, 133n16, 193–6, 192–202, 204–6, 209–11
Piaget, J. 39
Pierlejewski, M. 133n18
Pinker, S. 213n2
Pitts, W. 75, 101n1, 124, 127
PlayStation 207
post-Fordism 120
post-human 15, 42, 83, 189
Post-Traumatic Stress Disorder (PTSD) 43
presence 7, 11, 42, 47, 137–40, 147–56, 174, 203, 205, 214n8; *see also* absence
private sphere 119–22, 132, 138, 155; *see also* public sphere
profiling 54, 80, 85–6, 89, 136; *see also* psychological profile
propaganda 87–8, 137, 165
psychoanalysis 30, 39, 44, 49n4, 184n7; and algorithms 65; and the analogue 66, 69–70; aporias 14; and education 113–14, 161–4, 171–2; and gaming 173; informing digitality 5, 12–13, 18, 34, 52, 56–9, 71, 82, 97; McCulloch's critique 72–5; and politics 97, 211; psychologised 91; as a psy-critique 6–7, 12, 19, 41, 53–4, 211; and subjectivity 36, 77n17, 83–84, 93, 98, 167, 196, 210, 212; uselessness 13, 88, 98–101, 160, 182, 211
psychoanalytic pedagogy movement 161, 164, 169, 171–2, 182–3
psychological profile 10, 12, 82, 85–9, 167, 191, 195, 213n1; *see also* profiling
psychologisation: and biopolitics 132; and digitalisation 54, 63, 96, 98, 123–6, 128–9, 131, 143–6, 160, 203–5; of education 114–15, 120, 122, 141–2, 155, 164, 168; inextricable part of psychology 6–7, 53, 85, 95, 142; and interpassivity 196; and interpellation 122, 126, 142, 148, 163, 198–9; and neurologisation 121, 142; risk of 92; of torture 88
psychology: Gregory Bateson's use of 68, 70; cardboardesque 46, 95; choice of model 39, 65; critique of 6, 55; as a dangerous fantasy 81–3, 87–9; and education 115–17, 141, 143, 146, 170; essentialising 13, 165; explaining digitalisation 80–1, 201–2; Husserl's critique of 53–4; informed by digitality 5, 85–6, 160, 191; informing digitality 5, 18, 26–8, 34–5, 38–40, 42, 44, 56, 66, 75, 86, 90–1, 93, 95, 98, 100–1, 113, 131, 178, 206–7; and the machine 32; and (neuro)psychologisation 142; neuroscience 117, 129; Norbert Wiener's use of 59–60, 62; and psychoanalysis 7, 58, 88, 163, 210–11; and subjectivity 85, 147; too much for digitality 26, 48, 83–4
psy-critique 6, 17–18, 46, 52, 79, 101
psy-sciences 20, 45, 95, 116–18, 133n7&8, 146, 164–5; and education 96, 113, 115, 141, 170; explaining digitalisation 5, 80; and interpellation 196–200; and parenting 127; shaping digitality 46, 54, 59, 89, 123, 131, 138, 141, 144, 160, 201; structural problem of 28, 52–4, 87–8
public sphere 95, 119–22, 132, 155–6, 166–7, 169, 175; *see also* private sphere

Ramaekers, S. 145
Rand, A. 97
Real: Lacanian concept 84–5, 212
Red Vienna 161–3
reinforcement learning algorithms (RLA) 110–11
Rizzi, J. 114
robot: learning to recognize cats 110–11; learning to walk 110–11
Rogers, R. 82
Rose, N. 123, 145
Rousseau, J.-J. 170
Rouvroy, A. 83, 102n7
Ruder, D. B. 128

Saint-Jevin, A. 58
Salovey, P. 141
Saramago, J. 20n4, 113
Sartre, J.P. 152
school: history 113, 115, 119–20, 170, 180; Hans Zulliger 171–2, 177; under digitalisation 121–2, 130, 148–50, 155–6, 159, 175, 177–8, 181
Schröter, J. 192
Schugurensky, D. 170
search engine 81, 157
sex 76n2, 182; Turing Test 31, 33–5, 39, 41
sexuality: psychoanalysis 13, 70, 72, 82, 213n4; Turing Test 32–5, 37, 76n2
sharing economy 191
Shotter, J. 112
Silicon Valley 5, 8

Silver, M. 170
Simon, M. 110, 132n1
Simondon, G. 193
Skinner, B.F. 112
smart parenting 127, 130, 146
Snapchat 136, 138
Snyder, T. 29–30, 33–4
social media 9, 10–1, 79, 116, 122, 171, 208, 211; and the commodification of subjectivity 13, 54, 82, 84–6, 100, 206; and education 174, 177, 181; informed by psychology 6, 81, 86, 90, 138–9, 160–2, 182, 201, 204; informing psychology 46, 85; and parenting 114, 121
solipsism 175
Soros, G. 80, 214n9
speaking being 15, 29, 37, 43, 47, 63, 80, 147, 171, 183
spectacle: medieval 151, 154, 175
Spence, S. 11–12
Spreeuwenberg, R. 146
Spotify 192
Steiner-Adair, C. 125
Stephens-Davidowitz, S. 5, 82
Stiegler, B. 80, 90, 96, 102n8, 117, 147, 159–61, 169, 181–2, 193, 197
Stillwell, D. J. 82, 84–6
surplus enjoyment 43, 121, 207, 209
surplus value 65, 120, 206, 213
surveillance 128, 179
subject: split 47, 49n3, 75, 167, 174, 212
subject of the sciences 54, 119, 196

Tamagotchi 208–9
theatre: Descartes 102n10, 151, 182; and digitality 156; modern 151–4, 175
Thomas, D. 63
Thomas, S. 129
Thompson, C. 17
Thorndike, E. 97
Thornton, D. J. 133n20
Thrift, N. 80
Tindr 137
torture: involvement of psychologists 87–8
Totem & Taboo 172
transference 149, 177–8, 180
transubstantiation 131–2, 154, 160, 175
Trump, D. 82, 169
Turing, A. M. 25–42, 45–48, 52, 54–9, 62, 67, 71, 75, 76n2, 79–80, 92, 100, 101n1, 109–11, 123, 129, 160, 167, 174
Turing test *see* imitation game
Turing machine 47, 167

Turkle, S. 80
Twitter 38, 122, 153, 164

UbicKids 123, 130–1
uncanny 92, 189, 213, 214n19
unconscious 13, 58, 61, 75, 77n13, 83–4, 97, 132, 160, 163
Unheimlich *see* uncanny
universal machine *see* Turing machine
Urban, T. 14–18
Ur-Father 172–3, 184n8

Vandenbroeck, M. 115
Venturini, T. 82
virtuality 6, 31, 57, 131, 151, 154, 181, 200, 209, 214n19
virtualisation 10, 15, 131, 150
viva voce 40
Von Munchhausen 53, 76n1
Vroom 131–2
vulgar materialism 29, 48

Walker, R. 45, 124
Wang, Y. 31
Watson, J. B. 111
Web 1.0 153
Web 2.0 5, 64, 130, 153
Web 3.0 130, 153
Wiener, N. 19n3, 27, 54, 57–64, 66, 67, 71, 73, 74, 75, 77n7, 77n10, 123, 160, 214n15
Williams R. 166
Williamson, B. 123–5, 146, 130
Wilson, E. A. 75, 77n15&16, 79, 101n1
Winer, D. 168, 171, 210
Woolf, V. 166–7
World War I 161–2
World War II 60, 114, 120, 141, 161, 164, 170, 172
Wright, M. 86, 178
Wylie, C. 82

YouTube 102, 122

Zeiher, C. 76n4, 77n13
Zeitschrift für psychoanalytische Pädagogik 162, 172
zero-level of subjectivity 19, 65, 69, 133n18, 160, 167, 174, 182–3, 199, 209–10
Zeuxis 97–8
Žižek, S. 14–15, 19, 42, 79, 83, 97, 101n3, 140, 173, 179, 200, 204, 206
Zuckerberg, M. 9, 86, 136, 161, 205–6, 209
Zulliger, H. 39, 114, 162, 170–2, 175–8, 183